Myths and Misconceptions about Teaching

What Really Happens in the Classroom

Vicki E. Snider

Rowman & Littlefield Education
Lanham, Maryland • Toronto • Oxford
2006

Published in the United States of America
by Rowman & Littlefield Education
A Division of Rowman & Littlefield Publishers, Inc.
A wholly owned subsidary of The Rowman & Littlefield Publishing Group, Inc.
4501 Forbes Boulevard, Suite 200, Lanham, Maryland 20706
www.rowmaneducation.com

PO Box 317
Oxford
OX2 9RU, UK

British Library Cataloguing in Publication Information Available

Library of Congress Cataloging-in-Publication Data
Snider, Vicki, 1949–
  Myths and misconceptions about teaching : what really happens in the
classroom / Vicki Snider.
      p. cm.
  Includes bibliographical references.
  ISBN-13: 978-1-57886-345-7 (hardcover : alk. paper)
  ISBN-10: 1-57886-345-7 (hardcover : alk. paper)
  ISBN-13: 978-1-57886346-4 (pbk. : alk. paper)
  ISBN-10: 1-57886-346-5 (pbk. : alk. paper)
  1. Teaching. 2. Effective teaching. 3. Slow learning children–Education. I.
Title.
  LB1025.3.S65 2006
  371.102–dc22   2005028739

∞™ The paper used in this publication meets the minimum requirements of
American National Standard for Information Sciences—Permanence of Paper
for Printed Library Materials, ANSI/NISO Z39.48-1992.
Manufactured in the United States of America.

I would like to thank all the wonderful teachers I have known who provided me with anecdotes and inspiration for this book. I thank the friends and colleagues, especially those who didn't agree with me, who took the time to read early versions of my chapters and who made me think harder about what I was trying to say and how I was saying it: Don Crawford, Joanna Futransky-Lerish, Sarah Hadden, Carol Reid, Roger Tlusty, and Kathleen VandeLoo. I also want to thank my mentor, Dr. Sara Tarver, who taught me about the science of teaching. A special thanks to my husband, Ansel Brooks, for drawing my figures, for sharing his outside perspectives on education issues, and for encouraging me to keep going when I got discouraged by the enormity of my task. Finally, I wish to thank my father, a man of humble origins who was at home in a library and who taught me that you have to know something to be smart.

Contents

List of Tables and Figures

TABLES

FIGURES

Acknowledgments

I would like to acknowledge the University of Wisconsin—Eau Claire for granting me a sabbatical leave to complete this book. I also thank all the wonderful teachers I have known who provided me with anecdotes and inspiration for this book. I thank the friends and colleagues who took the time to read early versions of my chapters and who made me think harder about what I was trying to say and how I was saying it. I also want to thank my mentor, Dr. Sara Tarver, who taught me about the science of teaching. A special thanks to my husband, Ansel Brooks, for drawing my figures, for sharing his outside perspectives on education issues, and for encouraging me to keep going when I got discouraged by the enormity of my task. Finally, I wish to thank my father, a man who came from a poor, urban environment but grew up to be at home in a library. He taught me that you have to know something to be smart—not the other way around.

1

Introduction

Dear Mrs. Snider, I want to tell you that your the best teacher I've had in all the years I've been teached. It least you give us some work to do and that's a pretty darn good thing for a teacher to do.

—Jeff, fifth-grade student with mild disabilities

I have been a teacher my entire adult life, both at the elementary and college levels. I'm fairly certain that most of my students would agree that I gave them plenty of work to do, but I doubt if they were all as appreciative as Jeff. During my 35 years in the field of education, many things have changed, or perhaps I have changed; probably both. The more I learn about what *could be*, the more dissatisfied I am with what *is*. I am increasingly troubled by our low expectations and unwillingness to tackle difficult educational problems. I have come to the conclusion that our collective inertia is maintained by dogmatic beliefs that I call *teaching myths*.

My career path was unusual, but my experiences as a teacher were fairly typical. I fell into teaching by chance. My brother had a disability that today would probably be diagnosed as autism. Not surprisingly, I spent a lot of time around children and adolescents with disabilities and, because of my family's connections, I was lucky enough to spend my summers directing a day camp for children with disabilities for the Parks and Recreation Department in our community. I liked it well enough, and decided to become a teacher so that I could get a job in the emerging field of special education. I discovered that in order to become a special education teacher, I also had to get certified in elementary education. At that time, I had no interest in working with "normal" children, so I made the best of the situation by enrolling in the Cooperative Urban Teacher Education Program, which sent me to Kansas City for a semester to complete my methods classes while I lived in an inner-city neighborhood and taught in an all-black school.

During my first 8 years as a teacher, I taught children who were identified as mildly retarded, defined at that time as an IQ between 70 and 85 (today they would no longer be eligible for special education), and who came, for the most part, from low socioeconomic environments. Some of the children had real disabilities and some of them did not. A few came from dysfunctional families, many were on welfare, and almost all were poor. I visited their homes and I found that most parents were cordial and had the best interest of their children at heart. During my last 4 years in the public schools, I taught students with learning disabilities, and those children came primarily from working-class and middle-class families.

For several years, I worked in a school without walls designed to facilitate the innovative Individually Guided Education programs that were popular in the 1970s. We implemented inclusion before the word had any meaning in education. Most of the teachers I worked with were young and smart; a few were stodgy and worn out; all were dedicated and caring. Some of the principals I worked for were better than others, but I got along with all of them. I was lucky because special education was still so new that most administrators gave me a free rein as long as my troublesome students stayed out of their office. The point is, I have always taught students on fringes of general education, and have worked closely with general educators during my entire career.

I learned very little in my undergraduate teacher education program about how to teach; and for those first 8 years I relied on luck, trial and error, and the competence of colleagues for my professional development. I regret that I didn't know more from the beginning because despite my earnest efforts, my students didn't achieve as much as they could have. I knew very little about curriculum, effective teaching, or principles of classroom management beyond what I learned on the job.

After my graduate studies at the University of Wisconsin–Madison, I saw possibilities beyond what I had glimpsed in my limited personal experience. Between getting my master's and doctorate degrees, I taught a resource program for children with learning disabilities. With my new expertise, I "cured" several children of their learning disabilities. The number of students in my program shrank so dramatically that the district made my position half time and I had to split my time between two schools.

Now I run a clinic for underachieving children and adolescents where I get a chance to practice what I preach, and we get some pretty good results. I also supervise student teachers, so I spend a lot of time in schools. Sometimes I find myself in classrooms where well-meaning teachers engage in instructional practices that are, from my perspective, nothing short of "academic child abuse" (Engelmann, 1992). At other times, I find myself in classrooms where talented teachers bring out the best from students by using effective teaching practices. One would think that these successful teachers would express high levels of job satisfaction. Instead, they are frustrated by a complacent and unresponsive system.

My quarrel is with the system, not with individual teachers. The education bureaucrats—administrators, education experts, state Department of Public Education officials, curriculum consultants, and professors—determine policies. Teachers are the soldiers; they are on the front lines. If they have never received adequate training and do not have effective instructional tools, and most have not, they are understandably enticed by the teaching myths.

I worry about the enormous social, economic, and political costs of the large number of students who are poorly educated as a result of the myths. In my lifetime of work with children with mild disabilities and others who are at risk for academic failure, I have seen individual children written off as unteachable and entire groups of children denied valuable learning opportunities. I have felt helpless talking to tearful parents whose children have been victims of a flawed educational system. I have seldom encountered a student with learning disabilities who was taught well from the beginning. The educational establishment appears unconcerned about the consequences of educational failure, perhaps because the failures are hidden. Former U.S. Education Secretary William Bennett commented that "there are greater, more certain, and more immediate penalties in this country for serving up a single rotten hamburger in a restaurant than for repeatedly furnishing a thousand school-children with a rotten education" (cited in Finn, 1991). Educators just keep serving the same fetid food, and calling it a banquet.

Everything I have learned since I started teaching 35 years ago convinces me that student failures are not inevitable, and that educators have to change the way they think about teaching and learning. They can't continue to do things the same way and expect a different result. Based on my lifetime of experience and the results of a survey that I conducted with Rebecca Schumitch in 2004, I have identified six myths that adversely influence teaching practice. The first four myths impact teaching practices and often result in ineffective instruction. The last two myths provide a way to explain the predictable academic failures that result from the other myths.

Myth #1   The myth of process emphasizes what occurs during instruction and de-emphasizes what happens as a result of instruction. When activities and projects become an end in themselves, there is little accountability for learning outcomes. Actual achievement is less important than participation.

Myth #2   The myth of fun and interesting ensures that the process is not only emphasized but is entertaining as well. This myth ignores the fact that the initial learning of a skill or concept is rarely fun. It's the fluent performance and application in a new context that is enjoyable.

Myth #3   The myth of eclectic instruction refers to the practice of drawing on a variety of teaching methods and materials. Teachers believe that designing patchwork lessons is creative and makes learning more interesting. This haphazard approach, however, ignores the complexity of curriculum and restricts teachers' practice to what is intuitive.

Myth #4   The myth of the good teacher assigns most of the variation in teaching quality to the personal characteristics of the teach*er* rather than to the quality of the teach*ing*. Inspired teach*ing* not only depends on the person doing the teaching but also on his or her level of skill and access to effective curricula.

Myth #5   The myth of learning style refers to the popular idea that teaching methods should be matched to students' unique characteristics. Although individualization is desirable, learning style assumes that certain learner characteristics are intrinsic when they may in fact be the result of experiential factors that are amenable to instruction. As a result, teachers may inadvertently deny low-performing students opportunities to learn.

Myth #6   The myth of disability refers to the low expectations that are conferred on students once they are believed to have a disability or risk factors such as low socioeconomic or minority status. Rather than view them as students in need of more and better instruction, educators may view them as uneducable.

The premise of this book is that the myths stand in the way of developing a science of teaching. By *science of teaching*, I mean a set of empirically validated teaching practices and programs that work with most teachers for most students. Without a science of teaching, many students, especially those who come to school with a variety of risk factors, will continue to underperform and school leaders and teachers will be frustrated in their attempts to reach accountability goals.

As I describe the myths in more detail, I use the content area of beginning reading as a way to illustrate my points. I could as easily use mathematics or writing or social studies, but I have chosen to focus on beginning reading for several reasons. First, future academic achievement in every subject depends on being able to read. Children who fall behind early continue to fall further behind over time, and remediation becomes increasingly difficult. According to the National Reading Panel, "only about 5% of children learn to read effortlessly. About 60% find early reading difficult, and of that number, 20–30% really struggle. By fourth grade, the seriousness of the problem for these children becomes obvious" (National Institute of Child Health and Human Development, 2000, p. 34).

Second, a large body of research suggests that there is a way to teach beginning reading so that no child gets to fourth grade without knowing how to read. There are no other content areas where the evidence and the consensus are so strong.

Third, reading specialists resist change and tenaciously adhere to outmoded beliefs, even in the face of evidence that earlier practices, formerly called whole language and now called balanced literacy, were inappropriate and ineffective. Their intransigence provides a good example of how the myths limit children's opportunities for academic success.

I also pay special attention to problems at the elementary level, rather than the secondary level. My focus on elementary education is partially because that is where most of my experience lies, but it is also because the foundation for future academic success is laid in the primary grades. That is where low achievement begins, and it is where interventions must begin. The governors of 13 states recently announced plans to raise standards in high schools (Pear, 2005); Bill Gates supported them, calling high school education "obsolete and morally indefensible because it fails to prepare many students—particularly poor minorities—for college" (U.S. high schools, 2005). Unfortunately, the seeds of low achievement are sown in elementary school. Nearly 70% of high school freshmen read below grade level and similar numbers are ill-prepared in other subjects as well (Ravitch, 2005).

As children progress through the grades, the achievement gap widens. Keith Stanovitch (1986) referred to the cumulative effects of reading disabilities as *Matthew effects* in reading: the rich get richer and the poor get poorer. Children who get off to a good start in reading and spelling have the best opportunity for future success in all subjects. Children who don't learn to read, on the other hand, quickly learn to hate reading. Early unrewarding reading experiences lead to lack of practice, which further limits progress. Children who can't read, don't read; and children who don't read, can't succeed in school.

Lack of foundation skills has a cumulative effect, and secondary teachers inherit a problem that is not entirely of their making. If children do not learn basic reading, writing, and mathematics skills in elementary school, or if they do not acquire basic content knowledge in science and history, then they will be unprepared for the demands of middle and high school. The old problems remain and also create new ones. The content at the secondary level may be watered down, not because teachers are lazy or because they lack sufficient content knowledge, but because students lack the prior knowledge and basic skills necessary for academic success at that level.

Suppose that a builder puts up a house without taking the time to make sure the front door is square. That defect may easily be overlooked for a while, but as time passes, that small imperfection extends into the door's entire mechanism. The slight angle of the door creates areas of friction, excessive wear, and places where there is no contact at all, letting in the outside air. The closing mechanisms don't fit smoothly, creating an ill-fitting and wearing marriage of parts. As the worn spots get rougher and the closing mechanism gets looser, the door gets harder to shut. It has to be forced. Since the door doesn't fit the frame anymore, cold air comes in from the outside, requiring the furnace to run harder and inefficiently. It uses more fuel, which costs more money and wastes natural resources, and so on. All because the door wasn't square.

If I have a philosophical bias, it is that I am an empiricist. Instructional practices should be determined by results, both at the system level and at the individual level, and not by unsubstantiated beliefs. And if we don't get results, then we need to change beliefs.

2

The Problem

I think we have a chance to do something about education, very important. We should have done it years ago. It doesn't matter who does it—Democrats or Republicans—but it's long overdue. Our education system is a monstrosity. We need to go back and rebuild kindergarten and first grade and teach reading and writing to everybody, all colors, and then the whole structure of our education will change because people will know how to read and write.

—Ray Bradbury, interviewed in Salon (August 29, 2001)

Close to three million schoolteachers work an average of 50 hours a week (National Education Association, 2000–2001), but their efforts are not paying off. The media conveys the gloomy statistics:

- Large numbers of young children are unable to read or do mathematics at grade level.
- American students perform poorly on international comparisons in mathematics and science.
- SAT scores have declined and increasing numbers of students must take remedial courses in college.
- The achievement gap between poor and minority children versus white, middle-class children keeps widening.
- Increasing numbers of children need special education or prescription drugs to get them through the school day.

What's wrong? Why aren't hardworking teachers producing high-achieving students? The answer lies in the teaching myths.

Six compelling, but false, beliefs stand between mediocrity and excellence. These beliefs sustain our nation's educational malaise by lowering academic expectations and keeping the science of teaching outside the school doors. These myths have been woven into the culture of teaching over the course of a century, and they are now deeply ingrained in the fabric of American education. Mistaken beliefs about teaching obstruct educational reform efforts because beliefs that supersede science stand in the way of progress. Remember Galileo?

The story of Galileo Galilei is a cautionary tale about dogmatic beliefs prevailing over reason and scientific inquiry. He was a mathematician who lived in Italy during the last half of the 16th and first part of the 17th century. He built a refracting telescope that was superior to anything that existed previously, and with it he observed the night sky. The prevailing theory at the time, and the one favored by the Catholic Church, was that all the heavenly bodies revolved around the Earth. His observations, however, convinced him the Copernican system, which theorized that everything revolved around the sun, was correct. Late in his life he was tried by the Inquisition and imprisoned for heresy because he insisted Copernican theory was a physical reality. His lasting contribution to Western civilization was his use of the scientific method. He used logic and observation to reduce problems to questions that could be analyzed and solved. "I do not feel obliged," he said, "to believe that the same god who has endowed us with sense, reason and intellect has intended us to forgo their use." It would be well for educators to take his words to heart.

FIFTY YEARS OF ATTEMPTED REFORM

Widespread criticism of public education began after World War II with books such as Arthur Bestor's (1953) *Educational Wastelands*, Rudolph Fletch's (1955) *Why Johnny Can't Read*, and James Koerner's (1963) *The Miseducation of America's Teachers*. Since 1960, there has been a progressive loss of confidence in local control and a larger role for the federal government in education policy (Kirst, 2004). The most recent history of education reform, which dates from the publication of *A Nation at Risk*

(National Commission on Excellence in Education, 1983) spans four presidents, both Democrat and Republican, and two generations of school children. President Ronald Reagan commissioned *A Nation at Risk* in response to "the widespread public perception that something is seriously remiss in our educational system" (p. 1). The report began with an ominous appraisal: "If an unfriendly foreign power had attempted to impose on America the mediocre educational performance that exists today, we might well have viewed it as an act of war. As it stands, we have allowed this to happen to ourselves" (p. 5).

In 1989, President George H. W. Bush and the nation's governors held a national education summit at which they set goals for public education. In 1994, a compromise version of those goals was finally passed into law under President Bill Clinton as Goals 2000 (U.S. Congress, 1994). Goals 2000 provided funding for states to adopt their own content and performance standards and to develop assessments. The goals were ambitious, but the legislation contained little accountability and weak enforcement provisions. Although all states eventually complied by developing standards and assessments, there was great variability in how well they were done. In 1998, a group of business leaders, policymakers, and education reformers met and issued *A Nation Still at Risk* (Thomas B. Fordham Foundation, 1998), which advocated increased accountability and school choice as a means to move the nation toward those goals.

Legislative mandates for education reform culminated with the No Child Left Behind Act (U.S. Congress, 2001) (NCLB) under George W. Bush, which included tough accountability measures and consequences for failing schools. This radical mandate required schools to disaggregate data from annual assessments to show whether traditionally low-performing groups—children of poverty, individuals with disabilities, minorities, and second-language speakers—were making as much progress as more advantaged populations. It also required the use of research-based methods (the words "scientifically based research" appear more than 110 times in the law) for teaching reading and provided immediate funding for training reading teachers how to use validated teaching methods.

In the wake of NCLB, I have often heard teachers and administrators complain that expecting *all* children to learn is unrealistic, but that attitude reveals the naive perspective of individuals who believe in the teaching myths. I think that many of the abuses related to the implementation of

NCLB—teachers who cheat on tests, adolescents forced to drop out of high school to inflate test scores, instructional time wasted on test preparation—result from an inability to even imagine that more effective teaching practices could result in higher expectations and better outcomes.

Glenn Latham (2002) related a story about his high school golf team that is somewhat analogous to the situation that schools find themselves in with NCLB. Latham's golf coach, who was also the driver education teacher, knew nothing about how to teach golf. When the team lost their first game, the coach told them that in order to win any games they would have to shave a few strokes off their game. It was up to them, however, to figure out how to improve their technique. Schools find themselves in much the same situation with NCLB. The government has essentially told them to shave a few strokes off their game. Although the federal government has indicated that scientifically based research can help, generally the people in state Departments of Public Instruction, who are directly responsible for enforcing NCLB, don't know what that means. Scientifically based research in education is a foreign concept. It's difficult for educators to play the game differently than they have for past 100 years. It will be very difficult to improve test scores, especially for disadvantaged populations, as long as the teaching myths dominate educators' thinking and scientific research is ignored or misunderstood.

NCLB has politicized education and no doubt some people will misconstrue my motives as political, but my motivation is strictly professional. I believe in the goals of NCLB but, truth be told, I am a lifelong Democrat and a social liberal. The social and economic problems that depress academic achievement must be addressed in the political arena, but meanwhile educators need to examine and change the educational variables that are under their control—teaching methods, quality of curriculum, teacher preparation, use of time, leadership, school climate—and raise their expectations for the success of all children. They need to shed the myths and imagine other possibilities.

OTHER POSSIBILITIES

Data from the National Adults Literacy Survey (NALS) conducted by the National Center for Educational Statistics in 1992 (Kaestle, Campbell,

Finn, Johnson, & Mikulecky, 2001) provide a graphic illustration of literacy in the United States. The NALS assessed a broad cross-section of adults to obtain information about three different types of literacy. They used a very broad definition of literacy that went beyond traditional decoding and comprehension skills to include prose literacy, document literacy, and quantitative literacy. Prose literacy is reading nonfiction to gain information; document literacy involves locating information in common documents, forms, maps, and schedules that are common in the workplace and in everyday life; and quantitative literacy involves performing basic mathematical operations to figure out tips, keep a checkbook, plan purchases, and calculate interest payments. There were five levels of task difficulty in each category, with 1 being the easiest and 5 the most difficult.

A Level 1 task in prose literacy requires individuals to read a short passage, similar to one you might find in the newspaper, and answer a simple, literal comprehension question. Below is an example. The reader is to underline the sentence that tells what Ms. Chanin ate during her swim.

University of Maryland senior Stacy Chanin on Wednesday became the first person to swim three 28-miles laps around Manhattan.

Chanin, 23, of Virginia, climbed out of the East River at 96th Street at 9:30 p.m. She began the swim at noon on Tuesday.

A spokesman for the swimmer, Roy Brunett, said Chanin had kept up her strength with "banana and honey sandwiches, hot chocolate, lots of water and granola bars."

Chanin has twice circled Manhattan before and trained for the new feat by swimming about 28.4 miles a week. The Yonkers native has competed as a swimmer since she was 15 and hoped to persuade Olympic authorities to add a long-distance swimming event.

The Leukemia Society of America solicited pledges for each mile she swam.

In July 1983, Julie Ridge became the first person to swim around Manhattan twice. With her three laps, Chanin came up just short of Diana Nyad's distance record, set on a Florida-to-Cuba swim.

A Level 2 task asks the reader what age Ms. Chanin was when she began swimming. Levels 3, 4, and 5 tasks require individuals to read increasingly dense text and make more difficult inferences. For example, one Level 4 task requires individuals to summarize a newspaper editorial.

The simplest Level 1 task in document literacy is signing in the appropriate place on a Social Security card, and a Level 2 task requires individuals to fill in certain portions of a job application. Document literacy at Level 4 might require reading a bus schedule.

An example of a Level 1 task in quantitative literacy would be adding two amounts on a bank deposit ticket. Level 2 tasks require the individual to figure out that they must be added. An example of a Level 4 task would be figuring out a 10% tip on lunch. (Sample items can be found at http://nces.ed.gov/naal/defining/defining.asp.)

In other words, Levels 1 and 2 literacy tasks are very simple and even Level 4 tasks are not terribly difficult for an educated adult. Although the authors of the study emphasize that adults who scored in Levels 1 and 2 are not nonreaders, their literacy skills are certainly low. Adults who can only complete Levels 1 and 2 tasks may need a lot of help in the workforce and performing daily tasks.

The good news is that level of education makes a difference. The more education a person has, the higher his or her level of literacy (Kaestle et al., 2001). The bad news is that half of all high school graduates demonstrated low literacy (Levels 1 and 2) and that *only* half of college graduates demonstrated high literacy (Levels 4 and 5)! Figures 2.1, 2.2, and 2.3 show the percentage of *high school and college graduates* who scored at each level in each literacy category. It is important to note that these figures do not report results for the general population, only for those who have graduated from high school or college. An individual is said to score at the level where he or she can complete 80% of the tasks. For example, the first chart labeled *Prose Literacy* shows that 16% of people who graduated from high school scored at Level 1, meaning that they completed fewer than 80% of the Level 1 tasks, or that they could successfully complete Level 1 tasks, but not Level 2 tasks. The consistency across types of literacy is quite striking.

If the levels were renamed with more descriptive labels, high school graduates who cannot perform Level 1 tasks might be called *uneducated*; they graduate from high school with no literacy skills. In the current sample of high school graduates, they comprised about half of those in Level 1, or 8% (Kirsch, Jungeblut, Jenkins, & Kolstad, n.d.). The remaining individuals in Level 1 and all of those in Level 2 might be considered *undereducated*. They graduate from high school with low literacy skills.

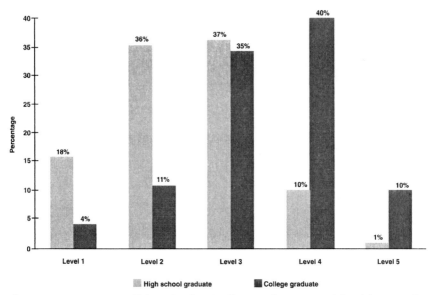

Figure 2.1. Percentage of high school and college graduates at each level for prose literacy

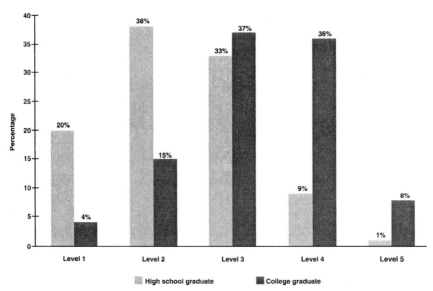

Figure 2.2. Percentage of high school and college graduates at each level for document literacy

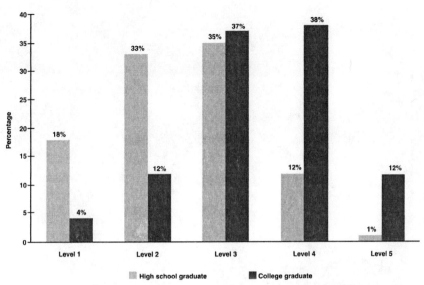

Figure 2.3. Percentage of high school and college graduates at each level for quanti-tative literacy

They can read simple passages for information, which is usually consid-ered functional literacy. High school graduates in Level 3 could be con-sidered *adequately educated* and those in Levels 4 and 5 might be con-sidered *well educated*. The 1992 data shown in Figure 2.4 is labeled as the "current achievement curve." That data indicated that 52% of high school graduates (Levels 1 and 2) are currently uneducated or undereducated and 48% (Levels 3, 4, and 5) are adequately or well educated.

What I propose, what I see as *another possibility*, is that more effective teaching practices could reduce the percentage of uneducated and under-educated individuals from 52% to 8%, as shown in Figure 2.4. The yard-stick of adequate literacy remains the same (defined as Level 3 or above). The hypothetical "better achievement curve" assumes that about half, though not all, of those currently at Level 3 would move up to Level 4. There will still be a few adolescents in the tail of the curve and there will still be a gap between the highest and the lowest performers, but instead of 48% of high school graduates being adequately or well educated, there will be 92%. Not everyone will be above average, that's statistically im-possible; but everyone who completes high school will be adequately or well educated. The fact that adult literacy is lower than it used to be or that

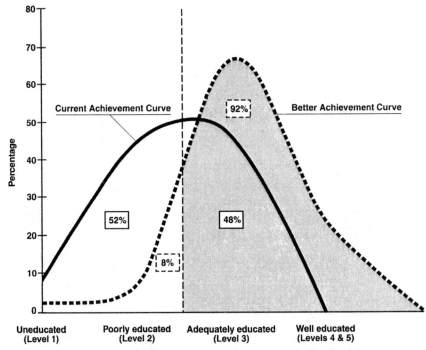

Figure 2.4.   Hypothetical better achievement curve for high school graduates

American children perform worse than children in other countries is be-
side the point. Individuals who have spent 13 years in school, even most
of those with disabilities, should be verbally and mathematically literate
(Level 3). Period.

We have the professional expertise, the curricula, and methods to move
individuals from Levels 1 and 2 up to Level 3. Researchers know quite a
bit about what works for teaching basic skills, especially in reading. The
most daunting task would be moving people who currently score at Level
3 up to Levels 4 and 5 because performance at that level involves sophisticated thinking skills and content knowledge that researchers still aren't
sure how to teach. To attain a better achievement curve, teachers would
have to use teaching practices that are known to work and researchers
would have to find ways to teach higher-level academic skills more effectively.

Could it happen? In a society as ethnically, economically, and socially
diverse as ours, could a high school diploma mean that a person was ade-

quately or well educated? Theoretically it could happen, but not until people stop *expecting* that low literacy is normal and acceptable. Not until all children acquire basic reading, writing, and mathematical skills in the primary grades. Not until we shed the teaching myths that constrain us and implement instructional programs and procedures that work.

WHAT WORKS

To understand why the question of what works is so controversial, it is important to understand something about the two competing philosophies of education—progressive and traditional education. Progressive education (also known as developmentally appropriate, holistic, implicit, and constructivist) is often referred to as child-centered, but I prefer the term *learner-directed* because *all* education philosophies are child-centered. Learner-directed methods foster children's innate interest in learning through exploration and discovery. Students are encouraged to work in small groups or individually and ideally the curriculum should follow the children's own interests. The teacher is a facilitator, guiding students in their development. Student progress is measured relative to themselves rather than to an absolute standard. Social and emotional needs are emphasized as much as cognitive growth.

Traditional education (also called explicit, direct instruction, positivist, and behavioral) is often referred to as teacher-centered or teacher-directed, but I prefer the term *curriculum-based* because all methods require teacher direction. Curriculum-based teaching stresses the need for all students to move through an established curriculum that emphasizes mastery of specific content in each subject area, although students will not necessarily move through at the same rate or in the same way. The teacher is the class leader, and he or she measures student progress toward specified standards in an objective way. Goals 2000 and NCLB implicitly favor curriculum-based approaches precisely because they require schools to measure students' progress against a standard of acceptability.

The dominant philosophy among educators is learner directed. People who adhere to a learner-directed philosophy believe that research comparing one instructional approach with another, derisively referred to as "horse-race research," is inappropriate because best practice is relative.

Teaching methods must vary depending on the context. The popularity of this philosophical perspective among educators has had the effect of limiting the amount of research conducted to find out what works and what doesn't, and has created some reluctance to accept what little research there is. In other words, the predominant educational philosophy is at odds with development of a science of teaching based on empirical research.

Despite this philosophical barrier, there is more that is known about effective teaching practices than most people realize. Some teaching practices can even mitigate risk factors such as disability or poverty. In the early 1970s, the federal government launched the largest educational experiment ever undertaken, called Project Follow Through, in order to identify effective ways to teach children of poverty in the primary grades. Observers had noticed that the cognitive gains students achieved in Head Start preschool programs seemed to dissipate when children went to public school. Project Follow Through was an attempt to identify which instructional practices best maintained the gains made in Head Start. The models represented the full spectrum of educational philosophies. At the end of third grade, standardized achievement tests indicated that the models that yielded the best results were those that emphasized direct teaching of basic skills (curriculum based), specifically Applied Behavior Analysis and Direct Instruction (Stebbins, St. Pierre, Proper, Anderson, & Cerva, 1977). Children who participated in these two models not only learned basic skills but they also surpassed children in the other models in higher-level thinking and self-esteem. Unfortunately, the results were largely ignored. In fact, the models that did most poorly, the conceptual-cognitive or self-esteem models that represented mainstream thought in the educational establishment, received the most additional funding. The programs that achieved the best results got the least funding (Watkins, 1997).

More recently, a number of professional organizations—the American Association of School Administrators, American Federation of Teachers, National Education Association, National Association of Elementary School Principals, and the National Association of Secondary School Principles—sponsored *An Educator's Guide to Schoolwide Reform* (American Institutes for Research, 1999). The resulting report rated school reform models in a *Consumer Reports* type of format. Three comprehensive school reform models—Direct Instruction, Success for All, and High Schools That Work—got the best reviews.

Procedures for monitoring progress, such as precision teaching, curriculum-based measurement, and curriculum-based evaluation (e.g., Howell & Nolet, 2000) have been shown to provide the accountability to help classroom teachers improve instruction, but they are seldom used, either. A generic set of explicit teaching practices referred to as teaching functions (Rosenshine, 1986) or the Hunter (1982) model was widely promoted in the early 1980s, but faded away. Much is known about general principles of classroom management that can prevent minor misbehavior and solve chronic behavior problems (e.g., Alberto & Troutman, 2003), yet most teachers never take a single course in behavior management.

Meta-analysis is a statistical technique that combines the results of all the studies conducted on a particular teaching approach to yield information about how well it works. Lloyd, Forness, and Kavale (1998) conducted a meta-analysis of methods used in special education and found that four instructional approaches had the most support—mnemonic training, reading comprehension instruction, behavior modification, and Direct Instruction. A separate meta-analysis also found that Direct Instruction programs improve achievement outcomes for all children (Adams & Engelmann, 1996), but most educators, among those who even know about it, dismiss Direct Instruction programs as too regimented. Success for All is a comprehensive school reform model that has 20 years of research backing its effectiveness (Slavin & Madden, 2001), but few districts are clamoring to adopt the model.

In two exhaustive studies, the late Jeanne Chall (1967, 2000) systematically reviewed and evaluated all the quantitative and qualitative research conducted this century on beginning reading. She compared the effectiveness of child-centered, progressive (learner-centered) approaches to traditional teacher-directed (curriculum-based), explicit approaches and made a very strong case that teacher-directed instruction produced higher achievement overall, especially for low-income children. Her conclusions have been supported by research conducted by the National Reading Panel (National Institute of Child Health and Human Development, 2000). Despite the abundance of evidence, educators resist explicit teaching.

Why do educators ignore teaching approaches that have been shown to be effective? Why do they cling to familiar, yet unproven, approaches? Why did administrators in my hometown, with the blessing of the school board, close the only school in the district that was closing the achievement gap in reading? They closed a low-income, high-minority school that had implemented the comprehensive school reform model Success for All. The school went from 55% of students scoring advanced or proficient on the third-grade reading test in 1999 to 94% in 2004, which exceeded the district average.

Why did the school district in Madison, Wisconsin, refuse $2 million of *Reading First* federal grant money associated with NCLB because accepting the money would mean replacing their existing learner-directed program, which was ineffective even according to their own data, with a program that was more effective? (Reading between the lines, 2004).

Why did the new superintendent in Rockford, Illinois, forbid a school that was 80% black and poor to use Direct Instruction, an approach that has been highly effective in urban areas, when that school outscored every other school in the district (except for the school that housed the gifted program) on the state reading test just one year earlier (Watters, 2005)? Why did the superintendent remove both the instructional program and the principal who oversaw those gains, even though the local newspaper raved that it was the "first school to prove that educating poor black schoolchildren . . . is not a lost cause" (Our view, 2003). How could that happen? The same blatant disregard of results in favor of ideology occurred in Chicago (Grossman, 2005), New York City (Wolf, 2005), and Memphis (Edmondson, 2001). Reasonable people must wonder, why do educators resist change?

WHY EDUCATORS RESIST CHANGE

Peter Senge, a systems-theory expert and advocate of "learning organizations" in business, relates an anecdote that reveals teachers' perspectives on change. He asked a group of educators if systems change occurs only in response to a crisis. Usually in business groups, three-quarters will agree that's true, but the response in the education group was different. When he asked the question, very few said yes. So he asked, "Does that mean you believe significant innovation can occur without crises?" but again no one raised a hand. He went on, "Well, if change doesn't occur in response to a crisis, and if it doesn't occur in the absence of a crisis, what other possibilities are there?" Finally someone from the audience responded, "I guess we don't believe significant change can occur under any circumstances" (cited in Smith, 2001, p. 30).

Throughout the 20th century, the lasting changes in education have been structural or organizational—things that could be added on to existing school functions. Examples include establishing kindergarten, special education, graded classrooms, middle schools, and vocational classes (Tyack & Cuban, 1995). Pedagogical changes, changes in the way teachers teach, have seldom lasted (Kirst, 2004). The "new math" that swept the country in the 1960s is a good example of a pedagogical change that didn't last. Instructional changes seldom take hold. The limitation of making organizational reform without instructional reform is illustrated by the following anecdote. Elmore (2002a) interviewed a high school social studies teacher about his attitude toward block scheduling, an organizational change that combines periods to provide longer instructional blocks of time. "I asked him, 'So what do you thinking of block scheduling?' He said, 'It's the best thing that's ever happened in my teaching career.' I asked, 'Why?' And he said, 'Now we can show the whole movie'" (p. 1).

Organizational reform without instructional reform is a bit like implementing universal health care in a country where the doctors still treat patients by bleeding with leeches. The research base for validated procedures in education is small in comparison to medicine, but we know something about effective school practices. Educators seem to resist any sustained or viable change in teaching procedures, and perhaps it is their stubborn adherence to the status quo that leads educators to insist that there is no reason to change.

In the preface to their book *Manufactured Crisis: Myths, Fraud, and the Attack on America's Public Schools*, Berliner and Biddle (1995) suggested that education reform is a conspiracy "led by critics whose political goals could be furthered by scapegoating education" (p. 4). Although most educators stop short of conspiracy theories, they simply refuse to admit that a problem exists. They maintain that (a) test scores show that American children, particularly in selected locations, are doing just fine; (b) test scores are meaningless, anyway; and (c) more funding will fix the problem (if in fact there is one). Although there has been some tinkering around the edges, no new ground has been broken. In response to Goals 2000, educators developed standards and aligned local curriculum to match those standards, but there is no evidence that students are making substantial gains in academic achievement; at best, they are treading water. The gap between black and white students is persistent and perplexing. Some people have come to the conclusion that school reform will never work. For example, the Edna McConnell Clark Foundation, a foundation dedicated to improving the lives of young people from low-income communities, restricts its giving to out-of-school programs, having come to the conclusion that large-scale school reform won't work (Temes, 2001).

I believe that the reason educators resist instructional change that might result in higher student achievement is related to the six teaching myths. To find out, Rebecca Schumitsch and I surveyed teachers and teacher educators in Iowa, Minnesota, and Wisconsin in 2004. We asked respondents to choose between two statements on opposite ends of a continuum and to indicate which statement was exactly or somewhat like what they believed. They could also take a position between the two statements, indicating that they were undecided or balanced between the two beliefs. Results for teachers can be seen in Table 2.1.

We found that teachers supported statements that emphasized the process over the outcome, but about half of them indicated that they were balanced or undecided between the two statements. For example, 35% thought that teachers should facilitate rather than teach directly and only 13% thought the opposite, but 52% were balanced or undecided. Teachers revealed stronger support for the process by placing more importance on "making learning fun and interesting" compared to producing high student achievement outcomes. It is understandable that teachers were reluctant to take sides, but we wanted their bottom line. A lot of teachers didn't seem to have one, which suggests they may be open to change.

Teachers reserved their strongest beliefs for eclectic instruction and the importance of learning style. These results are not surprising. Teachers' preference for eclectic instruction has been documented elsewhere (Baumann, Hoffman, Moon, & Duffy-Hester, 1998; Stahl, Osborn, & Pearson, 1994; Zalud & Richardson, 1994) and learning style is so well accepted among both educators and the general public alike that it is almost considered a fact. The danger of these beliefs is that they are idiosyncratic and leave little room for the inherent absolutes associated with the idea that scientific research can identify teaching practices that work for most students.

Our survey also revealed other beliefs that stand in the way of change. Teachers believe that experience is more important than education and

Table 2.1. Teachers' Beliefs Related to the Teaching Myths

Belief	Percent Agree	Belief	Percent Agree	Undecided or Balanced
Teachers should facilitate learning, rather than teach directly.	35%	Teachers should teach directly, rather than just facilitate.	13%	52%
A great teacher cares about students and makes learning fun and interesting.	45%	A great teacher cares about students and produces high student achievement outcomes.	11%	44%
There is no best way to teach all students; an eclectic or balanced approach to instruction is best.	78%	There is a best way to teach that will be effective with most students.	13%	9%
Individual learning styles should be an important factor in deciding how and what to teach.	80%	The concept of learning style has little relevance for deciding how and what to teach.	6%	14%
Experience is more important than education and training for becoming an effective teacher.	44%	Education and training is more important than experience for becoming an effective teacher.	7%	49%
Teaching is more of an art than a science.	46%	Scientifically conducted research is the best guide for determining what and how to teach.	19%	35%
Factors (e.g., home life, dyslexia) can prevent children from becoming functionally literate and mathematically competent, regardless of the school's best efforts.	52%	All children (excluding those with severe disabilities) can become functionally literate and mathematically competent.	29%	19%

training, and that teaching is more of an art than a science. In other words, teachers believe professional development and scientific research are relatively unimportant. Any change in instructional practices is unlikely without more rigorous professional development for teachers and more attention to scientific research. The most startling result of the survey was that over half of teachers believed that factors such as dyslexia or environmental factors could prevent students from becoming functionally literate and mathematically competent. Conservatively, that means that half of America's teachers write off about 40% of the school-age population. Statistically, that means that a fifth of the kids in school have no one to believe in them.

Results for education professors reveal similar results, with some differences as shown in Table 2.2.

The teaching myths are based on a number of faulty premises and much harm is done as a result of these unexamined beliefs. They perpetuate the use of teaching practices that are ineffective with large numbers of children. When students fall behind academically, they are labeled as having a certain learning style, a disability, or demographic risk factors. The serious consequences of this labeling trap for students can hardly be overstated. Without a clear focus on the goals of education and in the absence of a consensus about effective professional practices that work (for the most part) in all schools, with all teachers, and for all students, teaching failures are incorrectly identified as student failures. The teaching myths virtually guarantee that students who come to school at a disadvantage will remain disadvantaged. This situation can only change when a science of teaching replaces the teaching myths.

There are understandable reasons that educators believe in the myths. Their origins lie in the historical, sociological, and philosophical forces that shaped the field of education throughout the century. Education researchers have neglected the important question *what works?* and educators have ignored answers they didn't like. Professional development has not been rigorous, sustained, or valued. Teaching practices are frequently haphazard, the result of trial-and-error learning. The functional result is that well-meaning teachers underestimate and therefore undereducate too many American youth.

Teachers aspire to be professionals, but without a shared scientific body of knowledge they remain *bricoleur*, a term borrowed from French by an-

Table 2.2. Education Professors' Beliefs Related to the Teaching Myths

Belief	Percent Agree	Belief	Percent Agree	Undecided or Balanced
Teachers should facilitate learning, rather than teach directly.	48%	Teachers should teach directly, rather than just facilitate.	7%	45%
A great teacher cares about students and makes learning fun and interesting.	30%	A great teacher cares about students and produces high student achievement outcomes.	25%	45%
There is no best way to teach all students; an eclectic or balanced approach to instruction is best.	81%	There is a best way to teach that will be effective with most students.	11%	8%
Individual learning styles should be an important factor in deciding how and what to teach.	75%	The concept of learning style has little relevance for deciding how and what to teach.	14%	11%
Experience is more important than education and training for becoming an effective teacher.	11%	Education and training is more important than experience for becoming an effective teacher.	16%	73%
Teaching is more of an art than a science.	28%	Scientifically conducted research is the best guide for determining what and how to teach.	23%	49%
Factors (e.g., home life, dyslexia) can prevent children from becoming functionally literate and mathematically competent, regardless of the school's best efforts.	28%	All children (excluding those with severe disabilities) can become functionally literate and mathematically competent.	53%	19%

thropologist Levi-Strauss (1966). There is no precise translation for *bricoleur* in English, but according the translators note, they are a "Jack of all trades," not a handyman exactly, but a *professional* do-it-yourselfer. They cannot be called craftsmen because they work with whatever tools are at hand to solve whatever problems exist, nor do they have a specialized niche like craftsmen. They must be very intelligent and may, at times, achieve good results, but they are still constrained by their limited and finite assortment of tools and by the extent of their experiences. Contrast the *bricoleur* to engineers. Engineers have access to a range of tools designed for the specific job that needs to be done. They rely on the cumulative evidence for theoretical and technical knowledge, and use what is known to expand the boundaries of their professional knowledge. They rely on other professionals and specialists to help them do their job and to solve new problems. Engineers specialize—electrical, mechanical, biomedical, chemical, aerospace, naval, civil—and one type of engineer may assist the other, but would never be expected to do his or her job. An engineer is a member of a profession, but a *bricoleur* is just a clever person. Without a common body of knowledge about best practice, every new *bricoleur* teacher reinvents the wheel.

A profession that is guided by myths rather than by empirically validated principles and practices maintains its *bricoleur* status. The teaching occupation will become a profession only when educators replace myth with science and raise their expectations for the success of all students.

3

The Myth of Process

Let's get the job done here. I don't want to hear about the process.

—NFL Coach Bill Parcells on *60 Minutes* (October 3, 2004)

The myth of process suggests that engaging in the educational process is an end in itself. When the educational process is an end in itself, learning may or may not take place. Like all myths, there is a certain amount of truth to the myth of process. The experience of doing something may be valuable, regardless of the outcome. We've all heard the saying, "It's not whether you win or lose, but how you play the game." When the process is emphasized in education, however, there are no winners and losers because no one is keeping score. Actual learning may become secondary to participation. As the Charles Schultz Peanuts character Sally put it, "Going to our school is an education in itself, which is not to be confused with actually getting an education."

I don't want to overstate the case. Educators do not completely discount the importance of academic outcomes; it's just that the journey itself generally appears to matter more than the destination. The teacher facilitates the journey by providing learning opportunities in the form of activities and projects, often done in groups. These activities are often called "authentic" because they involve students in solving interesting, real-world problems. Teachers are, as the cliché has it, a guide on the side, not a sage on the stage.

Our 2004 survey found that teachers and teacher educators favored their role as facilitator (see Tables 2.1 and 2.2). Our results are consistent with other surveys that asked the question in different ways. When asked which of the following two statements was closer to their philosophy of the role of the teacher—"Teachers should see themselves as facilitators of learning who enable their students to learn on their own" or "Teachers should see themselves as conveyors of knowledge who enlighten their students with what they know"—78% of teachers, 87% of superintendents/principals, and 92% of education professors said that they see themselves as facilitators (Farkas, Johnson, & Foleno, 2000, p. 32). A survey by Public Agenda found that 86% of education professors said that it was more important for kids to struggle with the process rather than to end up knowing the right answer (Farkas, Johnson, & Duffett, 1997).

The myth of process explains the negative response many educators have to standardized testing. Eighty-four percent of teachers say schools place too much emphasis on test scores (Public Agenda: Reality Check, 2002). When educators say that learning can't be adequately measured with standardized tests, what they really mean is that the process can't be measured, which is true. If one believes, as John Dewey (1916) did, that "the educational process has no end beyond itself; it is its own end" (p. 59), then there is no reason to measure the outcome. A Public Agenda survey of new teachers found that 53% thought that standardized tests were a seriously flawed measure of true student achievement, but that 62% could live with them as a "necessary evil" (Farkas, Johnson, & Duffett, 2003, p. 13). Even though teachers saw the value in testing, they complained that standardized tests inevitably led to teaching to the test, did not assess what students needed to learn, and took some of the "joy and learning" out of their lessons (Johnson & Duffett, 2003, p. 14).

Education professors are even more adamant. Seventy-eight percent want less reliance on multiple-choice standardized tests that rely on right and wrong answers. Said a Boston professor, "Giving people tools is probably more important than all of that information—which they can now get on the computer. And [it's] more important than passing those doggone standardized tests, which probably are not showing what that student really knows" (Farkas et al., 1997, p. 10).

FAULTY PREMISES

The myth of process is based on the idea that learning will occur naturally if teachers give children the tools for learning. There is no need to impart information. This assumption presumes that critical thinking can be isolated from facts and information, which is questionable. It further presumes that academic learning is natural and that natural learning is preferable to the alternative, which I suppose is artificial learning. Both of these faulty premises are based on the misapplication of research in cognitive psychology.

Learning How to Learn

Educators who believe in the myth of process think that "learning how to learn" provides the impetus for lifelong learning. Many educators assume that teaching facts, information, and vocabulary is not a good use of time because, as they say, "you can always look it up." Teachers do not attach as much importance to knowledge of science, scientific facts, history, or geography as the general public does (Elam, 1989). Process-oriented teaching methods emphasize figuring things out and using higher-level thinking skills. Although this sounds good in theory, facts and concepts cannot be separated from higher-level thinking because they are mutually reinforcing. Higher-level thinking cannot occur in a content vacuum.

Importance of Background Knowledge

People need facts, information, and vocabulary in order to understand almost everything. They provide the means for memory and thinking by forming networks of related knowledge that psychologists call schema. Schemata are just facts, information, and concepts that are stored and organized so that they can be retrieved at a later time as background knowledge.

Every fact and concept that an individual commits to memory provides a "hook" for new learning. Without the hook provided by this background knowledge, there is no place to "hang" new information and it will quickly be forgotten. Background knowledge differs in terms of density — the more dense, the more places there are to hang new information. In other words, the more a person knows, the more he or she is capable of learning. A schematic representation is shown in Figure 3.1. The lowest density level is the general knowledge that is necessary to create and sustain interest in any topic. The next density level includes more and more specific prior knowledge that people need to learn about a subject—to "look it up" or to be a lifelong learner. Finally, the highest density is the wide and deep specific subject-matter knowledge that comes with specialization. People need this specialized knowledge in order to think critically and have original ideas about a subject. Higher-level thinking requires something to think about. Knowledge of a particular subject doesn't guarantee critical thinking, but it certainly increases the probability. It is virtually impossible to think critically about subjects one knows little about—just listen to call-in talk radio for the evidence.

Every time people add to their existing prior knowledge, thereby increasing the density, they *construct* new knowledge. The idea that learners construct new knowledge as they encounter new information forms the basis for a popular learner-directed teaching method called "construc-

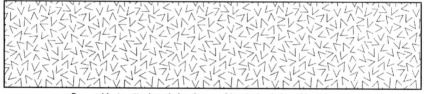

Deep subject matter knowledge that provides the basis for critical thinking

Prior knowledge that promotes further learning

General knowledge that generates interest

Figure 3.1. Levels of background knowledge needed to promote learning and thinking

tivism." Educators have interpreted this rather sound principle of learning and memory to mean that teaching should be nondirective and organized around authentic learning experiences that will facilitate the construction of knowledge. The problem is that a theory of learning does not necessarily translate to a teaching methodology. Learners construct just as actively from a good book or a lecture as from a "hands-on" activity or field trip. It's even possible that people construct more, and more accurately, when instruction is didactic or highly focused.

Educators also use this theory about how knowledge is constructed to suggest that instruction should build on a learner's existing interests so that new information will be meaningful. If students are allowed to follow their own interests, the theory goes, they will naturally acquire an increasing density of knowledge on a sufficient number of subjects to become well-rounded, educated adults. This idea, however, seems to ignore the importance of the first level, the general knowledge needed to create and sustain interest in a topic. Once the hooks on a particular topic are part of a person's general knowledge, independent learning and mere exposure may lead to new learning and an increasing density of background knowledge. The question is, how do the first hooks on any topic get put in place? Isn't that the function of formal education?

It seems to me that the trick is to present new facts, information, and vocabulary in an integrated way that highlights relationships and similarities so that the pieces fit together. When instruction is integrated, then it will be meaningful. This is an issue of curriculum, which will be discussed in chapter 5. Whether learning is implicit or explicit, activities or teacher-directed, is not the issue. The secret to increasing students' background knowledge is to make sure instruction is deliberate and integrated rather than disjointed.

Cognitive psychologists have established an extensive body of literature on the importance of background knowledge for comprehension and memory. Experts with extensive background knowledge about a subject not only understand and recall more of what they read but they understand the text differently and more deeply (Chi, Glaser, & Farr, 1988). General knowledge of a subject is often not enough for thorough comprehension of a subject as simple as, say, baseball. Research suggests that people who know a lot about baseball recall more information and more important information after reading passages about baseball than people without such prior knowledge (Spilich, Vesonder, Chiesi, & Voss, 1979).

Being able to look something up depends on already knowing enough about a topic to understand the explanation (Hirsch, 2000). Naive learners are easily overwhelmed by unfamiliar vocabulary, facts, and explanations. There may be more new information than a naive learner can assimilate, and much of the information may seem nonmeaningful even when it isn't. Someone with more prior knowledge can easily assimilate the new information because there is less that is new. An example will help illustrate. Looking up the word "tsunami" on the Internet yields the following definition:

> tsunami—A Japanese term which has been universally adopted to describe a large seismically generated sea wave which is capable of considerable destruction in certain coastal areas, especially where underwater earthquakes occur. Although in the open ocean the wave height may be less than 1 m, it steepens to heights of 15 m or more on entering shallow water. They have been incorrectly referred to as tidal waves.

To a person who knows the terminology and who has some background knowledge, this passage would be informative. A knowledgeable person might learn, for example, that tsunamis are not the same as tidal waves. To someone without background knowledge, however, the unfamiliar vocabulary and new information would make the passage difficult to understand. The reader must understand the meaning of *seismic* (not to mention the derivation *seismically*), what the abbreviation "m" means and how high a meter is, how high normal waves are, and why a shallower water produces larger waves.

People also need prior knowledge in order to evaluate what they read. Given the massive amount of information available on the Internet, critical reading is essential. The ability to evaluate depends on the use of strategies and reasoning skills, but it also depends on background knowledge. For example, I require college students in my methods class to find a persuasive article on the Internet about teaching reading or spelling. Then they must critique it by using what they've learned about the research base for teaching reading and by asking questions such as "What is the author's conclusion?" "What evidence do they use to support their conclusion?" "Do they use any faulty logic?" This is an extremely difficult assignment even for the best students. The reason that it is difficult, I think, is that undergraduate students lack sufficient background knowledge (even after my expert instruction) to think deeply and critically. All other things being equal, the more dense a person's prior knowledge about a subject, the more insightful the evaluation.

Insufficiently dense general knowledge results in the situation described by the late Al Shanker (1995), longtime president of the American Federation of Teachers. "The problem with many youngsters today," he said, "is not that they don't have opinions, but that they don't have facts to base their opinions on."

Importance of School for Building Background Knowledge

School experiences designed to teach facts, information, concepts, and vocabulary are particularly important for students who may have not acquired the background knowledge necessary for school success outside of school. Vocabulary knowledge is one form of background knowledge that is essential for success in school. Low vocabulary knowledge is endemic among children with risk factors and evidence suggests that they arrive in kindergarten knowing far fewer words than their more advantaged peers. In their landmark study of language development, Hart and Risley (1995) recorded the verbal interactions between adults and children in low-, middle-, and high-income families. For two and a half years, they observed 42 families for 1 hour each month. They found that by age 4, children from high-income families had heard 30 million more words than children from low-income families.

This early gap depresses the vocabulary knowledge of low-income children because they have fewer opportunities to learn new words than children from professional families. Before children learn to read, they can only acquire vocabulary by listening. Their deficits in language put them at a disadvantage from the first day of school. The vocabulary gap continues to widen in the early years in school. At the end of second grade, a 4,000-word gap already exists between advantaged students who score in the highest quartile (who know about 7,100 root words) and those who score in the lowest quartile (who only know about 3,000). Even by fifth grade, students in the lowest quartile have learned 7,000 root words, the same number that their more advantaged peers knew at the end of second grade (Biemiller & Slonim, 2001).

The high correlation between vocabulary knowledge and reading comprehension has been documented since the early 20th century (Anderson & Freebody, 1981; Thorndike, 1917). Put simply, readers must understand the words if they are to understand the ideas. Similar to the definition of tsunami above, if there are too many unknown vocabulary concepts in a text passage, reading comprehension decreases.

Becker (1977) was the first to notice that disadvantaged students who made adequate progress in beginning reading (decoding or word recognition) began to fall behind in reading in fourth grade and above when the nature of reading changes from learning to read to reading to learn (Chall, 1983). Furthermore, he observed that these same students continued to improve in mathematics, which led him to conclude that the problem with reading comprehension was lack of opportunity (to acquire vocabulary and background information outside of school) rather than lack of ability.

A longitudinal study confirmed Becker's observation that low-income children scored as well as their normative peers in all areas of reading, including word meaning, in second and third grades, but began to fall behind in fourth grade (Chall, Jacobs, & Baldwin, 1990). Chall referred to this as the "fourth-grade slump." A follow-up study of these students in seventh, ninth, and eleventh grades revealed that their scores declined compared to peers at every grade level. By grade 11, their reading scores were in the 25th percentile. These results are not surprising since text at the second- and third-grade levels contains words that are known to most seven- and eight-year-olds, regardless of socioeconomic status. Passages at the fourth-grade level and above, however, tend to contain words that are seldom encountered in everyday speech.

These studies illustrate the fact that at-risk populations are at a severe disadvantage in school, although it would be a mistake to assume that middle-class children are not also in need of vocabulary and other content knowledge (Hirsch, 2003). All students need explicit instruction to fill in the gaps so that they can successfully comprehend what they read and perform well in content classes. Furthermore, it's important to establish a solid foundation in the primary grades. Reading comprehension and listening comprehension are dependent on vocabulary knowledge, and they are also dependent on facts and information that a learner with risk factors is not likely to encounter incidentally at home or by participating in the "hands-on" activities or group work at school. This information must be taught intentionally and directly.

The rationale for emphasizing process over specific content is not justified by research in cognitive psychology. Strategies for learning how to learn are useless without content because lifelong learning and higher-level thinking depend on facts, information, concepts, and vocabulary. Many children, I would go so far as to say most children, do not acquire sufficient vocabulary and background knowledge incidentally or outside of school. They need deliberate and integrated instruction to make sure they acquire the general knowledge that will provide the potential for future and continued academic success.

Learning Is Natural

The second faulty premise that underlies the myth of process is that children learn naturally and that it is preferable to let them learn naturally than to interfere with didactic or artificial teacher-directed instructional methods. This way of thinking is summarized in the old Greek proverb "the bird sings sweetest who has not been taught" (Nikiforuk, 1994). The myth rests on the assumption that all learning occurs naturally, and it is best promoted in natural, or authentic, learning contexts.

Academic learning is presumed to be as natural as cognitive and physical development among infants. There is some truth to the idea that learning is natural. Humans do seem to have a natural instinct for primary learning (Pinker, 1994). Play helps develop basic cognitive activities such as spatial orientation, physical manipulation of objects, social relationships, speaking, and even elementary counting skills. These skills appear to unfold in a predictable sequence and they are transcultural and universal. All of this is learned through "discovery" and facilitated by casual adult-infant interactions. The problem is that school learning is secondary learning, not primary learning. Reading is not natural, and neither are mathematics, history, science, literature, and writing. If reading were natural, one billion adults or 26% of the world's adult population would not be nonliterate (Facts about illiteracy, 2001).

There are three fundamental problems with naturalistic learning. First, it is apt to lead to incorrect learning or no learning at all. Naturalistic learning involves discovery, a form of inductive learning, which is figuring out what is the same about a series of examples. For example, in beginning reading children must attend to many details to discern the sameness among words. They must figure out that certain letters and letter combinations make specific sounds. They must figure out that the order of letters determines the word; and that once the word is spoken, it can be recognized and understood. For example, c + a + t is the word "cat," a furry creature that goes meow. A discovery method assumes that children will figure all this out just by being exposed to books.

When children do not figure out what sound each letter makes and how to sequentially say those sounds to make words, they may "discover" their own strategies for reading. Instead of using the letters in a word to pronounce it, students "read" by guessing based on pictures, context, and prior knowledge. Although a few children might learn to read this way, most will not. It's not a very efficient way to read since one needs to recognize at least 12,000 different words to read high school textbooks (Carroll, Davies, & Richman, 1971). A more reliable alternative is to explicitly teach the letter sounds and show children how to blend the sounds together using text passages that discourage guessing. This approach is called explicit, systematic phonics and it does not rely on discovery.

A second problem with discovery learning is that it favors those with more background knowledge. As discussed earlier, the more one knows about a subject, the easier it is to learn more about it. Privileged children come to school with a lot of background knowledge about the alphabet. Marilyn Adams (1990) reflected on the literacy experiences of her son.

> Since he was six weeks old, we have spent 30 to 45 minutes reading to him each day. By the time he reaches first grade at age six and a quarter, that will amount to 1,000 to 1,700 hours of storybook reading—one on one, with his face in the books. He will also have spent more than 1,000 hours watching "Sesame Street." And he will have spent at least as many hours fooling around with magnetic letters on the refrigerator, writing, participating in reading/writing/language activities in preschool, playing word and "spelling" games in the car, on the computer, with us, with his sister, with his friends, and by himself, and so on. (p. 85)

Compare those experiences to a child who comes to school from a home where there are no books, or where the parents themselves are nonreaders.

A third problem with discovery is that it is inefficient at best, and ineffective at worst. It takes much longer to discover a new concept unassisted than with step-by-step instruction. The average person who has had to learn a new computer operating system or computer program can appreciate how inefficient discovery learning can be. Why withhold information that has been known for centuries and ask children to reinvent the wheel? The important discoveries that need to be made are those that remain undiscovered. We should do everything we can to accelerate young people's growth so that they are in a position to make new discoveries.

Between 1975 and 1995, the entire country embraced a discovery approach to teaching reading called whole language. Whole language relied on children to discover rules about the nature of the English language from simply being exposed to good literature. Teachers taught phonics "as needed," but instruction was not systematic or explicit and the amount of actual phonics instruction depended on the philosophical orientation and skill of the teacher. The widespread use of whole language occurred even though the theoretical underpinnings were not universally accepted and there was no empirical research supporting its effectiveness.

In 1988, the Department of Instruction, the State Board, and the Curriculum Commission in California adopted whole language as the mandated reading approach for all schools in the state. Schools were not allowed to purchase basal reading programs with state funds that did not adhere to a so-called "meaning-centered approach." By 1992, California's fourth-grade students ranked next to last among all states participating in the National Assessment of Education Progress (NAEP); and by 1994 they were dead last (Fry, 1996). Many defenders of whole language claimed that the large population of minorities in California's schools contributed to poor scores, but among white children, California scored last; and among children of college-educated parents, California scored second from last. Blacks scored fourth from last (Community Action Forum, n.d.). People also tried to excuse the dismal test scores by blaming Proposition 13, which decreased public funding of education, but per pupil expenditures in California were only slightly below the national average. The most surprising thing about this story is that even after 1994, districts across the country followed California's lead like lemmings to the sea.

Research in cognitive psychology has long supported the idea that a combination of direct explanation and practice are superior to discovery alone. Judd (1908) described one of the most famous studies 100 years ago. Children in the experiment had to throw darts at an underwater target. One group of students received instruction on how refraction of light can distort perceptions of where objects are located underwater. The other group received no explicit instruction. Both groups did equally well on the practice tasks which involved a target located 12 inches below water. On the transfer test, however, which involved a target 4 inches below water, the children who received instruction did much better—presumably because they understood the principle of refraction, which they could generalize from 12 to 4 inches of water. Twenty-five years ago Ausubel (1968) summarized the findings on discovery learning by saying that "actual examination of the research literature allegedly supportive of learning by discovery reveals that valid evidence of this nature is virtually nonexistent" (p. 497).

A more recent experiment reiterated the flaws in discovery learning. Researchers randomly assigned third- and fourth-grade students to a direct teaching or a discovery learning condition. The pretest required students to design experiments to study how ramp length affected how far a ball rolls after it comes down the ramp. The post-test required students to design an experiment to test the earlier factor (ramp length) and a new factor (ramp surface). Students who received direct teaching were successful 77% of the time and only 23% of those in the discovery condition were able to design scientific experiments (Klahr & Nigam, 2004).

The Chick-Sexing Experiment

An ingenious experiment with chick-sexing nicely illustrates the problems with naturalistic learning. It's extremely difficult to discern the sex of day-old chicks, and yet egg-producing farmers need to know which chicks are pullets (female) and which ones are cockerels (males) so that they don't lose money by feeding chickens that won't produce eggs. People actually go to chick-sexing schools to learn how to discriminate gender differences between day-old chicks and even after weeks of guidance from a mentor, trainees are lucky to attain over 80% accuracy. Very experienced chick-sexers can sex up to 1,000 chicks per hour with 98% accuracy. The Japanese invented chick-sexing in the 1920s and they still hold competitions to see who can identify the most chicks, the most accurately, in the shortest amount of time.

Two cognitive psychologists (Biederman & Shiffrar, 1987) devised an experiment designed to explore rates of learning on a difficult perceptual task like chick-sexing. Their research design also provided an ingenious comparison of explicit versus discovery learning. With the help of Mr. Carlson (a chick-sexing expert with over 50 years of experience sexing 55 million chicks), they developed a short one-page handout with five sketches and a brief explanation of how to identify the critical distinctive features of each sex. The handout described how to look for convex versus concave or flat features in order to determine the sex of day-old chicks.

People without any chick-sexing experience were shown 18 pictures of chicken genitalia and asked to sex them. On the pretest they all performed slightly above chance levels with about 60% correct. For the post-test, some participants were randomly assigned to a group that received the handout and the others were just asked to complete the task again. Individuals with the handout had about 1 minute to study it before performing the task again. (The pictures were shown in a different order.) Those who did not get the handout scored lower than they had on the pretest, about at chance levels. Those who studied the handout got 84% and their performance resembled that of retired chick-sexers who also completed the picture task.

This experiment has many implications for education, for surely academic subjects are at least as complex as chick-sexing. First, discovery learning resulted in no learning for the group who got no instruction. In all fairness, their performance would have been better had they received feedback, but the reality in classroom situations is that many students do not receive timely feedback. Second, the professional chick-sexers with a great deal of prior knowledge were able to transfer their knowledge to the picture task and perform well without instruction. Third, a relatively small amount of explicit instruction designed to focus learners' attention on the critical features of the task dramatically improved performance in a short period of time. An important, yet neglected, responsibility of those who design curriculum is to figure out what those critical features are and to figure out how to present that information clearly. The failure to do so is the result of the myth of eclectic instruction, which will be discussed in chapter 5.

Finally, instruction does not have to take place in an authentic context. Novice chick-sexers typically learn by handling actual chicks under the supervision of an experienced mentor. The "authentic" task requires manual dexterity in addition to the difficult visual discrimination task. Proficiency on the contrived picture task prior to attempting chick handling might speed the learning curve. This experiment illustrates that direct teaching can be more efficient and reliable than discovery in authentic contexts.

In one respect, naturalistic, discovery learning is cruel. The origins of the word kindergarten mean "children's garden." But what gardener would idly stand by while weeds crowded out young sprouts, plants drooped for lack of moisture, leaves were eaten by pests, and growth became stunted by poor soil? What lover of plants would refuse to interfere with the natural order of things?

THE HARM THAT IS DONE

The functional result of the myth of process is that the process becomes an end in itself, which leads to a lack of accountability. Without accountability, students get promoted without regard for performance, which can lead to a situation where students lack the foundation skills that will enable them to engage in the higher-level thinking skills that educators value so much. As with all the teaching myths, the negative effects are far more detrimental to students who possess a variety of risk factors that make school challenging.

Lack of Accountability

Teachers are understandably comforted by the de-emphasis on assessment because they have great difficulty measuring their effectiveness. Lortie (1975) observed that compared to other occupations, the goals of teaching are more intangible. Social and moral goals can be just as important as intellectual goals. The very idea of measuring a child next to an absolute standard is inconsistent with teachers' high regard for each child's individuality. Other professions can be judged more easily, the patient gets well or the engineer completes a bridge that doesn't collapse, but it is more difficult to measure whether or not a teacher's goals have been achieved. In addition, teachers have many different ways of measuring progress, many of them are quite subjective, and there is a lot of variation in how much progress is thought to be enough. "Critical, recurrent problems remain unresolved in the daily work of teachers—uncertainty stalks as they try to determine whether they are influencing students" (Lortie, 1975, p. 150). Given these ambiguities, it's understandable that teachers prefer to value the process and avoid absolute standards for academic outcomes.

That being said, however, a lack of accountability lies at the heart of the persistent criticism of public education. Under Goals 2000, states were required to write standards and indicate how they would reach those standards. Some states did a better job than others, but part of the reason that NCLB passed with such bipartisan support is that the lack of accountability in Goals 2000 legislation meant that nothing had changed (Cohen, 2002).

Outcome measures of early reading progress are objective and easy to administer. Teachers can assess word accuracy, rate, and comprehension on a passage by briefly listening to students read aloud. Once students can decode (usually by third grade), they can read passages independently and answer comprehension questions. It's not a perfect measure of reading skill, but it approximates the task of reading fairly well. Many reading specialists, however, have rejected these reliable measures of reading achievement as inauthentic. They "replaced them with measures of motivation, enjoyment, self-esteem. Attitude, not achievement became the outcome in the reading education research community" (Moats, 2000, p. 10). These psuedoassessments, which measure the process rather than the outcome, are often called "authentic assessment" because they assess reading in real-life contexts. Although they may be authentic, they are virtually meaningless for accountability purposes.

Teachers complain about "teaching to the test," but they *should* teach to the test because tests assess the basic skills and general knowledge that are necessary for students to engage in higher-level thinking and increasingly complex learning. Tests don't measure everything a student can do nor do they measure a teacher's full impact on a student's well-being. Test items measure the extent to which students have acquired the knowledge and skills that will give them the potential to learn more. If teachers don't teach to the test, then the test becomes a measure of ability, like an IQ test or a measure of opportunities outside of school. A good achievement test measures what is learned in school.

Arguably, lack of accountability has the potential to do the most harm at the preschool and elementary levels. Unfortunately, I have observed that the strength of teachers' belief in the myth of process is strongest among those teaching at the lowest levels. Early childhood educators are ardent believers in an approach called developmentally appropriate practices, which emphasizes the process. Ravitz, Becker, and Wong (2000) found that elementary teachers had stronger constructivist beliefs (which would be consistent with emphasizing the process) than high school teachers, and that English teachers were more constructivist than teachers of other high school disciplines. By emphasizing the process, by not holding students to any yardstick of achievement in elementary school, teachers practically guarantee that secondary teachers will have to water down the content because students will lack both the basic skills and the content knowledge to engage in complex verbal and mathematical pursuits.

Teachers need to be clear about their goals. They need to measure progress toward those goals by assessing pupils' academic performance (not attitude) in the classroom, and by assessing school performance through the use of standardized tests. If they do not, they risk losing many learners along the way and not knowing they're gone until it's too late to retrieve them.

Social Promotion and Self-Esteem

Another harmful by-product of the process approach is social promotion. When there is no agreed-upon outcome that can be reliably assessed, there is no choice but to keep moving children ahead regardless of their skill level. The push for standards and accountability may have had the effect of decreasing social promotion in recent years. The number of teachers who said their school automatically promoted children in their school dropped from 41% in 1998 to 32% in 2002 (Johnson, Duffett, Vine, & Moye, 2003). However, just under half of all teachers admit that they pass students to the next grade as long as they try hard and attend, and they have promoted students who should have been held back (Johnson, 2003).

When there is no accountability, students are unlikely to put forth their best effort. This is especially true at the high school level. It is the rare adolescent who is intrinsically motivated to do well in school, and those who lack the basic skills and background knowledge necessary for success are even less motivated. No one is intrinsically motivated to do things he or she is not very good at. Eighty-one percent of the American public said that students achieve only a small part of their potential (Johnson, et al, 2003; Rose & Gallup, 2001) and even students seem to recognize that fact. Public Agenda found that 71% of students readily admitted that they do the minimum to get by and 56% said that they could try a little harder (Johnson & Farkus, 1997) and a MetLife (Markow & Scheer, 2002) survey found that 73% of students agreed that students in their school do only enough work to get by.

No doubt many students would agree with Calvin in Bill Watterson's *Calvin and Hobbes* cartoon strip. Calvin decided that he could stop doing his homework because he didn't need to learn things to like himself. To which Hobbes replied, "So the secret to good self-esteem is to lower your expectations to the point where they're already met?" The myth of process probably bolstered the self-esteem movement. The idea that high self-esteem was a precursor to academic success enjoyed a rather long run of popularity in both educational circles and popular culture. A recent review of the literature on self-esteem research, however, concluded that self-esteem is more likely to be the result of high performance than the other way around (Baumeister, Campbell, Krueger, & Vohs, 2003).

Even though students may recognize that they aren't working up to their potential, good grades for doing very little cannot help but give students an inflated sense of achievement. They end up thinking they know a lot more than they do and why shouldn't they? It's difficult for individuals to know what they don't know. Students may feel better about their academic performance than they deserve to. In turn, their high self-esteem causes them to want to be entertained (Ruggerio, 2000), which makes the myth of process a trap that leads right into the myth of fun. Many smart college students admit to me that they did not study in high school and got straight As, but they faltered in college. For the first time in their life, they got Cs and sometimes even Fs because they didn't know how to study.

SUMMARY

Emphasizing the process results in a lack of accountability for student achievement and may lead to a situation in which students lack any incentive to work hard. No students are served well by the myth of process, but students who arrive at school less prepared for academic learning suffer the worst effects. Rather than diminishing differences among students, the myth of process exacerbates them. The myth of process is incompatible with a science of teaching because there is no way to determine if the process was effective unless the result is assessed.

One might think that de-emphasizing specific content in favor of thinking skills would benefit smart, curious youngsters regardless of their socioeconomic status or cultural background—but it turns out that's not true. Children who come from homes where education is not stressed or where the parents are undereducated themselves are less likely to acquire the background knowledge that they need to experience school success. One might think that lack of accountability would raise student confidence and self-esteem, but the effect is probably temporary. One might think that lack of accountability would help low-performing students save face, but with no yardstick to measure progress, it's easy to ignore achievement gaps that eventually lead to humiliation.

4

The Myth of Fun and Interesting

Most educators have bought the myth that academic learning does not require discipline—that the best learning is easy and fun. They do not realize that it is fluent performance that is fun. The process of learning, of changing performance, is most often stressful and painful.

—Ogden Lindsley (1992, p. 23)

The myth of fun and interesting is an extension of the myth of process. When the process is emphasized, the entertainment value of a lesson and the students' level of engagement becomes the measure of a successful lesson. Teachers derive their reward and sense of satisfaction from creating fun and interesting lessons rather than from attaining specified learning outcomes. The strength of this myth is surprising. Recall that 45% of teachers in our survey defined a great teacher as one who makes learning fun and interesting whereas only 11% believed that a great teacher produces high student achievement. Forty-four percent were in the middle, believing the best of both worlds is possible.

There is some truth to the myth that learning should be fun. I can understand why teachers feel compelled to make lessons entertaining. I, too, like to design activities that engage students, create excitement, stimulate discussion, and make students laugh. I also know that these reinforcing moments do not necessarily guarantee that students have mastered the content. The exhilaration of my great lesson is more than offset by the letdown when I assess retention and application of skills and concepts. Ideally, school should be interesting, but let's be realistic: Not every lesson will be interesting to every student.

The idea that learning should be fun is probably related to modern American society's almost pathological need to be amused and entertained. Frankly, I still adhere to the old adage that school is the work of childhood, and as such, doesn't need to be fun. My work isn't fun, even though I like what I do. It's challenging and stimulating and creative, but it's also frustrating and even tedious. Paddling a kayak or riding a bike on a fine day are my idea of fun, and even those activities can stop being fun in a headwind or on a series of steep hills.

It's easy to get fooled by terminology. I have talked to people who agree with me that learning need not be fun, but in the next breath they endorse authentic learning, active learning, brain-based learning, or hands-on learning. All of these terms are euphemisms for activity-based methods of instruction that make fun sound more serious and scientific. The fact of the matter is that instruction that is billed as authentic is often spurious, that all learning must be active and brain-based or else there is no learning, and that most of what goes on in classrooms involves "hands-on," even if it's just hands on a pencil.

FAULTY PREMISES

There are three faulty premises that support the myth that learning should be fun. A first premise is that learning should be effortless. The second premise is that entertaining activities will motivate students and reduce misbehavior; because so few teachers receive effective training in classroom management during their teacher preparation, this idea is appealing. A third premise is that hands-on activities will accommodate the learning style of those children who supposedly cannot benefit from didactic verbal or analytic classroom approaches.

Learning Should Be Effortless

The idea that school is the work of childhood, and that study, like all work, takes time and effort has gone out of favor. "Students don't 'work'—they learn," says popular education writer Alfie Kohn (1997). Rather than thinking that accomplishments are the result of effort and hard work, students and teachers seem to think that academic accomplishments require neither effort nor hard work. The new attitude seems to be that hard work and effort are not a responsibility; they are an option when a student is interested (Stone, 1999). A recent study of 90,000 high school students in 26 states found that 55% said that they study no more than 3 hours per week, and 65% of those students reported getting As and Bs (Friedman, 2005).

For some reason that I still don't understand, students (and their families) change their attitude about the need for hard work and effort as soon as they go from the school building to the football field. It always strikes me as ironic that our society places so much value on hard work and effort in sports and so little in education. One hears few complaints about the hours spent driving children and adolescents to sporting events, but endless complaints about the amount of assigned homework. I know parents who spend their weekends traveling to hockey or soccer games, who emphasize the need to practice skills and word hard in order to win, and who push their child to succeed in sports and who brag about their child's exploits on the ice or the field—and I have never heard these parents mention a word about academics. It seems as if they are working hard for something with no payoff. The chances of a child becoming a professional athlete are very slim. A college education seems like a goal with a higher likelihood of paying off.

I have often wondered why people accept the need for effort and hard work in sports and the performing arts but not in education. Perhaps effort has a more observable payoff in sports and the performing arts. Sports fans, peers, parents, and friends can detect lack of effort both in the skill level and in how the game is played. The improvement that comes from practice and hard work is more visible in sports and the performing arts. A person can count the number of free throws that go through the net and hear the melody played in key. These events can be seen and heard, whereas cognitive events like increasing reading fluency and word recognition remain unseen.

Perhaps sports and arts are intrinsically more fun than intellectual pursuits, and it's more fun to spend hours shooting free throws and playing scales than to practice reading or learning math facts. I'm not sure that's entirely true. Young children are typically very motivated to learn to read and will spend hours pouring over the trashiest supermarket paperbacks for beginning readers. Children and adolescents who are avid readers never consider time spent with a book to be wasted.

An important difference between school and sports or the performing arts is that after-school activities are voluntary whereas school is required. All students must go to school whether they want to or not, and whether or not they are any good at it! If an activity is voluntary, the motivation to do well is already built in, at least to some extent. Voluntary activities have the added advantage of encouraging competition. The prospect of beating an opponent is motivating. Maybe there is something innate that makes human beings enjoy the challenge of games. The involuntary nature of schooling makes too much competition inappropriate because the risk of ridicule and humiliation is high in a classroom with a wide range of ability levels.

As much as I hate to admit it, however, I think the real reason that hard work and effort are valued in sports and not in academics is that our society values sports more highly than academics. You don't see the girls clamoring to get a date with the guy who won the science fair. As American humorist Evan Esar (n.d.) noted, "America believes in education: the average professor earns more money in a year than a professional athlete earns in a whole week."

Regardless of the reason that hard work and effort are undervalued in school, the fact is that they are necessary. Educators need to take a lesson from the great coaches. Nobody doubted Vince Lombardi (n.d.) when he said, "Excellence is achieved by mastery of fundamentals." Mastery of fundamentals can only be achieved in one way—practice. There's no way to get around it. Getting good at anything requires practice. Jaime Escalante, the subject of the movie *Stand and Deliver* (Warner Brothers, 1988) is the closest thing we have to a Vince Lombardi in education. His class of disadvantaged high school students performed so well on the National Advanced Placement Calculus Examination that the Educational Testing Service, surprised by the high scores from students who lived in the barrio, accused them of cheating. When they took the exam again, carefully monitored by outside observers, the students still passed. But do you know what it took to bring those disadvantaged students to that high level of expertise? It took a lot of effort and hard work. Students came to school for one extra period before school and stayed an hour after school. They came to class on Saturday mornings and during Christmas and summer vacation for two years (Zigmond, 2005). Incidentally, after his brief moment of fame, Mr. Escalante did not enjoy accolades from his peers. The other teachers accused him of spending too much time on academics, and he was eventually scorned, punished, and removed from the departmental chairmanship. He moved to another school district to teach until he retired in 1998 (Lindsley, 1992).

Entertaining Activities Motivate Students

The assumption that fun and interesting activities motivate students and reduce discipline problems seems reasonable on the surface. Education professors believe it, many teachers believe it, and students believe it. But is it true?

The idea that fun and interesting activities reduce discipline problems is especially popular among education professors. A report for the Public Agenda (Farkas et al., 1997) found that 61% of education professors believed that when students misbehave it is because the teacher has failed to make the lesson interesting or engaging enough. "Underlying these attitudes seems to be a sense that children have an innate love of learning that can be used to harness any wayward or mischievous impulses" (p. 10). Anyone who believes that children don't misbehave when they're having fun either doesn't have any children or hasn't been out in public recently. Misbehavior may even occur more frequently in fun situations because they tend to be unstructured.

I can understand why teachers might believe that they need to entertain students. Activities that demand little of students, especially students who have never had much expected of them, can placate students, and tend to make classroom management easier (Jesness, 2000). Early in my career I worked in an open spaces school near a teacher whose students did nothing but color and complete inane worksheets all day long. Her classroom was a much more impassive place than mine, but none of the students in my room ever wanted to go to hers. If students are used to having little expected of them, they may rebel when a teacher pushes them to perform difficult tasks; however, once they get used to experiencing success with difficult tasks, they will find challenging activities motivating.

Not surprisingly, 67% of high schools students think that they would learn more from "a teacher who uses hands-on projects and class discussion," but they reported that only 22% of their teachers actually do that (Johnson & Farkas, 1997). It's hard to know exactly what these adolescents mean by "hands-on," but it may mean that they want activities with more entertainment value. Ruggiero (2000) suggests that the self-esteem movement made children and adolescents want to be entertained. The emphasis on self, both in school and in the mass culture, makes students feel like every moment should be enjoyed. He suggests that children expect fun and interesting presentations because a lifetime of media exposure, beginning with children's programming, has conditioned them to it. A survey of elementary and secondary teachers reported that all but 2 out of 65 teachers interviewed identified "sedentary activities" as "producing disinterest and, often, causing antagonism" (Zahorik, 1996, p. 557). Sedentary activities refer to lecture, explanations, giving directions, review, tests, reading, workbooks, and taking notes.

Teachers may feel some pressure to make learning fun and interesting in order to be well liked by students or just to get a response. The need to be well liked and popular is very hard to resist. Promoting high achievement and providing an interesting classroom are not, and should not be, mutually exclusive, but fun and easy tend to go together. Students would always prefer to be entertained in the short run. So would I. The rewards for being known as a demanding teacher, rather than a fun and easy teacher, are not immediate and overt feedback from students or parents is relatively rare.

The truth is that behavior management skills are a far more effective way to motivate student learning than fun activities. Teaching expectations for behavior, keeping students on task, maintaining a high rate of positive interactions with students, avoiding negative interactions that reinforce undesirable behavior, and making sure that students understand exactly how points and grades are awarded are just a few of the research-based principles that can help teachers motivate students even when the content is difficult and demanding. Applying principles of classroom management has the added benefit of increasing the amount of time available for actual teaching.

There is a lot of pressure on teachers to make learning fun and interesting, but it's doubtful that such activities actually motivate students in the long run. The motivation may be short-lived, and certainly not conducive to lifelong learning. Basic principles of classroom management are a far more effective way to motivate students.

Hands-on Activities Accommodate Learning Styles

A final faulty premise is that fun and interesting activities accommodate students' learning style. The topic of learning style will be discussed in more detail in chapter 7, "The Myth of Learning Style." Suffice to say that activities designed to appeal to so-called tactile or kinesthetic learners run the risk of irrelevance. In addition, like all instructional practices that emphasize the process, they adversely affect low-performing students— exactly the students that "hands-on" activities are supposed to engage. Hirsch (1996) summarized the problem well.

> Caution is especially required when the phrase "hands-on" is used to imply disdainfully that visual and verbal learning is artificial and unengaging. Antiverbal prejudices spell disaster for disadvantaged students, who have not been exposed to a breadth of verbal learning outside the school. In contemporary life, the verbal has a strong claim to being just as "lifelike" as the tactile. (p. 253)

The idea that learning should be painless is probably a vestige of the belief that the best learning is natural learning. Educators also seem to subscribe to the idea that fun and interesting activities will motivate students to learn; however, sound principles of classroom management will do a far better job of motivating students. Finally, there is some overlap between the underlying premises of the myth of fun and the myth of learning style because fun activities are presumed to accommodate a greater variety of learning styles.

THE HARM THAT IS DONE

There are four harmful effects that result from overreliance on fun and interesting activities. First, fun activities lead to a lot of wasted instructional time. Second, activity-based instruction can make it difficult for learners to focus on what it is they are supposed to learn. Knowing what to pay attention to is called selective attention in the psychological literature and it is often a problem for young or naive learners or those with learning disabilities. Third, rather than increase motivation to learn, activities with a high entertainment value but a low content value may actually decrease the probability that a child will become a lifelong learner. Fourth, without effort and practice, individuals cannot master any intellectual or creative endeavor.

Wasted Time

Research has confirmed the obvious relationship between achievement and instructional time. In a typical six-hour school day, about 47% of the time is allocated to noninstructional activities like announcements, recess, lunch, special events, and so on. About 43% is allocated to instructional activities, but 10% of the allocated time is wasted, which leaves students engaged in instructionally relevant activities for about one-third of the school day (Latham, 2002). This estimate seems generous to me because it assumes that the instructional activities are valuable. In fact, the myth of fun ensures that many of them are of questionable value.

Just allocating more time to academic subjects seems to increase student learning (Rosenshine, 1976; Rosenshine & Berliner, 1975); however, if instructional activities are only marginally related to the subject, then that time can't really be considered allocated time. For example, making log cabins out of Popsicle sticks and milk cartons (Reed, 1997–1998) can't really be considered time allocated to learning about the life of Abraham Lincoln. Building a shoebox-sized replica of the items in your school locker and then labeling them in Spanish for Spanish class can't be considered a good use of time since the total time for the project is about 20 hours and total number of words learned (maybe) is two dozen at the most (Sewall, 2000).

The second chunk of time is called engaged time. It is the amount of time that students actually think about the academic content. Engaged time is often called "time on task." In the above examples, the amount of time spent thinking about the life of our Civil War president is near zero, and in the second example the amount of time spent thinking about Spanish vocabulary is probably 15–30 minutes, or less than 2% of the time spent doing the activity.

I am not saying that projects and activities don't have a place in the school curriculum. I think projects that encourage students to delve deeply into a subject are valuable. They allow students to become experts in one small area, to increase their density of background knowledge, and to think critically. Activities are good when they are relevant and when there is some accountability for learning outcomes. Teachers have to weigh the relative merit of each activity in relationship to the time expended and make intelligent choices.

Knowing What to Pay Attention To

Selective attention is a term used by psychologists to describe the ability to attend to the salient aspects of a task. It is not the same thing as attention span. Attention span refers to the length of time that a person maintains attention, whereas selective attention has to do with knowing what is important to pay attention to in the context of a task. Rick LaVoie (1994) described the difference between selective attention and attention span like this: A person with poor selective attention pays attention to everything; a person with a short attention span pays attention to nothing.

Poor selective attention is influenced by both intrinsic and environmental variables. Young children and children with learning disabilities tend to have more difficulty than average children knowing what to focus on within the context of a particular task (Tarver & Hallahan, 1974). They tend to deploy their attention indiscriminately. As children mature, they become more economical in their perceptions and they learn what to pay attention to. How much a person knows about a subject also influences his or her ability to selectively attend to the important aspects of a task. The more one knows, the more likely it is that he or she will know what to pay attention to.

A classic example of how selective attention influences school performance is the tendency of young children to confuse the letters *b* and *d*. From the perspective of a naive kindergarten student, *b* and *d* look the same, but not because there is anything wrong with their eyes or visual perception. For their entire life they've been taught that the name of objects stays the same regardless of its position in space. A cup is cup, whether it's sideways, upside down, or right side up. It doesn't matter how it's held, it's still a cup. When children go to school, however, that rule suddenly changes. Now the way an object points changes the name; *b* does not have the same name as *d* even though they look exactly the same. A 6 does not have the same name as 9, even though they look the same. The only difference is their position in space. No wonder so many young children get confused! Children have to learn that when it comes to letters and numbers, position in space is important.

There are a number of instructional techniques that teachers can use to help children focus on the distinctive features, shape, and directionality, of letters and numbers. The worst thing that a teacher can do, however, is to bombard children with fun activities related to the letter *b* and then move on two days later to the letter *d*.

Consider the following instructional activities recommended in the *Land of the Letter People* (Reiss-Weimann & Friedman, 1997) for introducing the name and sound of the letter *b*. When students meet Mr. B (a knee-high inflatable balloon), the teacher asks them to guess his name by asking "What does Mr. B have all over him?" (He has buttons.) Then, Mr. B has an argument with Mr. Z over whether buttons or zippers are better. The teacher takes a poll of students to find out who has zippers and who has buttons and draws a graph using the words *more*, *fewer*, *most*, and *equal*. Finally, the class listens to a song and children pretend to button a button each time they hear the words *beautiful buttons*. Later in the week, they get to an activity that might actually help children understand that *b* makes the sound *buh* when the teacher brings in a large grocery bag with a picture of Mr. B on it containing numerous items that begin with *b* like *b*unch of *b*ananas, *b*erry juice for a *b*edtime snack, *b*rushes, *b*athrobe, a *b*ook and *b*ookmark, a *b*ear, and (of course) a *b*ox of *b*uttons. Other activities include blowing bubbles, illustrating a poem, decorating a bag with things that start with *b*, classifying buttons, making a class book about "How We Keep Warm in Winter," writing about why they feel good about themselves, making patterns using a computer program, making a graph to show how cold it is outside, making Mr. B's Berry Blizzard (a smoothie), and so on.

I understand the need for activities in kindergarten, but the two critical pieces of information that kindergarten children *must* learn for future success in reading and spelling are not at all obvious in the meeting with Mr. B. Those two important things are (a) how letter *b* looks (stick first then the ball, not the other way around), and (b) that it makes the sound *buh*. In the barrage of fun activities, it is unlikely that naive learners will acquire this critical piece of information. So much is going on that a naive learner may miss the point. Children who come to school already knowing the name of the letters or even the sound might do okay because the activities merely reinforce something they already know. Children who have had very little exposure to the alphabet and children who are not naturals with print are more likely than other children to ignore the critical features of directionality and sound. In a stimulating environment of games and activities with Mr. B, children who haven't a clue, won't get one, even though they might have fun. When Mr. D is introduced in short succession, confusion is inevitable.

Naive learners or learners with poor selective attention may miss the point when instructional environments are too much fun. A "busy" instructional context can create confusion and hinder learning, especially for students who have less prior knowledge.

Fewer Lifelong Learners

George Lucas, director of *Star Wars*, is quoted as saying, "My own experience in public school was quite frustrating. I was often bored. Occasionally, I had a teacher who engaged me, who made me curious and motivated to learn. I wondered, 'Why can't school be interesting all of the time?'" (Chen, 2001, p. 42). Lucas is chairman of an educational foundation that specializes in helping teachers use the Internet and innovative technology to improve education and, one assumes, to make school interesting all the time. This might be an unachievable, and even undesirable, goal.

An important factor in awakening interest is novelty (Zahorik, 1996), but the irony is that nothing can remain novel for very long. Rude (2002) suggests that interest that is spawned by novelty inevitably leads to boredom once the novelty wears off. Events and objects that initially spark interest eventually become boring unless they evolve. "PacMan was interesting, for example, when it first appeared. But if interest alone could keep that product going, why the constant barrage of new, wilder, more violent, more bizarre video games? The simple answer is this: Interest doesn't last. What alleviates boredom can, in turn, beget boredom" (p. 40).

Teachers also try to motivate students by using students' interests to guide instruction. This practice is central to the learner-directed philosophy. I'm not sure how frequently teachers actually do this, especially with state- and district-mandated standards, but it certainly seems to represent the ideal to most educators. Every nominee for any Teacher of the Year Award I've ever read about claims to use innovative methods to capitalize on students' interests or to allow their students to explore their interests.

At what point, I wonder, do teachers have a responsibility to introduce students to something they aren't interested in? When should teachers insist that students go beyond what they already know? How can a person get interested in something about which he or she knows nothing? How do students acquire new hooks for general knowledge if they only use the hooks they already have to learn more? These questions are particularly important for students who are unlikely to have any exposure to unfamiliar people and places through life experiences.

Rude (2002) suggests that the challenge for teachers is not to find what interests students, but to lay the groundwork for future intellectual pursuits. As described in chapter 3, a certain level of general information is necessary to create and sustain interest in a topic and to promote lifelong learning. For example, I had only one course in world history (actually European history) in ninth grade and I don't remember ever doing one fun thing in that class. Despite the fact that Mr. Wagner's presentation was somewhat dry, when I spent a summer in the British Isles several years after I graduated from college, I had enough general knowledge to spark an interest in the history of the British Empire. I started reading books and, although I never could quite get all those kings and queens straight, developed an interest that persists to this day.

People seldom decide to pursue a new intellectual area out of the blue; they become interested because they find themselves in a situation that reactivates some general knowledge that a teacher thought important years ago. If they have enough general knowledge, they can find out more through experience, by going to the library or looking on the Internet, or taking a class. The more specific knowledge they acquire, the more they are able to learn. Sometimes this positive reciprocal learning cycle leads to a depth of knowledge that allows a person to think critically and analytically. In other words, interest is the *reward of* learning, not the *motivation for* learning.

It's an interesting paradox that bears further consideration. I sometimes wonder if we aren't shortchanging students by trying to entice them into the world of ideas with gimmicky activities, rather than by igniting the pleasure of learning for its own sake. Sometimes it's just fun to know stuff. I have seen children beam when they use a new vocabulary word or share an interesting fact. Motivating students with fun activities eventually may lead to boredom rather than genuine interest. Adults without sufficient general knowledge are not lifelong learners, and they are unlikely to have many intellectual interests.

Competence Requires Practice

People forget that smooth and effortless performance in anything comes with a price. Nothing that is worth learning is learned easily. "All evidence . . . indicates that real competence only comes with extensive practice. By denying the critical role of practice, one is denying children the very thing they need to achieve competence" (Anderson, Reder, & Simon, 2000, p. 13). Teachers who stress practice of lower-level skills (the derisive term is "drill and kill") are considered drill sergeants, but practice is necessary to achieve fluency. Good teachers know how to provide necessary drill without killing motivation or dampening enthusiasm. We all recognize fluency in accomplished performers. They are able to make the right moves without apparent effort. When Ray Seigel, the host of *All Things Considered* (National Public Radio, 1997), asked the late Ray Charles what he played when he practiced, he answered, to Seigel's surprise, that he practiced the scales. He explained why. "You gotta practice. I mean, you gotta keep your fingers loose, you gotta keep your mind active, you know, because what your mind thinks of—the question is: what your mind thinks of, can your fingers play?"

Fluency goes beyond accuracy. It is accuracy plus speed. Our traditional reliance on accuracy only, in the form of percentages, does not distinguish between students who have learned a skill, but still perform it with hesitation, and those who are fluent. Failure to make this distinction underlies many educational failures (Binder, Haughton, & Bateman, 2002). Students "progress by building one non-fluent skill on top of another until the whole skill set becomes 'top heavy' and falls apart" (p. 3). At that point, learning a subject becomes too difficult to be enjoyable and students may respond to this stressful learning situation by becoming inattentive, misbehaving, or failing to complete homework and other assignments. All of these consequences are predictable. If the teacher responds by making the learning more fun and interesting or by reducing accountability, the problem is solved in the short term, but the real issue remains unaddressed and the long-term result is low academic achievement.

The ability to perform skills fluently is related to students' ability to retain information and skills so they don't need to be continually retaught. For example, students whose performance is fluent will retain information and skills over summer vacation. It is also related to the ability to apply skills in more difficult and creative situations. In other words, it facilitates generalization. The goal of fluency is not just to do something fast, it is to do something well and without effort in order to accomplish a task that is more complex and creative—or, in Ray Charles' parlance, to make sure the fingers can do what the creative mind tells them to.

Fluency is also called "automaticity" in the professional literature. Automaticity is achieved when an individual can process information without consciously paying attention. Automaticity in lower-level skills is important because it frees attention from thinking about lower-level skills and enables learners to think about more complex skills. Many physical skills must be learned at the automatic level—driving, keyboarding, walking. Anyone who engages in sports or the performing arts knows that many physical skills must be mastered at the automatic level.

A critical academic skill that must be mastered at the automatic level is decoding. In order for an individual to understand a text, he or she must be able to think about what the words *mean*, not what the words *are*. Slow, labored reading of the words indicates that a student is not an automatic decoder. There is only one way to move from accurate to fluent performance of a skill—practice. There are ways to make practice challenging and interesting to students. Setting goals and graphing improvement, varying the practice activities, creating friendly competition, and peer tutoring are but a few of the teaching procedures that have been very effective in motivating students to engage in repetitious tasks to achieve mastery.

SUMMARY

School doesn't need to be fun and interesting all the time, and it definitely doesn't need to be easy. Intellectual growth requires the same sustained hard work and effort as athletic or musical endeavors. Although teachers should try to make learning as interesting as possible, attempts to motivate students through entertainment may be misguided.

Although there is nothing wrong with making lessons interesting, too many activities or those of questionable value end up reducing opportunities to learn. The real issue is not whether lessons are active and tactile, but whether they are relevant. In addition, interest that is based on novelty may be short-lived. Lifelong learners need to have enough general information that they feel comfortable stepping beyond the confines of their everyday experience. Not only do lifelong learners need background information to engage in complex thinking tasks, they need to have mastery of lower-level skills that enable them to perform complex cognitive tasks with ease. The myth of fun and interesting dovetails nicely with the myth of process, making it incompatible with a science of teaching.

5

The Myth of Eclectic Instruction

What surprised [him] most early in his career were the legions of "lone rangers"—teachers who create their own curriculum and teach pretty much what they damned well please. "The problem is that the lone rangers are often the best teachers, creative and passionate," he says. "But American teachers act like independent artisans. There is no sense of clear cohesiveness."

—Interview with a retiring principal in the *Boston Globe*,
March 31, 2002

The myth of eclectic instruction refers to the practice of using a variety of methods and instructional materials instead of relying on a single instructional approach. Eclectic instruction is primarily an issue of curriculum. Curriculum can be defined in many different ways depending on one's perspective. My definition is that curricula are the means for achieving the outcomes specified in state standards. Curricula refer to instructional materials that contain lesson plans and other suggestions for teaching the content. Curriculum is the invisible lynchpin that holds instruction together, and its strength depends on how well it is designed, its level of specificity, and the extent to which it has been field-tested or validated. Curricula that have all three components provide the best opportunity for teachers to reach all children and they are fundamentally incompatible with eclectic instruction.

Curriculum can be teacher-designed or designed by experts and published as a comprehensive core program for teaching language arts or mathematics (developmental basal), textbook, supplemental or remedial instructional program. School districts almost always purchase developmental basals that provide the curricula for teaching language arts and mathematics in grades K–8 and textbooks for other content areas at all grade levels. Sometimes teachers design their own curriculum to meet standards and these programs are necessarily eclectic. More often, however, teachers create eclectic instructional programs by combining published programs with their own creative additions or combining more than one published program. A well-designed curriculum is more than the sum of its parts, but eclectic instruction tends to be a collection of loose-fitting pieces.

Think of it this way. Well-designed curricula are like compounds whose components form an entirely new entity, the way that sodium and chloride combine to make salt. On the other hand, the best eclectic combinations are mixtures, like salt dissolved in water. H_2O and $NaCl$ can be mixed, but each retains its own identity. Too many eclectic curricula, however, are like oil and water. The components are incompatible.

Curricula can also be more or less specific. More specific curricula dictate exactly what the teacher should do and say. A curriculum that is very specific is often referred to as a prescriptive curriculum. Less specific curricula leave more room for teacher improvisation and encourage teachers to pick and choose. Nonprescriptive curricula are much more conducive to eclectic instruction.

Finally, curricula can be validated or not. Validated curricula are part of the science of teaching. They are subject to field-testing as they are developed. The completed curriculum is then tested in classrooms and compared to other similar programs. Researchers assess student achievement to determine the curriculum's effectiveness. Few curricula are field-tested during development and fewer still undergo comparison research to evaluate their effectiveness. Eclectic instruction cannot be validated because it isn't standardized. Results will vary enormously depending on which components teachers use and how they use them.

I understand the appeal of eclectic instruction. If someone had asked me 30 years ago to explain my philosophy of education, I would have said

I was eclectic. I continued to be eclectic until I figured out that eclectic meant that I was too uninformed to believe in anything. At some point in my graduate studies, I learned enough about history, philosophy, pedagogy, psychology, and research to formulate a philosophy of teaching and establish some criteria for identifying best practices. In our survey, close to 80% of both teachers and teacher educators expressed strong support for eclectic instruction. Other studies also confirm that most teachers use an eclectic instructional program (Baumann, Hoffman, Moon, & Duffy-Hester, 1998; Stahl, Osborn, & Pearson, 1994; Zalud & Richardson, 1994). Despite the popularity of so-called eclectic instruction, reliance on an assortment of methods and materials rather than on one sound instructional program is not necessarily beneficial to students. Looking back on my own career, I am certain that my propensity to dabble, even after I got my master's degree, reduced my effectiveness.

Michael Feldman, the host of the radio program *Whad'Ya Know* (Wisconsin Public Radio, 2002) had the following conversation about eclectic instruction with a second-grade teacher from the audience. It went like this.

MF: Ya' know, I've noticed my daughter has become an excellent, she's in grade 2 now, she's become an excellent reader but she can't write. Isn't there a connection between reading and writing?

T: Yes, there's a connection.

MF: When does that kick in?

T: The connection kick in?

MF: The spelling part of it.

T: Well, it depends on how much of an intuitive speller she is. Some people are real intuitive and spell well.

MF: Not an intuitive speller. So why do we have teachers then?

T: We can inspire it, influence it, and support it.

MF: You can't make it happen? Well, what are we paying you for?

[They talk about phonics and the teachers confesses that she teaches whole language and phonics. Michael is surprised to hear that she teaches phonics.]

T: We have a very eclectic approach. We take the best of every different approach and combine them.

MF: And none of it works.

Michael Feldman seems to understand something that the teacher does not.

Eclectic instruction is particularly problematic at the elementary level where children must learn foundation skills in reading, writing, and mathematics that will serve them for the rest of their lives. Understanding how to teach beginning reading, writing, or mathematics is not obvious from the perspective of a skilled reader, writer, or problem solver. Researchers have only recently unraveled the secrets of beginning reading. We now know that effective beginning reading instruction is completely counterintuitive. The things that skilled readers do when they read, like skip over words or use context, are not the things that beginning readers should do when they are first learning to read. When teachers use an eclectic approach, they may inadvertently use teaching procedures that are not helpful.

There are understandable reasons that teachers use eclectic instruction. One reason is that most teachers don't know how to evaluate instructional programs wisely. I would put my younger self in this category. Being eclectic was a way of hedging, of not making a big mistake. If one approach didn't work, then another one might. I didn't know enough about curriculum to make confident decisions until after I attended graduate school. I had neither a philosophy of teaching nor a basis for judging which of the curriculum materials on my shelves worked and which ones didn't.

Another understandable reason for using an eclectic approach is that the curriculum on the shelves, the one the district has adopted or that the previous teacher ordered, may be incomplete or ineffective. Teachers may see eclectic instruction as a way to compensate for perceived weaknesses in one approach (Heward, 2003). They may need to bolster district-mandated curricula since textbooks are woefully inadequate by almost everybody's standards (Burress, 1989; DelFattore, 1992; Loewen, 1995; Schmidt, Houang, & Cogan, 2002; Schmidt et al., 2001; Sewall, 2003; Tyson-Bernstein, 1988). This is true in almost all subject areas.

Similar criticisms have been leveled at comprehensive basal programs in language arts and mathematics. Few basals have been subjected to empirical validation or even field-testing. The content of basal reading programs tends to be guided by what sells, rather than what works. For example, almost all reading basals were aligned with the whole language philosophy from about 1985 until 2000, even though the California fiasco and subsequent research revealed that they were ineffective with large numbers of students.

It's hard to know if eclectic instruction is popular because curricula are so uniformly inadequate, or if curricula are inadequate because teachers prefer eclectic instruction. Creating curricular concoctions seems to give teachers a sense of flexibility, control, and creativity, but it is also very time-consuming. Although eclectic instruction enjoys universal acceptance, it is based on a number of faulty premises that bear further examination.

FAULTY PREMISES

One faulty premise underlying the myth of eclectic instruction is that learning is natural, which I discussed in chapter 3. If one believes that learning is natural, an eclectic assortment of methods and curricula is sufficient because, as the second-grade teacher told Michael Feldman, teachers cannot make learning happen. They can only "inspire it, influence it, and support it." There is no urgency to develop a set of teaching tools, methods, and curricula to hasten or alter the natural trajectory of learning because *que sera, sera*; what will be, will be. The problem with this premise is that academic learning is not natural, and discovery is an ineffective and inefficient way to learn.

Three additional faulty premises will be discussed in this chapter. The first is that selecting appropriate methods and curricula depends more on student characteristics than on what is to be learned. I argue that decisions about how and what to teach are best determined by the nature of the content, and that the only student characteristic that is relevant for making instructional decisions is student performance. A second faulty premise is that teaching is not technical, and that attempts to make it so are demeaning to teachers and students. A final faulty premise is that no one approach works for all students. Educators often recite this mantra in defense of learning style, but it implies that all instructional approaches have equal merit, which is simply not true.

Student Characteristics Should Guide Instruction

One of the first things that preservice teachers are directed to do in their field experiences is to make a list of the students in a class they are observing and identify their diverse characteristics. The ostensible purpose of this activity is to accommodate student diversity in their lesson plans. This common assignment in teacher preparation programs illustrates the prevailing attitude about the importance of student characteristics for planning instruction. From a learner-directed perspective, especially the philosophy of constructivism, the content is only important in relationship to the learner because no two learners get exactly the same meaning from any given task. Content is relative.

I'm not sure how useful this activity is, however, because the primary *curriculum* question is "What do students need to learn and what's the best way to make sure they learn it?" *not* "Who am I teaching the skill to?" The first question is important because academic learning does not occur naturally. It occurs as a result of deliberate teaching acts designed to promote learning. All other things being equal, the better the curriculum and the presentation, the more all students will learn. The second question is less important because most student characteristics are irrelevant for planning instruction.

Everyone would probably agree that characteristics like height, weight, hair, and eye color don't matter, but what about race, IQ, disability, or socioeconomic status? Many people claim that student interest should guide instruction, but I argued in the previous chapter that interest can as easily be a result of instruction. Relevant preskills and background knowledge will influence success or failure on any academic task, but do those differences change the *way* content is presented? Or do they just change the starting point?

Performance deficits caused by lack of prior knowledge can be addressed by teaching missing preskills or background information, and low skill levels can be addressed by providing additional repetition, more examples, structure, encouragement, and motivation. High skill levels can be addressed by less practice, enrichment, and greater independence. These adaptations do not necessarily require a different curriculum. The organization of the content doesn't need to change. What both high and low performers need is a curriculum that is structured so well that most students consistently perform well when they possess adequate preskills and the teacher's presentation is engaging.

For example, one of the critical features that children must attend to in reading (among many others that are less obvious) is to associate an abstract visual symbol—for example, *b*—with a sound, *buh*. That's it. It doesn't matter whether one is teaching a low performer or a high performer, a child or an adult, a doll or a dog. The task is the same, and it's not a task that can be ignored. A person can do other things at the same time, like say the sound while tracing the letter in shaving cream or looking at the letter on a computer screen while the computer says *buh* or looking at an alphabet book that shows the letter *b* while an adult says the sound—but the relevant detail in any of those activities is associating the symbol with the sound. It's the task; everything else is just fluff. The more fluff there is, the more likely it is that children will miss the connection: the letter that looks like this—*b*—says *buh*.

On the other hand, one cannot expect naive learners to associate the sound and the symbol if the task doesn't demonstrate the connection. You can't make barbequed beef on a bun, or throw a big ball, or sing a song about bananas bouncing, or balance a box of beans on a bug, or have children twist their bodies in the shape of a *b,* or trace, glue, and sprinkle glitter to make *b* and expect children to associate the sound with the symbol because nothing in those activities associates the symbol with the sound. The presentation has got to make sense given the nature of the task, regardless of the student's unique characteristics. Teachers must monitor individual differences in performance, but first they should reflect on what it is they are trying to teach and consider if the presentation makes sense.

Teaching Is Not Technical

All subject areas—reading, mathematics, writing, biology, history, English, literature—are complex, and designing curriculum that teaches the content in a way that allows naive learners to both understand and remember is equally complex. This is particularly true at the elementary level where the most basic, but essential, curriculum components may not be obvious from the perspective of an adult. Although the myth of eclectic instruction suggests that curriculum is more artful than technical, writing curriculum in any subject and at any level is very technical.

Curriculum design relies on principles extracted from research in behavioral, cognitive, and social psychology. Different authors describe these principles differently, but the gist is the same. Ellis, Worthington, and Larkin (1994) described the following six principles relevant to instructional design:

a. provide scaffolded instruction,
b. address different knowledge forms,
c. use techniques to help learners organize, store, and retrieve information,
d. teach strategies to promote independence,
e. teach explicitly, and
f. highlight sameness within and across subject areas to promote generalization.

In a sense, the best curricula are eclectic in that they draw on the best available information about teaching and learning, but that is not the definition of eclectic that most people associate with eclectic instruction and it is not the definition that I am using here.

The best curriculum begins with an analysis of the content and works backwards to identify all the parts and how they all fit together. The content analysis helps developers extract the big ideas, develop strategies, and determine goals and objectives. They provide explanations and select examples that will communicate concepts and ideas unambiguously, integrate related content so that it is meaningful, and scaffold the presentation of new information so that it builds on prior knowledge and does not overwhelm naive learners. Different types of knowledge are best taught in specific ways. For example, the teaching procedures are different for simple facts versus rule relationships versus concepts (Kameenui & Simmons, 1990). Lower-level forms of knowledge must be systematically integrated over time to form cognitive strategies, which are in turn combined to facilitate generalization. The details are important, and they cannot be left to chance if all children are to succeed. If it seems complicated, it's because it is!

The reason that curricula must be specific is because designing them is so complex. Every procedure, every skill, and every fact should be included for a reason. It's like a blueprint. It must be very specific, and if the teacher doesn't follow it exactly, then the actual outcome will be different from the intended outcome.

Good curricula are based on complex theories of learning, but they are only theories. As programs are designed, they should undergo field-testing by classroom teachers who observe student performance and provide feedback to the authors. Ideally, the curriculum undergoes independent evaluations to determine if it is effective. Instructional programs that follow this process are extremely rare, but there is no reason they should be.

The chick-sexing experiment described in chapter 3 provides a very simple illustration of instructional design. Based on his knowledge of chick-sexing, Mr. Carlson analyzed the task and figured out that it essentially involved identifying convex versus concave or flat shapes. That was a big idea. Then he communicated the specific critical features to naive learners in five sketches and a brief explanation. The curriculum was effective because it immediately boosted performance of naive learners from 59% to 84% on the chick-sexing task. Content analysis in reading, mathematics, or history is considerably more complicated, but the process should be similar.

A small number of curricula have been developed that use this process of analysis and research, but most educators shun them. Teachers want to be facilitators (myth of process) and eclectic instruction feels more "facilitative" than sticking to one prescribed curriculum. The focus on process rather than outcomes promotes exploration and improvisation, which is more consistent with eclectic than deliberate curriculum choices. The continuing need for novelty (myth of fun) creates a need to draw from a variety of sources to renew motivation. Eclectic instruction also provides an outlet for teachers' creativity. They get bored sticking with one prescribed curriculum, no matter how effective.

Teachers accept district-mandated basals and textbooks with the implicit understanding that they are only guides. In fact, most curricula invite teachers to pick and choose and teachers have been conditioned to think of curricula as optional because, on the whole, they are of poor quality. Certainly all curriculum decisions must pass through a teacher's brain, but curricula that are carefully designed, very specific, and validated understandably work best when teachers follow them exactly. Picking and choosing or combining to create an eclectic mixture will nullify all the careful analysis, design, and research that has gone into creating the original effective curricula.

Educators believe that teaching is a creative endeavor that should not be standardized in any way. They vigorously resist the idea that there is anything technical about teaching and they reject prescriptive practices and procedures as insulting. But I don't think that teaching is any different from any other profession in that manner. Standardized procedures, and repeated practice with using them, ensure that the client will be well served. The creativity comes from solving unforeseen or difficult problems, not from deviating from procedures that work or inventing new ones that may not.

Technical expertise results from performing a task over and over the same way. Not everything can be creative all the time. I don't want my surgeon to get creative in the middle of a procedure. Imagine the scene in the operating room. "Hey, let's try something really creative today. Has anybody here ever done an appendectomy by going through the back? Flip her over. Let's give it a try!" (Sprick, 1992, p. 11). I don't want my auto mechanic getting creative, either. Something as mundane as the spark plug gap can affect a car's performance, just as something as mundane as the sound of the letter *b* can affect student performance. I don't want the people I go to for professional services to be having too much fun. I want them to have technical expertise. Teachers provide a professional service to children and there is nothing wrong with following standardized procedures for teaching *if they work*.

The fact that teachers have a negative attitude toward anything that seems too "technical" is further evidence of their *bricoleur* status. No other profession rejects the technical expertise that provides the tools for solving problems the way education does. Chronic underachievement, especially among certain groups of students, will continue until a shared body of technical expertise is known, accepted, and incorporated into published curriculum, and until teachers view such curricula as useful tools rather than a ball and chain.

No One Approach Works for All Students

It may be overstating the case to say that a single curricular approach works for all students (there is more than one particular program that works and no doubt there are some student exceptions), but some teaching practices work better than others. Nowhere is this clearer than in the area of beginning reading. After screening and reviewing research on beginning reading, the National Reading Panel (National Institute of Child Health and Human Development, 2000) issued recommendations about best practices in teaching beginning reading. There are five critical components for teaching beginning reading to all children—phonemic awareness, phonics, fluency, vocabulary, and comprehension (Armbruster, Lehr, & Osborn, 2001).

The National Reading Panel recommended that phonics instruction should be explicit and systematic. They also cautioned that encouraging children to use picture and context clues, or to guess or to skip words, was inadvisable since it distracted children from the more difficult task of interpreting the alphabetic symbols. Once decoding is effortless, the focus of the reader will shift and the focus of instruction should shift to reading for meaning. This is true for all children, not just those with certain learning styles or other characteristics.

All five components should be emphasized from the beginning, but I'll just focus on one of the five components—phonics—to make it easier to illustrate the fact that some approaches work better than others. Just because a curriculum *includes* phonics doesn't mean that it actually *teaches* phonics. It's also important to remember that just because a curriculum teaches *phonics* doesn't mean it teaches *reading* because all of the other components need to be effectively taught and fit together with the others to make an integrated whole. I'll describe three curricula that teach phonics ineffectively, one that teaches phonics effectively, and a group of curricula that doesn't teach phonics at all.

Whole language is a failed approach to reading instruction that became widely popular in the 1980s. It was implemented in California with disastrous results, as described in chapter 3. Whole language was based on the idea that learning to read and spell was natural, just as learning to talk is natural, and that skills such as phonics (as well as spelling and punctuation) could be learned naturally. Some people mistakenly think that whole language teachers did not teach phonics. Not true, they just didn't teach it well. They taught phonics "as needed" in the form of mini-lessons. The amount and nature of phonics instruction was pretty much left up to the teacher, although too much phonics or phonics in isolation was thought to be harmful. It was a truly eclectic approach. Teachers encouraged beginning readers to use strategies that seemed intuitively correct from their perspective as a skilled reader, but that we now know were counterproductive. Teachers encouraged children to use context and pictures clues, to skip words, and to guess. Looking carefully at the letters or sounding out was discouraged, even though researchers now know that it is important for children to attend to letters and letter combinations during the early stages of learning to read.

Before whole language, however, there were many popular curricula associated with very different philosophical perspectives that taught phonics more explicitly but just as badly. When I arrived at my very first teaching position in 1971, there were three reading curricula on the shelves. All three taught explicit phonics. The first was called *Programmed Reading*, a self-paced linguistic series that used word families to teach phonics. Students answered items in a workbook independently and checked their answers by sliding down a cardboard strip in the margin. Workbook items were fill-in-the-blank and multiple-choice. The program also provided some small hard-cover storybooks that narrated the adventures of Sam and Ann. Although some modest reading gains were reported in the literature (Aukerman, 1971), the high degree of independence coupled with the temptation to peek at the answers reduced the effectiveness of the program and it disappeared fairly quickly.

The second curriculum was the *Initial Teaching Alphabet*, popularly known as i/t/a, in which phonetic orthography was used to make English completely regular. For example, *a* as in face was written as *ae*, *a* as in father was a, *a* as in ball was *au*, and *a* as in cap was *a*. The i/t/a represented 40 sounds with absolute consistency. The idea was intriguing, but the problem came when children had to make the transition to the regular English orthography at the end of a year. Although testimonials and some limited research studies indicated that children learned to read using the i/t/a orthography, there was little evidence that children transferred their knowledge to the traditional English orthography (Aukerman, 1971). It, too, faded away.

Luckily for me, I had a third curriculum on my shelves that actually taught phonics well. The third curriculum was DISTAR, which stands for *Direct Instruction Systems for Teaching Arithmetic and Reading*. One of the reasons that DISTAR was so successful was that it not only taught phonics in a systematic and explicit way (30 years before the National Reading Panel issued its report), it also included the other components necessary for decoding. It taught phonemic awareness ("say the sounds in *man* the slow way, then say it fast"); explicit, systematic phonics (pointing to the letter *a*, "this letter says *aaaaaa*"), and fluency (timed checkouts were included every fifth lesson). It has been revised and updated and is now called *Reading Mastery* (Engelmann & Bruner, 2003).

Reading Mastery was designed using the process of analysis and research described earlier in the chapter. It is often cited as one of the few beginning reading programs with a long record of research that supports its effectiveness (Adams & Engelmann, 1996; Stebbins et al., 1977; White, 1988). I feel fortunate to have stumbled into a classroom that had DISTAR. Because I had an effective curriculum, I felt like an effective teacher. That first year established an expectation that all children, even those with disabilities, could learn to read.

Programs that don't teach phonics at all simply don't teach children to read. They are neither validated through research nor theoretically sound. They do not even contain the components recommended by the National Reading Panel. In my early eclecticism, I dabbled in something called "process approaches" to beginning reading. The underlying premise of process approaches is that learning problems are caused by perceptual problems, especially visual perception, and teachers must remediate the perceptual problems before children can learn academic tasks. The perceptual programs I used addressed reading problems by having students do exercises and walk on balance beams, hit a Styrofoam ball suspended on a string with something that looked like a rolling pin, complete eye training exercises and paper-and-pencil activities like copying shapes or finding embedded figures or connecting the dots.

These approaches seem silly now, but were widely used in special education well into the 1980s. In 1986, the Council for Learning Disabilities issued a statement that specifically advised educators to shun process approaches. Interestingly, the past decade has seen a resurgence of interest in vision training despite a policy statement issued jointly by the American Academy of Pediatrics, American Association for Pediatric Ophthalmology and Strabismus, and American Academy of Ophthalmology indicating that "no scientific evidence exists for the efficacy of eye exercises ('vision therapy') or the use of special tinted lenses in the remediation of these complex pediatric neurological conditions" (Policy statement, 1998).

Newer process approaches keep making their way into American classrooms. Other process approaches to treating reading disabilities include

Irlen lenses, the Tomatis method, Davis Correction method, DORE Achievement Centers, and Brain Gym, to name just a few. The list of unproven methods that try to remediate perceptual difficulties presumed to be the root of reading disabilities is endless. These are not obscure. I often see them used as part of an eclectic approach when I am out in the schools supervising student teachers.

Not all curricula are effective; some are ineffective and some are downright criminal. A validated curriculum won't work the *same* for all students and for all teachers, but there is a high probability that it will work better than other alternatives. Effective instructional programs are painstakingly designed based on an analysis of the content followed by field-testing and independent research. Eclectic instruction tends to be based on irrelevant factors such as student characteristics and designed with more whim than technical expertise. This haphazard approach leads to some predictable problems.

THE HARM THAT IS DONE

When teachers design their own instructional programs or when teachers combine approaches or separate parts from the whole program, the result may be ineffective instruction. This can happen for a number of reasons. As is usually the case, use of eclectic instruction differentially affects low-performing students because they are ones most in need of clear and consistent instruction.

Components From Different Approaches May Be Incompatible

Whole language advocates were understandably unhappy with the recommendations of the National Reading Panel because whole language is essentially incompatible with the recommendation to use explicit, systematic phonics. Under pressure to support research-based practice but unwilling to reject their ideology, reading teachers have advanced a "balanced approach" to reading instruction that retains whole language teaching practices while appearing to incorporate the research-based conclusions of the panel. The balanced approach is neither balanced nor desirable. Louisa Moats (2000) summarized the problem.

[Direct, systematic phonics] is not equivalent to an eclectic combination of whole language and phonics. Whole-language approaches by definition minimize or omit direct, systematic teaching of language structure (phoneme awareness, spelling patterns and rules, grammar, and so forth) in the name of preserving an unbroken focus on reading for meaning. To the onlooker, these points may sound trivial; in the classroom, however, such distinctions have profound consequences. (p. 6)

Explicit, systematic phonics means that the sounds of the letters are pronounced in isolation (the letter you are looking at says *aaaaaa*) and they are presented in a deliberate sequence. Explicit phonics is fundamentally incompatible with whole language, which emphasizes teaching phonics in context (not in isolation) and as needed by the learner (rather than in predetermined logical sequence). This hasn't stopped whole language advocates from suggesting that "phonics in context is both systematic and explicit" (Dahl, Scharer, Lawson, & Grogan, 2001, p. ix). It isn't!

Balanced literacy also emphasizes meaning from the very beginning, which means encouraging students to use context and pictures, and to guess. Children are encouraged to skip a word if they don't know it and read to the end of the line to see if they can figure it out. This is incompatible with explicit, systematic phonics instruction because when children begin learning to read, they must attend to the letters. Attention to the letters is critical for automatic word recognition because skilled readers recognize familiar word patterns and groups of letters (Adams, 1990). To encourage beginning readers to use context clues sabotages all phonics instruction.

Consider the following example of teaching phonics in context taken from *Rethinking Phonics* (Dahl et al., 2001, p. 6). A child, Daniel, misreads the sentence *Five tigers clawing* as *Four tigers scratch*.

MRS. ORLICH: That's what the picture shows. (She then points to the word *clawing* and keeps her finger there.)

DANIEL: C, L, c-l (pauses).

MRS. ORLICH: What does *a-w* say? *aw*.

DANIEL: *Cl-aw*, four tigers clawing.

MRS. ORLICH: Look at the picture.

Daniel looks at the illustration of five tigers and then back at the word *five*, but does not correct his mistake. Possibly he can't count any better than he can read. Mrs. Orlich leads Daniel back to the picture, which is same strategy that got him into trouble in the first place. Looking at the picture caused him to substitute the word *scratch* for *claw*. The words are not visually similar at all. The next time Daniel encounters the word *claw* or *four*, he is unlikely to know the word.

Whole language and explicit, systematic phonics are incompatible. They are like oil and water. An eclectic approach that tries to combine two such approaches is doomed to failure.

Teachers May Not Choose the Effective Parts of a Program

Picking and choosing appropriate components of different curricula is a risky strategy because it requires a deep understanding of both content and teaching methods, especially in beginning reading. Most elementary teachers are unprepared to teach beginning reading (Moats, 1995; 1999) and over 40% of new teachers reported that they felt unprepared to teach reading (Meister & Melnick, 2003). The nature of beginning reading is not intuitively obvious. Skilled reading happens too fast and too automatically for readers to be aware of how our brains make sense of the squiggles on the page. Skilled readers focus on reading for meaning, but the processes involved in beginning to decipher the code are essentially non-meaningful.

In an attempt to integrate phonemic awareness and phonics into a basal reading program with a weak phonics component, teachers often turn to supplementary texts and workbooks. This can present problems with the sequence of instruction. For example, there is a hierarchy of phonemic skills that starts with blending (teachers says *mmmmm-aaaaa-nnnnn* and the students says "man") and segmenting (teacher says "man" and the student says *mmmmm-aaaaa-nnnnn*) and ending with phoneme manipulation tasks (teachers says the word monkey, and asks what word will be left if you take away the *kuh* sound). Researchers agree that blending and segmenting are critical skills for future success in reading and spelling, but aren't sure about the role of phoneme manipulation tasks (Adams, 1990). Teachers without sufficient background knowledge may decide to teach difficult phoneme manipulation tasks that are of questionable value. When picking and choosing from supplementary materials, teachers are more likely to select fun activities like rhyming games (which require phoneme manipulation) or riddles and stories that use alliteration rather than the overt segmenting and blending described above that many children need to become proficient.

Traditional phonics worksheets are another way that teachers often try to squeeze phonics into an eclectic reading program. These worksheets typically show a picture and require a child to choose or write the beginning sound. (For example, a goat is pictured and the child writes or circles the letter *g*.) The first problem with these worksheets is that in order for them to be beneficial, a teacher or someone else must have the child say the word out loud emphasizing the first sound. It is virtually impossible to teach phonics, a fundamentally auditory task, with a paper-and-pencil worksheet that is completed independently. A second problem with these worksheets is that it is a form of implicit, not explicit, phonics. The child must segment the sounds in the word (*guh-oooo-tah*) in order to find the sound at the beginning. If the child has not yet developed phonemic awareness, the ability to segment sounds in words, the phonics activity will be worthless.

Picking and choosing parts of programs wisely depends on teachers' understanding of the content they are trying to teach. Teachers may unwittingly pick and choose activities that, although they are not harmful, do not yield a valuable learning outcome. They may turn out to be a waste of instructional time.

Isolated Components May Not Be Effective

Teaching letter sounds in isolation is a fairly common practice, but it may not be effective unless coupled with other important beginning reading activities. Children easily learn that *b* makes the sound *buh* as in bat, but so what? To them it's just another one of those things that adults make them memorize—like the names of the colors or their address or that sheep go baa or that apples are fruit. Information about letter sounds is only useful when children (a) understand that words are comprised of sounds (phonemic awareness) and (b) understand that letter sounds can be used to read and spell words (sounding out). Otherwise, they're just sounds.

Teachers need to present early reading skills in an integrated fashion to facilitate generalization. For example, once children have learned the sounds of *m*, *s*, *a*, and *d*, they can read the words *mad*, *sad*, *sam, am,* and *dam*. By the time they know 12 common letters (*a, m, s, d, f, o, t, c, n, i, g,* and *u*) along with irregular words (*is* and *the*), they can begin reading short stories that are completely decodable. For example, "Sam is a cat. The cat is fat. Tag is not a cat. Tag is a dog. Tag and Sam sit in the sun and dig." It's not great literature, but to a young child, using the sounds he or she has learned to read a text passage is enormously motivating. It helps children understand why sounding out is important, and it also provides opportunities to use their developing word attack skills. Without the application, children are likely to fall back on word recognition strategies that are easier and more familiar, like guessing or using picture clues.

When skills are taught in isolation as part of an eclectic approach, teachers risk fragmenting instruction in a way that either neglects important preskills or lacks sufficient context to ensure that students will know how to generalize the newly learned information.

Skills Might Be Taught at the Wrong Time

Some parts of a program may only be effective at a certain point in the learning process. The use of context clues provides a good example to illustrate this point. The National Reading Panel makes it very clear that beginning readers should *not* be encouraged to use context in order to figure out how to pronounce a word. Use of context—syntactical and pictures clues that lead to guessing—is not an effective word identification strategy. "This finding is one of the most consistent and well-replicated in all of reading research. It has been found with all types of readers, in all types of texts, and in a variety of different paradigms" (Stanovitch, 1993, p. 282). What's more, less skilled readers tend to overrely on context because they lack the necessary decoding skills to read the word based on its spelling. This contrasts sharply with the appropriate use of context—after a word has been decoded. Skilled readers do make use of context, but appropriately, after a word has been identified, to figure out the meaning or to confirm that a word was identified correctly.

The eclectic or "balanced" approach to phonics often leads children back to context for word identification. The following example is typical.

The teacher and student are reading the sentence *Lamb had no mother* (Dahl et al., 2001, p. 56).

MARTY: (reading slowly) Lamb heard on mother.

MRS. ORLICH: Does that make sense?

MARTY: Lamb heard NO mother.

Mrs. Orlich points to the letters of *had* to focus attention. She keeps her fingers under the word.

MRS. ORLICH: Does that make sense?

MARTY: Lamb HAD no mother.

By asking if the word makes sense, the teacher leads Marty back to a strategy (use of context) that is not useful for word recognition. Besides, *had* is a regular word that should be decodable once children know the most common sound of the letters *h*, *a*, and *d*. To lead Marty back to context by asking if the sentence makes sense does not teach him anything about letter-sound correspondences or sounding out.

In another year, however, after Marty is a fluent reader, it would be appropriate for Mrs. Orlich to help him use context to figure out the *meaning* of words. For example, "Sarah ate only a *morsel* of food. She wasn't very hungry." The context provides clues as to the meaning of the word *morsel* if the reader does not know the definition after having pronounced the word. It would be appropriate to ask Marty, "What do you think *morsel* means?"

A danger of eclectic approaches is that teachers will use a perfectly acceptable teaching procedure before or after it is developmentally appropriate, rendering it ineffective. This, once again, highlights the need for teachers to understand of the scope and sequence of their content area, which may not be entirely obvious, especially in the primary grades.

Using Multiple Explanations May Confuse Naive Learners

A common misconception is that using a variety of explanations and teaching procedures will increase the likelihood that every child "gets it." The rationale is that different explanations or teaching procedures will make sense to different children depending on their learning styles. It reminds me of firing a barrage at a target and hoping one will hit rather than carefully aiming for the bull's eye. There are two errors in this way of thinking. First, tailoring instruction to the learner rather making it fit what is to be learned is inadvisable, as described earlier. Second, multiple explanations are more likely to lead to confusion than to clarity. Naive learners have difficulty recognizing synonyms because of their poor vocabulary knowledge. When the teacher uses different language to re-explain a concept, the naive learner does not recognize the synonyms and instead assumes the teacher is on a new topic. Naive learners may hear five different versions without ever picking out the similarity among them or understanding the explanation.

To the naive learner, listening to five different explanations of the same thing is like listening to a jazz rift and trying to pick out the melody. If listeners know the melody, they can identify the melody in the improvisations of the musicians; if they don't know the melody, it's hard to hear it once it's been embellished.

Take the seemingly simple task of learning the most common sound of the letter *b*. Below are just a few of the many different explanations and teaching procedures that one can find in various basals and supplementary phonics programs. Switching terminology will leave naive learners wondering what in world the teacher is saying.

1. "What consonant stands for the final sound in *tab* and *rib*?" (Students may not know the meaning of "consonant," or that "final" means "end.")
2. Brainstorm lists of words that begin (or end) with *b*. Then play a guessing game by asking riddles such as "I'm thinking of a word that means the opposite of small." (Adding a vocabulary exercise to an activity designed to teach the sound of *b* may make the whole activity beyond the conceptual grasp of low-performing students.)
3. Have children say the name of each picture (*box, bat, Bill, big, bee, boy, bag*). Tell students to circle the lowercase letter and draw a line under each uppercase letter. (Using the terminology *uppercase* and *lowercase* will surely confuse learners.)

Teaching vowel sounds provides even more opportunity for confusing terminology.

4. Some words have the short *a* vowel sound, as in *cat*. (short *a*? vowel?)
5. Find the long *a* words on the page that name things you would find at home. (long *a*?)
6. Tell the students that Mr. B wants to introduce his friend, Ms. U, who is a letterlight. (Letterlight is another word for vowel.)

These examples show how easy it is to confuse children when teaching a very simple skill. There is an almost endless number of ways to confuse children when teaching more sophisticated concepts. Here's a novel idea. What if the teacher just showed the lowercase *b* (skip uppercase for the time being) and said, "This [point] says *buh*. What sound?" Do that until children know the sound of *b*. During initial instruction, keep it simple, stick to the melody. Don't embellish.

Altering a Well-Designed Curriculum May Render It Ineffective

Using only parts of a well-designed curriculum or using it too briefly may render it ineffective. This final harmful effect of using eclectic instruction doesn't happen very often because it is only a danger for those few teachers who are using an effective, validated program. An effective curriculum won't work if it's not used correctly and in its entirety. *Reading Mastery* (Engelmann & Bruner, 2003) is a program that is used quite a bit in special education, so I get an opportunity to observe teachers who use this program when I supervise student teachers. I have watched in horror as teachers massacre this highly effective program by skipping parts of the lesson, not using the program every day, not adhering to mastery criteria, or by improvising. In other words, by using it as part of an eclectic approach.

Using only parts of the *Reading Mastery* basal reading program renders a highly effective program completely ineffective. Teachers may omit parts of a lesson because of time considerations, but in my experience they are more likely to leave out the parts that are difficult for students. One day I was watching a student teacher teach reading to a group of first-grade students. I noticed that she left out the part in which students were supposed to say the sounds in a word, like *mat* (mmmm aaaaa tuh). When I asked her why she skipped that part she replied, without missing a beat, "because the kids can't do it." Segmenting sounds in words is a critical early reading skill and the fact that they *can't* do it is the very reason they *should* do it. This young teacher did not understand the critical relationship of phonemic awareness to phonics.

Although effective, well-designed instructional programs and textbooks are few and far between, when teachers find one they should use it correctly and consistently in order to maximize the benefit. A teacher who understands the content area can enhance published programs with a variety of carefully chosen supplemental activities, but teachers should avoid skipping parts or doing the lessons inconsistently.

A NASCAR Analogy

Curriculum should be valued, and well-designed, specific, validated curriculum should be prized. Even the best teacher cannot overcome the handicap imposed by a bad curriculum because it is the vehicle for learning. Seigfried Engelmann, lead author of *DISTAR* and *Reading Mastery*, described it this way.

> [Curriculum] is the difference between failure and success. When the curriculum fails, the teaching will fail. Period. This is not to say that if an excellent curriculum is in place, the teaching will automatically succeed. It means simply that the curriculum is like an automobile. The teacher's behavior is like driving that automobile. If the car is well designed, the teacher has the potential to drive fast and safely. If the curriculum is poorly designed, it will break down no matter how carefully the teacher drives. (Engelmann, 1992, p. 7)

The word *curriculum* derives from words meaning "run a (race) course" (Schmidt et al., 2001, p. 2), so an analogy to stock car racing seems appropriate. Any NASCAR (National Association of Stock Car Automobile Racing) fan can tell you that a driver is only as good as his car. The best driver cannot overcome a car with a mechanical problem. Effective and well-designed curricula empower teachers. Ineffective, poorly designed curricula make even the best teachers feel frustrated. Every driver in every NASCAR race has the ability to win; the drivers know how to drive or they wouldn't be there. The driver who wins is the one with the best car.

What's more, NASCAR drivers rely on the engineers who build the cars. Although the drivers know a good deal about engineering and mechanics, they don't build their own cars. Many educators bristle at the suggestion that teachers be confined to a specific plan designed by someone else. They say that teachers who use systematic (meaning "engineered") curriculum are "robot teachers" (Sizer, 1997) and that forcing "them to teach someone else's prescribed plan . . . cheapens them" (p. 1). It is another way of saying that they "cannot be trusted with their own craft" (p. 1). I would argue that it's not realistic to expect teachers to design instruction and to implement it any more than it would be reasonable to expect racecar drivers to design and build their own cars. The drivers rely on the specialists and no one would accuse Dale Earnhardt Jr. of being a "robot." Designing curriculum is, arguably, as complex and time consuming as designing cars.

Teachers need to understand their curricular vehicles; they need to know how to make repairs, but spending too much time tinkering with the engine means less attention to the more interactive and creative aspects of teaching. Relying on published curricula, if they're well designed, specific, and validated, does not diminish the art of teaching. It frees teachers from the burden of figuring out the details of what content to teach and how to best present the information. It gives them the opportunity to focus on the human richness and diversity of the classroom, to address students' unique academic and social/emotional needs, and to ensure the success of every student. It does not detract; it enhances.

The teacher is the driver, the artist who must react quickly and strategically to situations, and accelerate or decelerate as appropriate, but the teacher is not the engineer. Rather than spend time building primitive combustible engines, teachers need to demand cars that will allow them to drive fast and safely; cars that will allow them to attend to their craft. Teachers can't be expected to design instruction *and* implement lesson plans skillfully and artfully, manage classroom logistics, as well as engage in delicate human relations with students, parents, and colleagues. I think most teachers would welcome more effective curricula, but these curricula are so rare that most teachers are not aware of what they're missing.

SUMMARY

I know something about eclectic instruction not just from my knowledge of curricula for teaching beginning reading but also from teaching college classes. I know that I am most successful as a teacher when I use a textbook that is very well-designed and specific. I have two classes that I've taught over 20 times and I love teaching both of them. Many of the same students take both classes and they are both upper-division classes. In one class, I use an excellent, detailed text and in the other I have never found a text I like. I use the excellent text exactly as it is written and in its entirety. For the class without a good text, I rely on eclectic instruction and desktop publishing. Of course, I do supplemental activities and assign additional articles in both classes. Over the course of 15 years, I have observed that students in the class with the good text do better on tests, get better grades, and give me better evaluations than in the other class. And here's the interesting thing. Many people might think that such a specific textbook would make it easy for another person without my expertise to teach the course, but that is not true. When other people have taught the course using the same text, student learning and satisfaction are never as good. My subject matter expertise is important even when the curriculum is very prescriptive. Well-designed and specific curriculum materials provide a better opportunity for learning, but they do not diminish in any way the importance of subject matter knowledge or teacher expertise.

The popularity of eclectic instruction is understandable. It may even be desirable as a way to individualize instruction once good curricula are in place. Prescriptive curricula do not eliminate the need for teachers to understand their subject, but simply allow teachers to devote more attention to the interactive aspects of teaching. When the faulty premises are stripped away and the harmful effects considered, it seems reasonable to conclude that children and adolescents are best served by a more deliberate, coherent, and scientific approach to curriculum than eclectic instruction can provide. Rather than embrace eclecticism, educators should demand well-designed instructional programs with proven records of effectiveness.

Eclectic instruction can never be scientifically validated, so it cannot be part of the science of teaching. There is evidence that curriculum matters. The superiority of one curriculum over another has been documented in reading (American Federation of Teachers, 1998; Oregon Reading First Center, 2004; Stebbins et al., 1977), mathematics (Crawford & Snider, 2000; Schmidt et al., 2001), and U.S. history (Crawford & Carnine, 2000). The U.S. Department of Education is beginning to provide scientific evidence on specific curricula on the What Works Clearinghouse (http://www.whatworks.ed.gov) in order to help teachers and administrators make better curriculum decisions. If educators are serious about raising student achievement, attention to the quality of curricula bears the same intense scrutiny as attention to teacher quality.

6

The Myth of Good Teachers

Teaching is the only major occupation of man for which we have not yet developed tools that make an average person capable of competence and performance. In teaching we rely on the "naturals," the ones who somehow know how to teach.

—Peter Drucker (n.d.)

The American public relies on the natural teachers but, unfortunately, there aren't enough "naturals" to teach the 54 million students in public schools. Everybody knows there are some great teachers and some dreadful ones. The question is, how did they get that way? And what is the relative contribution of the teach*er* versus teach*ing*?

The fourth myth is that good teachers are the most important variable in students' eventual success. A good teacher outweighs everything else— methods, curriculum, school climate, organization, and leadership. This myth attributes most of the variation in teacher quality to intrinsic qualities of the teacher, but attributes very little of the variation to the teaching methods or the curriculum, which are alterable factors that can be taught and replicated in many classrooms. These factors comprise the science of teaching.

The view that methods and curriculum are less important than personal qualities is a popular one. Professor Ryder at the University of Wisconsin-Milwaukee summarized it like this: "The most potent factor in teaching children to read is a good teacher. A teacher who's highly dedicated to an approach is going to have success" (Teachers to learn, 2003). Although it's a nice sentiment, the statement doesn't make sense. By his logic, a teacher could believe that the zaniest kind of snake oil teaches reading, and it would work. If believing made it so, we wouldn't have an epidemic of high school graduates with low literacy skills since most teachers are "highly dedicated" to what they're doing.

Teacher quality is an elusive concept. The government defines teacher quality in terms of educational attainments—content area expertise, grade point average, and a liberal arts education. NCLB defines a qualified teacher as one who has met the certification requirements of the area in which he or she teaches. Neither definition is very useful. I don't know anyone who thinks that a piece of paper from the Department of Public Instruction makes a person a good teacher. It seems that defining "good teacher" is a little like defining pornography. As Supreme Court Justice Potter Stewart remarked, he was not able to define pornography, but he knew it when he saw it. Indeed, in my years as a teacher and teacher educator, I have found that there is usually high agreement about who is an excellent teacher, even among educators with very different philosophical perspectives. The cream rises and it's easy to see.

For the purposes of this discussion, I'll define a good teacher as one who consistently promotes learning and raises student achievement. I propose that there are three components to being an effective teacher: (a) having desirable personal attributes, (b) knowing how to teach, and (c) having access to effective curricula. Personal qualities generally thought to be desirable include intelligence or verbal ability, leadership, self-confidence, willingness to work hard, ethics, persistence, a pleasing personality, and the ability to establish rapport with students, colleagues, and parents—to name just a few. The educational jargon for personal attributes is *dispositions*.

Observable teaching behaviors are the *how* to teach. They include things like maintaining student interest, grouping students for success, monitoring student responses and progress, using techniques for actively engaging students, organizing the classroom and managing behavior. The educational jargon for *how* to teach is pedagogy or methods.

What to teach is the content included in instructional programs. As discussed in chapter 5, the vehicle for teaching content is curricula. Curricula may either be designed by teachers or by the "experts" who publish and sell materials, and they may be more or less effective depending on the extent to which they are well designed, specific, and validated. The *how* and *what* comprise the science of teaching. To use the NASCAR analogy from chapter 5, the driver's intuition is similar to teacher *dispositions*, the person's driving skill is similar to teaching *methods*, and the car is the *curriculum*.

The myth of good teachers suggests that dispositions influence teacher quality more than the science of teaching. Although there may be some truth to that statement now, it is only because the knowledge base for teaching is so limited or because what little knowledge exists is not conveyed in teacher education programs. I would argue that dispositions are a necessary, but not sufficient, condition for teacher quality. Good teachers do have desirable dispositions, but highly effective teachers, those who can get the most out of even the least impressive youngsters, also use effective methods and curricula. Effective teaching requires application of the science of teaching.

FAULTY PREMISES

The myth of good teachers rests on two widely accepted premises. The first faulty premise is that teaching is an art, not a science. This belief places little importance on establishing a consensus based on experimental research about *how* or *what* to teach. The failure to accumulate and to value a professional body of knowledge about effective teaching practices contributes to low student achievement, especially among students who are difficult to teach. The second faulty premise is that good teachers are born, not made. In the absence of a scientific body of knowledge, educators tend to rely on the power of personal qualities in combination with experience rather than on knowledge and skills that can be taught in a teacher certification program.

Teaching Is an Art, Not a Science

It's hard to know if educators believe this statement because, in the absence of a science of teaching, they're forced to rely on the art, or whether they have failed to develop and promote the science *because* they believe this statement. I think it might be both, which makes it self-reinforcing.

Forty-six percent of teachers in our survey believed that teaching is an art, not a science; and only 19% thought that scientifically conducted research was the best guide for deciding how and what to teach. As practitioners untrained in research methods, I was not surprised that so few teachers believed in a science of teaching because they have not been trained in research methods. I was disappointed, however, that only 23% of education professors believed that science should guide decisions about best practice.

I should not have been surprised, however, that so few education professors believed that science should guide decisions about how and what to teach. Education professors' philosophical preference for learner-directed methods creates a focus on individual differences (e.g., student interests and learning styles) rather than on unifying principles or practices that apply to all children. The fact that every student has unique characteristics leads to the mistaken idea that every learner must be taught differently. Content is perceived to be relative to the individual rather than independent or fixed. Skepticism of a science of teaching is also related to education professors' belief that teaching and learning are too complex to be reduced to simple cause-and-effect relationships. These beliefs seem to obstruct any attempt to objectively define and examine the relationship between teaching and learning as it applies to the general population of students. As a result, the field of education is heavy on theoretical research and light on classroom research.

Ellis and Fouts (1993) proposed a model of how education research should be conducted that is very useful for understanding the problems associated with establishing a science of teaching. They proposed that there are three levels of research that differentiate theoretical, applied, and validation research. Level 1 is theory-forming research. Education researchers often draw on developmental, behavioral, cognitive, and information-processing research in psychology to design teaching procedures. Sometimes educators draw on the work of linguists and psycholinguists, and recently, they have also drawn on brain research in neurobiology.

Equipped with data from Level 1 theory-forming research, education researchers can move to Level 2 classroom study in which instructional procedures based on theoretical research are tried out in the laboratory or in a few classrooms. This is the level where instructional variables that affect achievement or behavior can be examined separately before they are combined into an instructional approach or program. Level 2 classroom research often gets results because the teaching is done by the researchers themselves or other exceptional teachers whose skills make it successful, so it is necessary to have replication of Level 2 research as well as Level 3 research. Level 3 research involves large-scale implementation and data collection of a particular method or program across a broad cross-section of environments in an empirical study where plenty of ordinary students and regular, everyday teachers are assigned to the experimental condition and other students and teachers are assigned to a control condition.

The recent emphasis by the federal government on the need for scientifically based research encourages Level 2 and Level 3 implementation studies to adhere to what is often referred to as the "gold standard" of research. That is, students and teachers should be randomly assigned to an instructional approach in order to minimize the effect of confounding variables that might distort the results. Data of this type are extremely rare in education. Of 84 program evaluations and studies planned by the U.S. Department of Education in the year 2000, just one involved randomized trials (Cook, 2001). What's more, people outside the field of education conduct almost all the randomized experiments in education (Cook, 2001). Even in special education, where the need for powerful interventions is most urgent and researchers generally have a favorable attitude toward empirical research, few experiments have used a strong research design to assess reading and mathematics interventions. Seethaler and Fuchs (2005) found that of 806 relevant articles published in leading special education journals during the past 5 years, only 5% used a group design to evaluate reading and mathematics interventions and only 4% used random assignment.

When someone says that a particular instructional approach is research based, it seldom means that it has Level 3 large-scale implementation research or even a consensus based on many Level 2 classroom research studies. What it usually means is that the theory is reasonable, or it has Level 1 theory-building research. There is an abundance of Level 1 theory-building research, but few findings have been translated into teaching principles that have been tested in Level 2 classroom studies, and practically none have been subjected to full-scale Level 3 implementation research.

Many students could benefit if education researchers could get beyond their preoccupation with theory and conduct implementation research.

These are the results that matter most for improving teaching and increasing student achievement. Both behavioral and cognitive theories have acquired substantial empirical support, creating a knowledge base that includes research consistent with both the learner-directed and curriculum-directed philosophical camps (Ellis, Worthington, & Larkin, 1994). At this point, however, very few instructional approaches or programs have been subjected to Level 3, or even Level 2, research to establish which ones offer the most promise for increasing student achievement.

Teaching may *appear* to be more of an art than a science because teachers are forced to rely on art in the absence of science. Education researchers have conducted few classroom studies designed to answer the question "What works?" In order to increase achievement among all students, teachers need access to effective methods and powerful curricula. Furthermore, it's unrealistic to expect them to acquire these insights through trial and error without the benefit of meaningful education and training.

Good Teachers Are Born, Not Made

Teachers' attitudes toward education and training seem to be fairly negative. Only 7% of the teachers in our study believed that education and training were more important than experience, whereas 44% thought that experience was more important, and about half were in the middle. A survey of teachers in Canada revealed that teachers' most important source of teaching skills was on-the-job experience and their most trusted source of information about education issues was other teachers (COMPASS, 2003). It could be that teachers disregard their education and training with good reason—they didn't learn how to teach from their teacher certification programs. Interestingly, although 16% of education professors favored education and training over experience, three-quarters indicated that they were balanced or undecided about the relative value of experience versus education and training, suggesting that even those who are educating the teachers place a high value on experiential learning.

Teacher attributes and the ability to profit from experience might be considered traits that teachers are *born* with, whereas teacher preparation is what *makes* a teacher. Research suggests that none of these factors have a consistent measurable effect on increased student achievement. That is not to say that student achievement is unrelated to teacher behavior or experience, just that the variables related to academic achievement are difficult to tease out. It simply doesn't seem logical to me that teaching might be the only skilled occupation or profession whose members don't benefit from training and experience.

Teachers Are Born

Evidence that innate personal attributes influence student performance is limited. Consistent, but relatively weak, links seem to exist between teachers' performance on tests of verbal ability, like the ACT or SAT tests, and higher-achieving students (Ehrenberg & Brewer, 1994; Goldhaber, 2002). The failure to document the relationship of teacher characteristics to student achievement is not too surprising. There are so many personal traits that affect teacher performance and most of them (personality traits) are difficult to measure. What's more, I have observed that a certain baseline of what I call "average, above-average" intelligence is a necessary for excellent teaching, but beyond that, high intelligence is not necessarily advantageous. Other qualities become equally or more important.

Teachers rely on experience for professional development more than almost any comparable job with such heavy responsibilities. This trial-and-error learning begins in teacher education programs through field experiences that culminate with student teaching and continue with a trial by fire as teachers make an abrupt solo flight in their first year of teaching. Several studies reveal a small positive relationship between teacher experience and student achievement. At the elementary level, there seems to be an increase in student achievement for every year of experience, but that levels off after the first 3 years or so. Murnane and Phillips (1981) found that experience had the most effect during the first few years of teaching among teachers of inner-city children. Possibly a small effect for experience re-emerges at the very highest levels of experience, such as more than 14 years (Rice, 2003), but that is uncertain. At the high school level, experience seems to exert a more sustained effect extending longer into a teachers' career (Rice, 2003). The fact that experience has little effect after the first few years of teaching makes sense because there is only so much that a person can learn about teaching from trial-and-error learning, especially if he or she remains in the same classroom situation.

It could be that the reason experience in teaching does not show a strong relationship to teaching competence has to do with the trial-and-error nature of teachers' experience. Experience is not viewed as an *addition* to a firm foundation of professional knowledge, it is a *substitution* for professional knowledge or, even worse, a way of *acquiring* professional knowledge. I can't emphasize this crucial difference enough. Experience would have a more pronounced effect, I think, if it involved practice or application of knowledge and skills that form a common knowledge base for teaching or if experience involved meaningful continuing education. Targeted mentoring and coaching also seem like promising ways to increase the benefits of experience. Experience alone is an unreliable and inefficient teacher.

Teachers Are Made

Very few studies have been conducted that actually address the question of whether or not teacher certification is important, and many of the studies suffer from serious methodological flaws. Teachers do learn something in teacher education courses, but what they learn may or may not make them more effective teachers (Rice, 2003). Most of the studies that show a relationship between teacher certification and student achievement show small positive effects that are specific to certain contexts, such as teaching mathematics or science (Goldhaber, 2002). Longer teacher preparation programs have a positive effect on retention—teachers remain teachers for a longer period of time—but they have no clear effect on teacher performance. Advanced degrees seem to have no positive effect at all. In fact, getting a master's degree actually has a negative effect on student achievement for elementary school teachers (Rice, 2003).

Many reports on teacher quality have emphasized the importance of subject matter expertise. Although there is moderate support for the importance of subject-matter knowledge, the amount of coursework needed is unclear, and there may be a point beyond which college subject-matter coursework is superfluous (Allen, 2003). Teachers who take more courses in both content and methods—for example, college courses in science and science methods—seem to have a positive effect on the achievement of middle and high school students (Allen, 2003; Rice, 2003), but it is less clear that there is any effect at the elementary level (Rice, 2003).

I suspect that the difficulty with documenting a relationship between teacher preparation and student achievement is the lack of standardization in teacher preparation. Teacher educators have been unable to agree on a professional body of knowledge that can be called a science of teaching. Standardization is further hindered by the pervasive belief among teacher educators that any kind of knowledge, including teaching methods, should be discovered rather than transmitted. Field experiences provide the means for discovering effective teaching methods, but that process is limited by the quality of the placement and the ability of the cooperating teacher to facilitate discovery of essential teaching knowledge and skills.

It is even unclear whether teachers who have National Board Certification produce higher achievement than other teachers. National Board Certification requires experienced teachers to keep a portfolio in order to demonstrate how they translate theory into practice and to analyze their teaching through videotaped lessons. They also must produce evidence of student learning. A panel of experts evaluates each portfolio, and teachers must also complete a set of tasks that take place in an assessment center over the course of a full day. It costs teachers over $2,000 to participate, and many states reimburse candidates for successful completion. Vandevoort, Amrein-Beardsley, and Berliner (2004) reported favorable results for National Board-Certified teachers compared to noncertified teachers and maintain that the training is a powerful contributor to student achievement. Critics charge that the value-added achievement gains of National Board-Certified teachers compared to other teachers are extremely small and that board certification is not worth the time, effort, or money (Cunningham & Stone, 2005).

The picture that emerges from the research on the effect of teacher preparation programs on student achievement is discouraging. The problems of teacher education are widely known, even among teacher educators. Professional coursework in teacher education is faulted as intellectually thin (Keller, 2003), lacking important content (Steiner & Rozen, 2004), and ignoring research-based teaching practices in reading (Moats, 2000; Steiner & Rozen, 2004).

Conservative critics suggest that teacher certification programs serve no regulatory purpose and alternative certification should be encouraged (Walsh, 2001) and teacher educators defend their ground, citing data that show that certified teachers are more capable than uncertified or alternatively licensed teachers (Darling-Hammond, 2002). There doesn't seem to be much doubt, however, that schools of education could do better. Even insiders admit that problems exist. The Holmes Group (1986, 1990, 1995), which consisted of deans and education faculty, issued three reports addressing the low quality of teacher preparation. Although some of their recommendations have been implemented, such as establishing teaching standards for certification and working more closely with the public schools, these changes have not had a discernable impact on teacher quality as far as I can tell.

Once teachers are on their own, they quickly recognize what they should have learned in teacher education courses. Veenman (1984) analyzed 83 international studies to find out what beginning teachers perceived to be their weaknesses. Although this data is old, it rings true based on my own experience with alumni surveys. The rank order for various problems is listed below.

Rank	Problems
1	Classroom discipline
2	Motivating students
3	Dealing with individual differences
4.5	Assessment students' work
4.5	Relationship with parents
6.5	Organization of class work
6.5	Insufficient materials and supplies
8	Dealing with problems of individual students
9	Heavy teaching load
10	Relationships with colleagues

The striking thing about this list is that the first six items have to do with *how* to teach or teaching methods. They are the management skills that could and should be taught in teacher preparation programs. What's more, they are all areas in which there is some consensus about best practice and a substantial amount of Level 2 classroom research. Over the past 30 years, teachers have consistently reported that they did not learn enough about how to teach in their teacher preparation programs, especially how to manage student behavior (Farkas et al., 2000; Kagan, 1992; Latham, 2002; Meister & Melnick, 2003).

People who call themselves professionals should be able to do things as a result of their education and training that ordinary people cannot do. There seems to be a general perception among the public that anyone can teach, and maybe that's true. One study found that people recruited off the streets to teach high school social studies, electronics, and mechanics were just as effective as certified teachers (Popham, 1971). Effectiveness was measured by assessing students' achievement on specific content outcomes. Imagine if someone reported that any college graduate could do the work of a general practitioner with a medical degree. It would make a person think twice about going to the doctor, wouldn't it? Sure, anybody can go into a classroom and stay there for the day, but very few can produce high student achievement with hard-to-teach youngsters. It is the rare person, indeed, who can figure out how to teach and what to teach on the basis of trial-and-error learning. I didn't.

There is no occupation or profession that I can think of, especially none as complex as teaching, in which people are expected to perform without adequate training and to rely so heavily on experiential learning. The fact that educators put so much faith in personal qualities and trial-and-error learning once again exposes its *bricoleur* status. Just because teacher preparation *doesn't* matter, doesn't mean that it *shouldn't* matter and *couldn't* matter. As yet, we haven't even tried to adequately prepare teachers. Logically, better education and training for teachers would increase achievement among students, especially among traditionally underperforming groups who are difficult to teach.

THE HARM THAT IS DONE

In the 1970s and 1980s, Madeline Hunter's (1982) Instructional Theory into Practice (ITIP) became a nationwide fad. I remember hearing her speak in a large auditorium on one of our teacher in-service days. Her training model took well-established principles in educational psychology, and translated them to an instructional approach that was accessible to teachers. The ITIP model included stating objectives, activating prior knowledge, teaching for transfer, conducting frequent assessment, and providing appropriate practice. These are all learning principles that I heartily endorse. Although Hunter and her graduate students were able to raise student achievement using her methods in the lab school at the University of California in Los Angeles, her model did not achieve results in Level 3 full-scale implementation studies. When data was finally collected from places that had attempted to implement ITIP, they found that although there were some initial gains for her model in the initial years, they were not maintained over time (Mandeville & Rivers, 1991; Slavin, 1987; Stallings, 1985; Stallings & Krasavage, 1986). ITIP faded and went to the graveyard of educational innovations.

There are three things observers can learn about the science of teaching from Madeline Hunter. First, it's not a good idea to implement innovations nationwide until the instructional approach has been tried out on real kids in real schools through Level 3 implementation research. Educators' penchant for unsubstantiated innovation leads to pseudoscience and unending faddism. Second, even if an instructional approach has some limited or initial effectiveness, teaching teachers how to use an instructional approach requires more than a one-shot, in-service, training day. Teachers need more effective training models. Every powerful teaching procedure that I know requires practice over a period of time under the supervision of a coach or mentor. Finally, generic instructional approaches that are not tied to a specific curriculum leave a lot to chance and pose considerable risk of failure.

Psuedoscience and Faddism

Cook (2001) suggested that educators suffer from *sciencephobia* because of their aversion to randomized experiments. Perhaps it is their *sciencephobia* that leads them to engage in pseudoscience. Pseudoscience is dangerous because its scientific appearance (to the casual onlooker) gives it more credibility than it actually deserves. Pseudoscience in education occurs when educators borrow theories from psychology (or some other field) and use them to support their own philosophical biases or theories. They don't use data to form a theory. They make existing theories fit their beliefs. Then, they say that those beliefs and the instructional practices that accompany them are "supported by research." It may be supported by theory-building research, and it may sound like it is supported by large-scale implementation research—but it is not.

The whole language method of teaching reading that swept the country in the 1980s and 1990s was based on what turned out to be a misinterpretation of Level 1 research. Goodman (1965) observed that young children misidentified words when they appeared in word lists, but read them correctly when they appeared in passages. He incorrectly reasoned that reading was a "psycho-linguistic guessing game" and that beginning readers should be encouraged to use context rather than to sound out words. Later on, researchers found out that young and unskilled readers rely on context because they don't know the words, but that skilled readers do not use context for word recognition. Relying on context actually inhibits the process of becoming a skilled reader (Stanovich, 1984; Stanovich, West, & Freeman, 1981). There was very little classroom research conducted on whole language and what little existed was either not empirical or not favorable. There was no large-scale Level 3 implementation research until fourth-grade students in California demonstrated on the National Assessment of Education Progress that they couldn't read, as described in chapter 3. Had large-scale research been conducted *prior to* nationwide implementation of the whole language approach, the understandable flaw in logic would have been discovered sooner.

A more current example is the popularity of constructivism. Constructivism is based on a well-accepted psychological theory of learning and memory. Simply put, the theory is based on the observation that people's memories do not come out in exactly the same way that they went in. They are "constructed" based on a person's prior knowledge and beliefs. (Hence, the unreliability of eyewitness accounts.) From this psychological theory with Level 1 research support, educators extrapolate an approach to teaching in which knowledge cannot be explicitly transmitted, but can only be constructed by the learner on the basis of experiential learning. The first problem with this prevalent theory is that it is a misinterpretation of the psychological literature. There is no evidence that learning and memory are impaired when learners are explicitly taught (Anderson, Reder, & Simon, 2000). The second problem has to do with developing curricula. When learning is so personal, it becomes difficult to specify a series of experiences that will allow all students to construct the kind of knowledge that will help them become literate and well-educated adults. A small amount of classroom research on constructivist mathematics curricula has been conducted, but much of it is either poorly done or not supportive. There is no large-scale implementation research yet.

Another example of pseudoscience is the application of the neurosciences to education. Neuroscientific research is Level 1 theory-building research, and much of it is conducted with rats, not humans. One of the findings that has received a lot of attention in educational circles is that raising rats in more complex environments increases the density of synapses per neuron in the *visual* areas of their brain (Bruer, 1998). Educators have used these results to promote constructivist practices, such as providing "enriched" environments that promote active learning through a variety in classroom activities. There are many more examples of the premature application of neuroscience to education.

These leaps of faith are a complete distortion of science. First, educators may misinterpret existing theory to make it fit their version of the truth. Second, even if the theory fits, the instructional practices themselves are not tested or validated to find out if they actually work, if they actually increase achievement for all students in the hands of all teachers. All three levels of research must be completed before it is safe to say that an instructional procedure or program works. Third, and most troubling, insufficient research leads to faddism.

Robert Slavin (1989), author of Success for All, a reading program for the primary grades that has a large amount of large-scale Level 3 implementation research support, suggested that teaching practices will not improve as long as education is dominated by fads that swing back and forth in popularity, like a pendulum, without ever moving the field forward. During the upswing of an educational innovation, an innovation is proposed and piloted somewhere (Level 2 classroom research); however, the data from the pilot is never widely available. Then the program is introduced in innovative districts, which is to say districts run by administrators anxious to be on the cutting edge. The program becomes a "hot topic" for district in-service meetings and its popularity expands rapidly. Articles appear (not research studies) in popular education journals, giving teachers the impression that the program has more credibility than it actually does. Finally, at the end of the upswing cycle, some evaluation studies begin.

As the pendulum begins to swing the other way, administrators in innovative districts move on to the next innovation without ever admitting that there was anything wrong with the last fad they promoted. Eventually, complaints begin to surface in the professional literature because anecdotal evidence is disappointing. Interestingly, the promoters of the approach or program almost always claim that the failures were due to improper implementation by the teachers. Finally, interest in the new approach diminishes and last, but not least, controlled evaluation studies (still Level 2 classroom research) are published in the professional literature.

The complete upswing and downswing are only accomplished for very popular innovations. Lesser innovations never even reach the stage where controlled evaluations studies are ever published. They just fade in popularity. Sometimes the cycle can be completed in a year or two. Other times it takes a decade, as in the case of whole language. The point is that research to examine whether or not an approach works occurs after implementation, not before it has impacted millions of schoolchildren.

Fads in education are harmful. The lack of commitment to an approach with a proven track record creates discontinuity. Teachers never have an opportunity to get "up to speed" with one innovation before they have to move on to the next one. Large-scale Level 3 implementation research efforts should focus on instructional innovations that show promise, and if they pan out, then a concerted effort to train teachers how to use the innovative instructional approach should begin. Listening to one innovator after another insist that their approach is supported by research causes teachers to distrust real research and leads them to believe that either you can prove anything with research or nothing with research. This cynicism stands in the way of needed reforms based on Level 3 implementation research. Most importantly, unlike fads in fashion, in food, and in many other areas of daily life, educational fads can cause lasting and permanent damage to children.

Inadequate Training Models for Teachers

The role of teacher certification programs should be to teach teachers *how* to teach (methods) and to make sure they have deep subject-matter knowledge, whether it is history or beginning reading. Deep subject-matter knowledge will allow teachers to evaluate, select, and effectively use curricula, and to make appropriate modifications for individual differences. Speaking from my own experience, I'm not convinced that most teacher preparation programs accomplish these goals.

I have found that many pedagogy courses place a heavy emphasis on identifying student characteristics and creating units of instruction without sufficient attention to how to teach, what content to include, and how to determine if learning has occurred. For the most part, supervision of field experiences is either left to the teachers in the schools or relegated to the faculty lowest on the totem pole. Portfolios are increasingly popular as a way for aspiring teachers to reflect on what they've learned, but for the most part, they look more like scrapbooks than evidence of teaching competence.

Undergraduate education courses need to familiarize teachers with the science of teaching in sufficient depth that they are able to apply it. The failure to do so can set teachers up to reject effective teaching practices. Take teachers' number one concern, behavior management, as an example. Alfie Kohn (1993) has made a living out of criticizing the use of punishments and rewards, claiming that it diminishes intrinsic motivation and self-esteem. The problem is not behaviorism, as Kohn claims, but the misapplication of behavioral principles by people who don't understand them. If teachers are simply given a bag of tricks without understanding what makes them work, they cannot use them effectively. The only problem with principles of classroom management is that too many teachers have a superficial understanding of them and misapply them in simplistic ways to complex behaviors. Failure to adequately train teachers in methods of classroom management results from inadequate teacher training.

The same is true in reading. The process of skilled reading is very different from beginning reading and the linguistic requirements of beginning reading are not obvious to the untrained observer. "The knowledge base for teaching reading is hidden, extensive, and complex" (Moats, 1999, p. 11). Beginning reading teachers need to know, for example, that it's important to teach rhyming, but they need more than a menu of fun and interesting rhyming activities; they need to know how rhyming fits into the entire scope and sequence for beginning reading. They need to know why rhyming is important (it is a phonological skill that requires segmenting sounds, an important preskill to reading success), when to teach rhyming (after students can blend and segment syllables and simple words like *piiiiic-niiiiic* or *mmmmm-aaaaa-ttttt*), how to teach rhyming (always model first using onsets and rhymes), how to assess rhyming (students must be able to rhyme accurately and quickly), and what to do if students can't rhyme in a reasonable period of time (and what is a reasonable amount of time). And that's just rhyming! Louisa Moats (1999) had it right: "Teaching reading is rocket science."

The most vexing problem in teacher education is the disconnect between course work and classroom reality. If university course work suddenly improved to include information about the science of teaching, the disconnect would be even greater because best practice and common practice are miles apart. Prospective teachers need to spend time in classrooms where teachers know *how* to teach and use effective instructional programs—and there just aren't enough of those classrooms. The same problem exists regarding mentoring programs for beginning teachers. Mentorship programs are only as good as the mentors, and right now there are not enough highly qualified mentors to go around. Coaching is a model in which consultants or peers provide intensive training in specific instructional techniques. Schools can bring in coaches and develop their own "homegrown" coaches. This model holds promise for professional development; however, teachers and teachers' unions are somewhat skittish about peer evaluation.

In my ideal world, teacher certification would consist of four components: (a) rigorous initial course work that emphasizes scientifically based teaching practices, coupled with (b) related field experiences with teachers who modeled exemplary teaching practices, (c) mentorships and coaching during the initial 3 years of teaching, and (d) advanced, more specialized, professional development throughout a teacher's career. Initial certification would not need to be longer (teachers already go to school for 5 years to earn a bachelor's degree in most certification programs) than it currently is, just different.

I run a clinic in the summer that provides a small-scale example of how I envision exemplary teacher training. Students who participate as teachers in the clinic take the prerequisite courses in assessment, behavior management, teaching, and reading methods before they participate. The content of the courses is rigorous, emphasizes the science of teaching, and is consistent with what they will learn in the clinic. They have previously participated in numerous field experiences, and some graduate students already have years of teaching experience. Before children and adolescents arrive, teachers receive a day of training on how to use the curricula (we use the Direct Instruction program *Reading Mastery*) and assess student progress, and for the first 3 weeks they work with coaches who model teaching and correction procedures, assist with any student attention or behavior problems, observe, give feedback and advice, and provide written evaluations. I can usually pick out the teachers who will be "naturals" on the first day. After a day of training and about a week of working with an experienced coach, the "naturals" quickly learn how to use the curricula and students learn at an amazing rate.

We often get excellent results in a very short period of time and I wonder how much could be achieved if those efforts were sustained over the course of a year. Last summer we had a group of four kindergarten children who were all considered at-risk for failing to learn to read in first grade based on our testing. One was emotionally disturbed, another had been kicked out of Montessori preschool, and a third was being evaluated for learning disabilities. At the end of the summer, by well-accepted objective measures (Dynamic Indicators of Beginning Emergent Literacy Skills or DIBELS), they had acquired the prereading skills they needed to be successful in first grade—after only 30 hours of instruction.

Some clinic teachers need a lot of help and coaching. They are awkward in their first attempts, but eventually they do improve and they become better teachers than they would have been without intensive training and coaching, which means that children learn to read. Most are somewhere in the middle. I have worked with a lot of teachers who were average at first, but with training, they turned into excellent and highly effective teachers who came back to the clinic in future summers to coach other new teachers.

The two most effective models for comprehensive school reform at the elementary level, Direct Instruction and Success for All (American Institutes for Research, 1999), both have a very strong training component that is similar to what we do in the clinic. Trainers and consultants oversee the initial implementation and schools are encouraged to develop a system of homegrown coaches so that teachers can assist each other.

Some people have suggested that alternative certification programs are a way to get around the persistent problems in schools of education. It's worth exploring, but my experience is that alternative certification quickly becomes a synonym for "quick and dirty." I fear that those who promote alternative certification programs do not appreciate the depth of knowledge and the specialized knowledge that teachers need to be effective, especially with low-performing students. New teachers don't need less teacher training and they don't need more. They need *better* teacher training. "Training is everything," wrote Mark Twain (1899) in *Pudd'nhead*

Wilson, "The peach was once a bitter almond, a cauliflower is nothing but cabbage with a college education" (p. 49).

Generic Teaching Methods

Generic teaching methods consist of principles that can be applied to a variety of content areas and curricular programs. These teaching methods (how to teach) are usually gleaned from observing teachers who are able to produce high achievement among their students, but they entirely ignore the issue of curriculum (what to teach). This body of literature, often called the effective teaching literature, is an important body of research, but it has some limitations.

More than 25 years ago, the effective teaching literature revealed that providing more opportunities to learn resulted in increased achievement (Cooley & Leinhardt, 1978; Rosenshine & Berliner, 1975). Providing opportunities to learn seems like common sense, but the devil is in the details. One can't just say to new teachers, "You've got to provide lots of opportunities to learn if you want your students to achieve," and expect it to happen. Opportunities to learn are a function of management skills (how to teach) plus curriculum (what to teach). Effective teaching requires attention to how and what to teach, but neither one can stand alone.

A teacher who has good management skills is one who knows how to use time wisely; how to keep students engaged, motivated, and successful; how to assess student progress daily and weekly to ensure high levels of success; how to organize and manage people and materials; and how to prevent and solve behavior problems. A teacher who has content knowledge has a deep understanding of developmental reading, mathematics, and writing (at the elementary level) or their subject area (at the high school level). Teachers who have deep content knowledge will be able to evaluate and select well-designed curricula, individualize instruction, provide enrichment and opportunities for generalization, and generally make the content come alive.

When curricula are ineffective, students won't learn regardless of *how* dynamic or well-organized the teacher presentation is. On the other hand, an effective curriculum is utterly useless in the hands of a teacher who cannot manage the classroom environment or who doesn't understand what he or she is doing. No instructional program is teacher-proof. To put it in terms of the NASCAR analogy, teachers who are good drivers don't go faster unless they have well-built, powerful cars. Fast cars won't reach their maximum speed with an unskilled driver behind the wheel.

SUMMARY

I have been asked, "Which is more important, the teach*er* or the teach*ing* approach?" It's not a choice I want to make. The late Jeanne Chall, long-time advocate of teaching phonics and using teacher-directed approaches to reading instruction, reflected on the importance of good teaching at the conclusion of her classic book, *Beginning to Read: The Great Debate* (1967).

> Indeed, as we learn more about the teaching of beginning reading, we may find that a poor method in the hands of a good teacher produces better re-sults than a good method in the hands of a poor teacher. But this is not the point. This inquiry did not find that good teaching is obsolete. Good teach-ing is always needed. But a good method in the hands of a good teachers— that is the ideal. In fact, if my visits to classrooms during the present study and my contacts with thousands of teachers over the past twenty years have taught me anything it is that the good teachers are constantly searching for the good methods. (p. 308–309)

Here is the way that I would explain it. The quality of teachers proba-bly forms a normal curve of some sort, with a few terrible teachers at the bottom and a few stellar teachers at the top. Most teachers probably are in the middle and they do an adequate job. It's not enough to just screen out potentially "bad" teachers because that would still leave a lot of mediocre teachers. If teacher education programs actually taught teachers how to teach, and if publishers provided well-designed instructional programs that gave teachers good curricular vehicles, every teacher would be a lit-tle better and all children would learn a little more than they do now. There would be still a normal curve as shown in Figure 6.1, but more rig-orous education and training would skew the curve of teacher quality so that there would be fewer poor teachers and more excellent teachers. Higher quality teachers means higher student achievement.

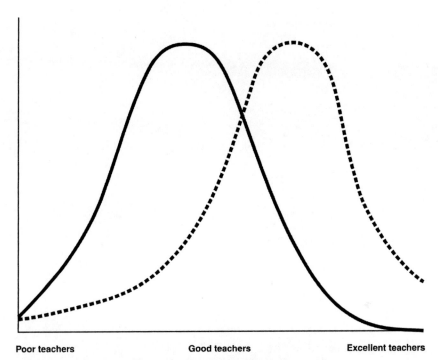

| Poor teachers | Good teachers | Excellent teachers |

Figure 6.1.   The effect of better teacher training on teacher quality

It is *not* a myth that we need more high-quality teachers. The myth is that knowing *how* and *what* to teach is intuitive and that teachers can figure out how to teach *well* in the absence of rigorous and relevant coursework, positive models, practice, and feedback from skilled mentors. The myth is that any reasonably smart, competent person can walk into a classroom and *teach well*—not just babysit, but inspire all students to meet high academic standards. The myth is that student achievement will increase substantially before researchers collect large-scale implementation data on the effectiveness of instructional approaches. The myth is that anything can change until educators value the science of teaching.

7

The Myth of Learning Style

The greatest danger of all is that what has been learned about teaching and learning from educational research and practice may be abandoned in the rush to study the effects of various neurological factors. . . . Some pupils may not learn to read and write well, not because they are right-brained rather than left-brained, but because they may not have been taught well, or were not sufficiently motivated at home and/or school.

—Jeanne Chall and Allen Mirskey (1978, p. 376)

CHILDREN ARE LIKE SNOWFLAKES. EVERY ONE IS DIFFERENT.

The myth of learning style emphasizes children's differences. Individuals differ in important ways, that much is true, but are they different in ways that are instructionally relevant? The phrase *learning style* refers to the idea that people learn in different ways and that teachers can, and should, recognize and accommodate each individual's learning style. Although a few experts suggest that it is important to make children more well rounded by strengthening their weak learning styles, the more popular view is that teachers should teach to learning style preferences. The assumption is that when people are able to learn in their own way they learn more, learn more easily, and feel better about learning.

It's a very seductive notion because all people have personal interests and preferences. People are most comfortable doing things that they do

106

well and enjoy. The fundamental problem with learning style is that it presumes that all individual differences are intrinsic differences, when in fact individual differences in academic readiness are very often the result of lack of opportunity or inadequate instruction. Although it is extremely important to recognize and foster an individual's strengths, using children's so-called learning style often results in pandering or ignoring skill deficits that are critical for academic success. It is ironic that an approach so cloaked in nurturing, learner-friendly rhetoric can have the unintended effect of denying educational opportunity. Once again, low-performing students are the ones most likely to suffer from the teaching myths.

The popularity of learning style in education has steadily grown. It was first popular in special education. A study by Arter and Jenkins (1977) found that 99% of special education teachers believed that a child's modality strengths and weaknesses (i.e., visual or auditory) should be a critical factor in selecting instructional methods. Ten years later, the idea of learning style became popular in general education, especially as it pertained to reading instruction. Our 2004 survey found that 80% of all teachers thought that "learning style was relevant to deciding how and what to teach," only 6% thought it was irrelevant, and 14% weren't sure. Belief in learning styles was just as strong among general as special educators, strongest among elementary teachers, and stronger among females (84%) than males (65%). A Google search for "learning style" yields over 12 million hits. Interest in learning styles continues to grow, and it is especially strong now among college educators and people interested in adult learning.

It's easy to define learning style in a general way, but difficult to define it precisely. Definitional problems are further complicated because the term *learning style* as it is used in the professional literature is slightly different than the quasi-learning style approach common among classroom teachers.

DEFINITION

There is no single definition of learning style. Curry (1983) described 21 different models of learning styles. I estimate that six models currently enjoy some popularity in educational circles. The oldest and least popularized version of learning style is Witkin and Goodenough's (1981) psychological construct of field independence and field dependence, referred to as cognitive style. Field-independent people are analytical and separate misleading background information from relevant information in order to solve problems, whereas field-dependent people tend to be more holistic in their approach to problem solving.

Another version of learning style has to do with personality types and is based on the theories of psychologist Carl Jung. The Myers-Briggs Type Indicator (Myers, McCaulley, Quenk, & Hammer, 1998) categorizes people along four dimensions: introversion/extroversion, intuition/sensation, thinking/feeling, and judging/perceiving. People are believed to favor one dimension over the other, resulting in 16 possible types. I, for example, am an "INTJ" type (Introverted, Intuitive, Thinking, Judging)—a perfectionist who can be rather hard on people (but that's not news to my family, friends or students).

Several learning style frameworks are organized around hemispheric preferences, for example, Kolb (1985) or McCarthy's (1987) 4 MAT. The 4MAT system identifies four types of learners. Two types prefer the left-brain mode and tend to do fairly well in school and on tests and the other two types prefer the right-brain mode and are more free-spirited.

The fourth learning style variation, and the one that has gained the most followers in education, has to do with perceptual preferences. People are believed to be visual, auditory, or tactile/kinesthetic learners. Leading promoters of this approach are Dunn and Dunn (Dunn, Dunn, & Price, 2000) and Carbo (1982). Combinations also exist. The notion of hemispheric preferences, especially the simplified version of left-brain/analytic learners versus right-brain/holistic learners, is often combined with perceptual preferences. It is also worth mentioning that all the authors mentioned have a copyright on a learning styles assessment instrument. Learning styles are not just educational, they are a lucrative business.

Pediatrician Mel Levine (2002) popularized a combination learning style approach in his popular book *A Mind at a Time*. Although he cites no scientific evidence in the book, he suggests that every child has a unique neurodevelopmental profile or "partly hidden spreadsheet of personal strengths and weaknesses" (p. 35). Interestingly, the medical profession has been much more critical of his ideas than have educators. In addition to book sales, Levine advocates an intervention called Schools Attuned, and he was recently awarded a $12.5 million contract by the city of New York to train teachers how to use his program (Herszenhorn, 2004).

A final variant on the learning style theme is Howard Gardner's concept of multiple intelligences described in his books *Frames of Mind: The Theory of Multiple Intelligences* (1983), *Multiple Intelligences: The Theory into Practice* (1993), and *Intelligence Reframed: Multiple Intelligences for the 21st Century* (1999). Gardner's basic idea is people are intelligent in different but equally important ways. He defines eight kinds of intelligence, including linguistic, mathematical, spatial, musical, kinesthetic, interpersonal, intrapersonal, and naturalist. In essence, what Gardner has done is to redefine talents as intelligences (Willingham, 2004). Gardner's idea has gone from being a disputed theory to a crusade to a foregone conclusion. His theories have spawned a cottage industry of handbooks and curricula that look a lot like applications of learning style and that have put a lot of people on board the cash train.

In my experience, most teachers adhere to a more informal interpretation of learning style that I call quasi-learning style. It combines various models and relies on teacher observation for assessment, but it suffers from the same questionable assumptions and harmful effects. I'll talk about quasi-learning styles in more detail later in the chapter.

FAULTY PREMISES

All versions of learning style are based on the same faulty premises that limit their practical application to education. The first assumption is that learning style is intrinsic and the second is that learning style can be assessed reliably. The third assumption is that learning style works. That is, academic achievement is higher when students' learning style is matched to a particular teaching style or method of instruction, and that a mismatch results in low achievement or even school failure. Repeated investigations have failed to support the efficacy of matching instruction to learning style.

Learning Style Is Intrinsic

Learning styles are presumed to be intrinsic and unchanging, something we are born with, like eye color. Presumably, they cannot be altered through experience, maturation, or education. However, the scores on tests of learning style do change. A person's assessed learning style appears to be influenced by maturation, background knowledge, and specific skills, especially reading. What appears to be a learning style may actually be a response to a particular situation.

Children's preference for a particular learning style seems to change as they get older. Even learning style advocates admit that some of what is measured as learning style is normal developmental change. For example, children and middle school students express a preference for tactile/kinesthetic learning, whereas high school students are less tactile and prefer auditory learning (Dunn, 1982). High school students need less structure, are more "self-motivated" (as opposed to peer-motivated) but more "unmotivated" than younger students, and have less need to work with peers than elementary students (Dunn, 1982, p. 145). These changes seem fairly predictable and more the result of maturation than some intrinsic way of processing information.

Traits identified as learning style do not necessarily represent static, intrinsic personality characteristics. What is called a learning style may actually be behavior that is situation-specific or related to factors that have nothing to do with the way a person processes information. Since there are no neurological tests for learning style, assessment depends on what a person does, or reports he or she might do, in a particular situation. Such expressed preferences do not necessarily represent intrinsic differences because tasks are not categorized so simply. Consider the following two situations as an illustration.

One day my keyless entry system (the remote transmitter than unlocks/locks the car doors) quit working. The first thing I did was look up "key" in the owner's manual. The manual gives a description of the problem, the probable cause (dead battery), battery specifications, and instructions, including two diagrams, on how to replace the battery. I figured it out by myself. Calling the dealership for an expert opinion or driving out there for a hands-on demonstration of how to replace the battery would be silly. Learning style advocates would say that my response to the problem (reading) makes me a visual learner.

On the other hand, if something electrical went wrong with the car—windshield wipers quit working, moon roof wouldn't close, headlights went out—I'd be hard-pressed to even diagnose the problem as a blown fuse. Thirty years ago I took a course with the degrading name of *Powder Puff Mechanics*, in which I learned about basic auto mechanics. Theoretically, I should have some background knowledge that would help. However, you might as well ask me to build an entire engine as to replace a fuse. The owner's manual provides five full pages of directions, including many diagrams complete with helpful arrows, but in this case I couldn't do it with the manual alone. I would need a person to assist me as I engaged in the hands-on activity so that I could ask questions and receive feedback. That makes me a tactile/kinesthetic learner.

I didn't change from a visual learner to an auditory/tactile/kinesthetic learner, the *task* changed. The second situation is one with which I am so unfamiliar and utterly lacking in background knowledge that reading alone is insufficient, even though I am a very good reader. I suggest that this is the case for many learners as it pertains to academic tasks. Students may require structure and assistance (hands-on learning), not because they're tactile/kinesthetic learners, but because they are *naive* learners or because the task is very difficult for them. In other words, the tendency to identify individuals as tactile/kinesthetic or hands-on learners has less to do with perceptual process than it does lack of background knowledge or weak academic skills.

The critical variable is not learning style, but whether the instructional method is appropriate for the task to be learned and whether individuals have sufficient background information to complete the task independently. What's more, people who report that they never like to use handouts or textbooks are probably not skilled readers, which is a very different kind of problem.

Learning Style Can Be Assessed

The second questionable assumption underlying the myth of learning style is that learning style can be assessed. I can't deny that learning style tests are fun to take. There are many online learning style inventories. They are appealing for the same reason horoscopes are appealing. The items give us an opportunity to think about our favorite subject, ourselves, and the results are vague enough to sound like us. For example, "In a classroom setting, you benefit from listening to lecture and participating in group discussions." What else is there? "You learn best when interacting with others in a listening/speaking exchange." As opposed to what, mind reading?

Assessing an unseen and poorly understood psychological construct is problematic. Paper-and-pencil assessments generally suffer from problems with reliability and validity. Reliability means consistency or the tendency for an individual's scores to remain stable or to be consistent with other tests that measure the same thing. High reliabilities suggest that the score a person obtains on a test is pretty close to what their "true" score should be. In other words, the test didn't make a mistake. If tests are not reliable, it means that they are poorly designed and/or the thing being measured is not a stable, intrinsic trait, or both. Validity means truthfulness, or the extent to which a test actually measures what it says it is measuring. The highly contextual nature of learning style makes it difficult to determine just exactly what is actually being measured, which reduces validity. Tests give teachers a false sense of objectivity, but they are no more scientific than informal observation.

A recent experiment compared students' scores on a standardized learning style test to teachers' perceptions of student learning styles. Researchers gave the Learning Style Inventory (Dunn et al., 2000) to nearly 500 students in grades 3 through 8 to determine if they were auditory, visual, tactile, or kinesthetic learners. After teaching the students for one semester, students' teachers were asked to predict the students' learning style. Teachers predicted only about 30% of the students' learning styles correctly, which is just above chance levels of 25% (Holt, Denny, Capps, & DeVore, 2005). It's hard to know whether the results of the standardized test were more or less accurate than the teachers' observations. The point is that behavior can be easily misinterpreted, whether it is based on self-report, on a standardized test, or on teacher observation.

One morning I sat down at the computer and took several learning style inventories available on the Internet. Every time, I came out a visual learner. That's good reliability, or consistency, among the three tests. But what about the validity? I went back to the items and took a closer look at them. On closer examination, it seems that I am visual learner because I can read and write well. Is that a learning style or a learned skill? Take one example, "I understand better by reading the newspaper than listening to the radio." First of all, when I read that item I compared reading the paper to listening to a news show like *All Things Considered*, but that was an inference. Other people who read that item might compare reading a newspaper to listening to a newsbreak on a rock station or call-in talk radio. Newspapers aren't comparable to radio headlines or call-in shows. But assuming the comparison is between getting news "visually" versus "auditorially," further analysis still reveals problems with validity. Reading is not just visual, it is qualitatively different than listening. Reading, because the print persists on the pages, gives one time for skimming, selective reading, rereading, and reflection. Reading can provide more depth and it's also faster. Minute for minute, a person can get a lot more information by reading than by listening. On the other hand, the newspaper is not as rich in human interest as radio news. You can do other things while you are listening to the radio, but it's hard to do more than drink coffee when reading the paper. The comparison involves much more than visual versus auditory processing.

Consider another item from the same learning style inventory. "I would rather have someone explain a computer problem than to figure it out by reading the manual." In this case, explanation has several advantages over reading the manual (or accessing the "Help" function on a computer) that have little to do with modality. An explanation may be easier to understand. It's quicker. Depending on how much background knowledge a person has and the nature of the problem, the manual may be incomprehensible. Explanation also has the obvious advantage of allowing for questions and clarification if the explanation is unclear or incomplete.

A person's answer to the above items reflects a fundamental difference in the nature of the task more than a preference for a particular way of processing information. Learning style inventories lack validity because they don't measure ways of processing information as much as responses to particular tasks and situations. It is doubtful whether such tests would accurately predict choices learners would make under different circumstances, let alone whether or not that information is of any practical value.

Learning Styles Can Be Matched to Instructional Styles

The third faulty premise is that matching learning style is an effective instructional intervention; that is, higher achievement results from matching learning style to a particular method or curriculum. Numerous experimental studies reveal that when instruction is matched to learning styles, students do *not* learn more than they would have otherwise.

One of the first experimental studies to examine the efficacy of matching teaching methods to learning style was conducted more than 30 years ago. Bateman (1971) gave a test to four classes of children going into first grade to determine if they were visual or auditory learners. The experimental children were compared to four classes of children who were not assessed for learning style (control classes). Half the classes used an auditory method of teaching reading (Lippincott, considered to be a phonics program in which *hearing* sounds was important) and half used a visual method of teaching reading (Scott Foresman, which stressed *visual* whole word recognition).

Among both the experimental and the control classes, children who were taught with the auditory method scored significantly higher than children who had been taught with the visual method. This was true *regardless of their learning style*. What's more, children who had been identified as auditory/phonics learners scored significantly higher than visual/whole word learners, regardless of how they were taught! These results clearly indicated three things. First, the auditory/phonics method of teaching reading was more effective. Two, auditory learners had an advantage over visual learners for learning how to read. Three, learning style was irrelevant. Subsequent research has verified these conclusions.

Tarver and Dawson (1978) reviewed 15 studies that investigated teaching to children's modality strengths (auditory versus visual learning styles). They, too, found that matching method of teaching reading to modality strengths did not improve reading achievement. They concluded that researchers have placed too much emphasis on analysis of the learner, but have paid no attention to analysis of the complex task of reading. Their conclusion seems prescient since our current understanding of how to teach reading has resulted from scientific study of skills that are essential to the task of beginning reading.

Thirty years of research have failed to support the relevance of learning style in reading. Kavale and Forness (1987) reviewed 40 studies and found an overall effect size around zero. I reviewed the literature on beginning reading and learning style in the early 1990s and concluded that matching learning style to reading methods was not only ineffective but also potentially harmful! Matching instruction to learning strengths ignores the phonological deficits of children with reading disabilities, penalizing them even further in their effort to learn to read (Snider, 1992). Stahl and Kuhn (1995) reiterated those conclusions and concerns. They stressed that children need to learn letter sound correspondences, which is now an unassailable fact. Liberman (1985) summarized it nicely.

> I think it is likely that most children who have difficulty learning to read are probably those who have been using a whole-word strategy already, never managing to see the alphabetic principle on their own, and thus falling farther and farther behind their more insightful classmates. To lead them back again to the same strategy, as the learning-style advocates would do, seems to me quite indefensible. (p. 101)

Great harm can be done in the name of learning styles. The danger is that by focusing on the *learner* instead of *what is to be learned*, teachers deny children the opportunity to acquire essential skills that they need for future success. Nowhere is this more apparent than in beginning reading. Researchers have reached a consensus on how to teach beginning reading. In 1997, *Time* magazine concluded, "the value of explicit systematic phonics instruction has been well-established. Hundreds of studies from a variety of fields support this conclusion. Indeed, the evidence is so strong that if the subject under discussion were, say, the treatment of mumps, there would be no discussion" (Collins, 1997, p. 81).

The problem with learning style is that it focuses solely on the characteristics of the learner (and assumes those characteristics are intrinsic and unchangeable) and completely ignores the nature of the task that needs to be learned. This distorted perspective can result in teaching procedures that don't make any sense.

Years ago, I attended a conference session in which a prominent learning style advocate described a procedure for "tripling" reading progress (Carbo, 1990). This feat could be accomplished simply by having tactile/kinesthetic learners listen to tape-recorded books and ride stationary bikes while looking at a book mounted on a stand over the handlebars. She insisted that youngsters who did this activity learned to read "100% better." No one would ever think that learning to ride a bicycle had anything to do with reading. It's completely irrelevant!

Several years ago, the satirical national paper *The Onion* did a hilarious spoof of exactly this kind of thinking. They captured the absurdity of using learner characteristics to determine instruction in an article entitled "Parents of Nasal Learners Demand Odor-Based Curriculum" (2000). The article admonished school districts for their failure to provide fragrant textbooks for nasal learners and the picture showed a despondent child struggling with an odorless textbook. Both smell and movement, and to some extent vision and hearing, are irrelevant because learning to read is primarily a language activity that requires interpretation of an abstract symbol system, the alphabet.

Learning style is described many different ways in the professional literature, but all of the variations suffer from the same problems. Learning style is not a well-defined or stable trait, which makes it very difficult to assess. Matching a method to an illusory characteristic has not resulted in higher achievement. Close examination of an activity like reading reveals that the characteristics of the task may make a learner's presumed learning style irrelevant. Besides, teachers don't have the luxury of prescribing 20 to 30 unique methods or curricula for every student or student type. Why are teachers so firmly committed to learning style when it isn't realistic and doesn't achieve the desired results?

QUASI-LEARNING STYLES

Looked at in the best possible light, learning style is just a way of acknowledging children's and adolescent's individual differences. I have listened carefully when teachers talk about learning style and I have asked them to explain what the term means to them. Generally, they say something like this: "Some students learn best when they hear about things, others need visuals to learn, and others need to see and hear things to learn. Many students learn best in small discussion groups and need hands-on experiences." In other words, teachers provide a very broad description of learning style usually focusing on perceptual preferences.

Teachers generally assess learning styles informally, through observation, rather than with self-report inventories. Informal assessment suffers from the same problems as the paper-and-pencil inventories discussed earlier. Tasks may appear to be visual, auditory, tactile, or kinesthetic, but the superficial exterior usually hides a more complex cognitive task.

Children cope with their inability to read in ways that might superficially seem like a learning style, but that actually reflect poor reading skills. It's easy to misinterpret certain behaviors. Consider the following examples.

1. Sometimes elementary teachers say that poor readers are auditory learners because they can't track words with their finger. It's more likely that their tracking problems occur because they can't read the words. Usually these auditory learners can keep their eyes riveted to a television or videogame screen for hours.
2. Sometimes elementary teachers say that poor readers are visual learners because they memorize and rely on picture clues rather than sounding out words. It's more likely that they revert to visual clues because they can't read the words. Without knowledge about of the underlying sound structure of the language, they have little choice but to rely on memorization and guessing.
3. Sometimes high school teachers say that poor readers are auditory learners because they need the text read aloud or explained to them.
4. Sometimes high school teachers say that poor readers are visual learners because they need pictures, graphics, and visual displays to explain the text they cannot read.

In all of these examples, the source of the observed behavior is poor reading skills. To ignore the basic problem in no way benefits the students. The same is true when students are labeled as tactile/kinesthetic learners. They need hands-on experiences, group work, and activities to learn, not because of their learning style but because they need structure, assistance, and feedback on difficult or unfamiliar tasks.

I have observed that high school teachers don't generally match a learning style to a particular instructional approach. Rather, they use eclectic, multisensory, or hands-on approaches. They hope that by presenting information in a variety of ways, they will reach everyone's learning style. This practice may or may not be a good idea depending on the task.

The *New York Times Magazine* (Nelson, 1993) described a learning style approach to teaching tennis. Using a test developed by a management consulting firm in Boston, aspiring tennis players were classified as watchers, thinkers, feelers, or doers. The watchers saw a video in which a pro modeled various tennis moves. The thinkers were given technical information about the game. The feelers did things like hold the ball in the crook of their elbow to learn the proper position for serving. The doers went out and practiced hitting the ball. The interesting thing was that sports teachers used all four techniques with everyone. In this case, all four techniques made sense to teach the game of tennis. Any one technique alone, however, would not make sense. In fact, the learning style assessment was irrelevant. The approach worked, not because the instructors catered to every type of learning style, but because the combination of activities all made sense given the task of tennis. Teaching procedures should be determined by the task, not the characteristics of the learner. The task determines the nature of the assessment too. Any meaningful assessment of tennis skills would certainly have to be tactile/kinesthetic by necessity.

There is also a strong element of student choice in the way teachers apply the concept of learning styles to their classrooms. To individualize according to learning style, teachers may allow students to choose how they want to learn (e.g., watch a movie or read a book) and how they want to be assessed (e.g., design a diorama or write a report). Giving students options is only a good idea if all the options make sense, given the task.

Human nature being what it is, students are likely to make choices that reduce accountability or that are easy and convenient. I know that when I was in high school, had someone given me a choice about how to complete the unit on tennis in physical education, I would have chosen the video. (This would have a number of advantages from my perspective. I could avoid the humiliation of exposing my poor coordination to peers and I wouldn't have to take a shower or wash my gym clothes.) If I could have chosen how I was assessed, I might have chosen a multiple-choice test on how to keep score. None of which makes a bit of sense if the goal is to play tennis.

Most meaningful assessments of academic skills involve reading or writing and sometimes speaking. For example, if a teacher wanted students to demonstrate that they understood the causes of the Civil War, it might be appropriate to have them write reports or essays, engage in debate, or write journal entries from the perspective of Northerners and Southerners. However, students could not possibly demonstrate that they understood the causes of the Civil War by making a diorama in a shoebox. Giving options to children and adolescents guarantees that only some students will achieve the desired outcome.

Looked at in another way, quasi-learning style is a very nice way of saying that some kids have not been successful academically. Rather than say, "Bill's a good football player, but he'll never make it in college," teachers can say "Bill has a kinesthetic learning style!" Rather than say, "Sandy needs to have an outline and a graphic organizer because she can't read and understand the text on her own," teachers say "Sandy is a visual learner."

Several years ago I visited a classroom where students were clustered in various parts of the room working on group projects. One student, however, was darting from group to group, knocking over chairs, and generally making a nuisance of himself. When I inquired about this child, the teacher casually told me, "Oh, he's a kinesthetic learner." Surely that was putting the best spin on what was clearly a behavior management problem. When expectations are lowered, even when it is inadvertent, learning style has the potential to diminish, rather than enhance, school experiences.

THE HARM THAT IS DONE

We know that tests of learning style are not reliable or valid. We know that individuals' scores change depending upon their age, the situation presented to them, and their skills. We know that matching instruction to learning doesn't lead to higher achievement. The belief in learning styles simply seems to result in teachers presenting information in a variety of ways. So what's the harm in that? Belief in and use of learning styles has two harmful effects. One, it prematurely, and subtly, sorts students into categories that may diminish their educational opportunities. Two, it provides an excuse for the failures of schools and teachers by blaming the victim for their failure to learn. The effect on students can be devastating.

The Sorting Hat

In J. K. Rowling's (1998) first Harry Potter book, she described how children put on the Sorting Hat at Hogwarts School of Witchcraft and Wizardry. The Sorting Hat reached deep into their souls to discover the personality traits that would assign them to the house of Gryffindor, Hufflepuff, Ravenclaw, or Slytherin. In American schools, teachers divine that information in less magical, and less reliable, ways. Since learning style doesn't necessarily reflect intrinsic traits, sometimes children get unfairly sorted in ways that are harmful.

The need to provide a different kind of school environment for some students may be a vestige of the differentiated curriculum that was a legacy of the progressive movement in the early 20th century. Poor, immigrant, and nonwhite children were believed to need courses in vocational education, not mathematics or English. The unstated assumption was that immigrant children, who comprised over 50% of those in school at the turn of the century, were not smart enough for the academic studies enjoyed by children from established families. This sorting philosophy of public education has dominated public schools in the twentieth century.

Despite the egalitarian rhetoric, compulsory school laws did not create upward mobility. They sorted children into those who were capable of benefiting from higher education and those who were not. Learning styles gives the sorting machine a kinder, gentler appearance, but they serve the same function.

The appeal of learning styles is enormous, not just to teachers but to parents, too. They would prefer to label their first grader a visual learner rather than a poor reader or their popular, star quarterback son as a tactile/kinesthetic learner rather than an underachiever. There is nothing inherently wrong with most of the children who struggle with school tasks. What teachers and parents do not understand is that just because children do not acquire certain academic skills naturally or without effort does not mean they are incapable. Labeling them with a learning style excuses their difficulty and ensures that they will come out of the sorting machine without the academic skills they need to become successful adults.

Blaming the Victim

Although all learning styles are considered equal theoretically, some learning styles are associated with low achievement. Students who are judged to be auditory, analytic, left-brain learners get good grades and do well on tests; and those who are considered to be tactile/kinesthetic, holistic, right-brain learners perform poorly on academic tasks. By giving those characteristics a name under the guise of learning style, however, the characteristics appear to be intrinsic, unchanging, and unavoidable when, in fact, they may well be the result of lack of exposure or ineffective instruction.

The fact that certain learning styles or types are associated with higher academic achievement is obvious at the college level when the cumulative effects of a lifetime of learning (or not learning) have the most effect. The Myers-Briggs Type Indicator (MBTI) is positively correlated to IQ (Myers et al., 1998) and other academic indicators. St. Louis University required all incoming freshman to take the MBTI in order to track and improve student retention (Kalsbeek, 1989). They found that IN types (introverted and intuitive, the most abstract and reflective type) tend to have higher SAT and ACT scores as well as higher grade point averages during the first semester of college. Forty-six percent of high-risk college students were ES types (extroverted and sensing, which means they are concrete, active learners) whereas only 8% of high-risk students were IN (introverted/intuitive) (Kalsbeek, 1989). In other words, high-risk college students had a high-risk learning style.

Sixty percent of college students preferred the sensing mode to the intuitive mode on the Myers-Briggs Type Indicator. The list of characteristics of those who prefer the sensing mode will help the reader understand why employers are upset about the quality of college graduates entering the work force. Sensing people are concrete and practical, they need structure, lack confidence in intellectual abilities, are uncomfortable with abstract ideas, have difficulty with complex concepts, have a low tolerance for ambiguity, do not have original ideas, and have difficulty with basic academic skills such as reading and writing (Schroeder, 1993). Is underachievement unavoidable because there are an increasing number of children who of ES types, or could it be that the lack of academic skills is the result of their inadequate school experiences? Might there be fewer ES types in college if students were more confident of their academic abilities?

Students with reading or learning disabilities and attention deficit hyperactivity disorder (ADHD) are often judged to have learning styles associated with low achievement. They are categorized as right-brain, holistic, and tactile/kinesthetic ("hands-on"). An interesting spin on ADHD promoted by the director of the National Reading Diagnostics Institute is that children diagnosed with ADHD are "simply kinesthetic learners [who] need to engage in gross motor (large-muscle) activity to learn best" and that once they "learn through the proper methods their inattentive behavior disappears" (Linksman, 2000, p. 1). Brand, Dunn, and Greb (2002) suggest that teachers can accommodate the learning style of students with ADHD by teaching them in the afternoon under soft illumination using tactile/kinesthetic and multisensory methods of instruction under parental, rather than teacher, supervision. Translation: pacify students with a fun activity and bring in their parents to supervise so that if they misbehave they'll "catch it" at home. This approach hardly seems like an intervention that will teach students how to manage their behavior.

Carbo, who has written volumes on reading styles, insists that poor readers, including those with dyslexia or learning disabilities, are global, tactile/kinesthetic learners and that once teachers stop trying to teach them phonics and match instruction to their learning style, they will learn to read (Carbo, 1984, 1987a, 1987b, 1987c). Unfortunately, school tasks tend to require analytic and auditory/visual strengths and bypassing phonics instruction only ensures that students will never become skilled readers. In other words, the learning style approach accommodates students' academic weaknesses rather than providing instruction that will address their problems. Teaching practices that accommodate learning style may guarantee continued school failure.

Some researchers have promoted the idea that minorities, especially African Americans, have a particular learning style. African Americans have been identified as having a holistic learning style, especially field dependent and people oriented. This is often contrasted with the dominant white culture, which tends to be more analytical, field independent, and competitive. If anyone doubts that certain learning styles carry value and judgment, consider the literature on multiculturalism and learning style.

The multicultural literature is replete with studies that examine the learning style of particular minorities, especially African Americans. Despite the widespread misconception that African Americans have a holistic, more nonverbal learning style, a careful examination of the literature suggests that is not true (Frisby, 1993; Irvine & York, 1995). Interestingly, when learning styles are applied to African Americans, the dangerous stereotyping inherent in learning styles is transparent. Several years ago, a passage in a booklet published by the New York State Board of Regents provoked controversy because a section on learning styles suggested that students who were at risk for dropping out of school—especially blacks, students with disabilities, or those with limited English proficiency—have been shown by research to learn *differently* than white, majority students. Differently? How can a race learn differently? Substitute "not as well" for "differently" and you can understand why some individuals viewed the statement as blatant racism.

Learning style blames the victim because it labels the symptoms of academic failure as a condition inherent to the individual. It pigeonholes students rather than addressing academic weaknesses. There are many reasons that students have difficulty in school, and many of them are beyond school control, but schools have a responsibility to teach academic skills and content. If students have difficulty reading or writing, difficulty with abstract concepts, or working independently, then it is the responsibility of the school to address those problems. The need for support is often related to low achievement and low achievement is amenable to instruction. Ascribing a label and prescribing watered-down instruction will not help students acquire critical academic skills or content.

The obvious appeal of learning style is that it acknowledges individuality. In the name of learning style, however, much harm has been done because it provides an explanation for failure. Teachers care, but they don't know how to help children who don't learn easily or naturally. The myth of process, fun and interesting, eclectic instruction, and the good teacher blur their vision. Most of the time, however, when children fail it is because the instruction failed. The most profound example of this is the teaching of reading. Millions of adults have low literacy skills, not because they didn't have the right learning style, but because they didn't have teachers who knew how to help them unlock the alphabetic code.

Learning style is a way to blame teaching failures on student failures, and to do it in a way that doesn't make it sound like anybody has actually failed. It is harmful and unjust to students because undeveloped verbal or analytic skills are falsely presumed to be intrinsic. It is detrimental to the field of education because teaching failures get excused, which eliminates any incentive to develop and use more effective instructional practices.

SUMMARY

Suppose that learning to play tennis was as important to success in life as learning to read. Throughout our school years, we spent many hours becoming skilled tennis players. People couldn't get jobs unless they played tennis well. It's easy to imagine that some youngsters might have trouble learning how to serve; not everyone will be a natural Pete Sampras or Billy Jean King, but they could lob the ball and do other things, like keep score. If teachers accommodated children's learning style by not teaching them how to serve, children might end up with some appreciation of tennis but they could never play tennis on a level with everyone else. They would be at a distinct disadvantage because they couldn't serve. The serve sets up the point. You can't overcome a bad serve. The task of reading also requires fundamental skills that must be learned well. When teachers fail to provide explicit guidance in "breaking the code" because students are not auditory or analytic or linguistic learners, it is like telling them to play tennis without a good serve. They will always be at a disadvantage. The same is true of other academic tasks.

Ultimately the analogy that children are like snowflakes succeeds because snowflakes are more alike than different, as are children. The differences among snowflakes, though wonderful, are not substantive. Snowflakes are made of the same substances. They crystallize under similar conditions, which are governed by the laws of physics. What is the same about children is their innate capacity for language, to learn to read and think inductively and deductively. In fact, what is the same about all children is that they will learn when provided with appropriate instruction. They may learn at different rates and may need different amounts of structure and practice to master academic skills and concepts, but they can learn. Our challenge as educators should be to design and deliver instruction that will maximize opportunities to capitalize on the sameness among all children—the capacity to learn to read, write, and think logically with both words and numbers.

People are different and teachers must be keenly sensitive to individual differences. Good teachers should observe and modify the instructional environment every day to meet individual needs, but they should not label and sort children by categories that have no instructional value. Individual differences in readiness to learn are best addressed with effective instruction at the student's instructional level. As with all the myths, the belief in learning style leads to lower expectations for many students and it devalues the need for curriculum and methods that work for all teachers and with all students, regardless of their so-called learning style.

The Myth of Disability

Few tragedies can be more extensive than the stunting of life, few injustices deeper than the denial of opportunity to serve or even hope, by a limit imposed from without, but falsely identified as lying within.

—Stephen Jay Gould, *The Mismeasure of Man* (1981, p. 28)

The sixth and final myth is that children who can't seem to learn and apparently won't behave have some kind of a disability (e.g., learning disabilities, attention deficit disorder) or some kind of a condition (e.g., low socioeconomic or minority status). Once the condition is labeled, it explains why students have failed in school. Labeling provides an excuse for the teaching profession, but it is a dangerous trap for students. It is the logical culmination of all the other myths. Without a clear focus on the goals of education and in the absence of effective professional practices that work in all schools, with all teachers, and for all students, teaching failures may be incorrectly identified as student failures.

Years ago, a colleague gave me a Tony Saltzman cartoon that I still display in my office. It shows a teacher lying on a psychiatrist's couch. The psychiatrist is saying, "Your feelings of insecurity seem to have started when Mary Lou Gurnblatt said, 'Maybe *I* don't have a learning disability—maybe you have a teaching disability.'" Maybe Mary Lou Gurnblatt had it right.

Not all teachers share the optimism implied by the No Child Left Behind slogan, although their level of optimism depends on how the question is asked. When educators are asked point blank if all children can learn, about 80% of teachers and 89% of principals agree (Markow, Fauth, & Gravitch, 2001). Interestingly, the level of optimism decreases as experience increases, from 86% agree for those with less than 5 years' experience to 73% for those with more than 25 years' (Markow et al., 2001).

When the question is asked in a more specific way, however, teachers are more pessimistic. Our survey found that half of all teachers believed that factors (such as home life or dyslexia) could prevent children from becoming functionally literate and mathematically competent, regardless of the school's best efforts. Less than a third thought that all children (excluding those with severe disabilities) could become literate, and the rest were unsure or balanced between those two beliefs. These statistics are disheartening because the effect of expectations, or more precisely the damage that can be caused by low expectations, has been well documented. When teachers believe that a label suggests that children are low performers, they will be low performers. This self-fulfilling prophecy of labels is devastating to students who already possess a variety of risk factors that make school challenging.

Go into any teachers' lounge across America and listen for comments like the following:

- A lot of students in my class flunked the last exam. I must not have taught the content very well.
- James seems to be having a lot of trouble keeping up. I think I'll do some informal assessments to find out where the problem lies.
- Sam is always interrupting and it's getting worse. I wonder if there's something I could do so that he gets less attention for his outbursts.
- Mary just doesn't get it. Maybe I could find a way to give her a little more practice.

You won't hear very many. You're more likely to hear things like.

- A lot of students in my class flunked the last exam. They never study for the test. They just go home and watch TV.
- James seems to be having a lot of trouble keeping up. I think he's got a learning disability.

- Sam is always interrupting and it's getting worse. I wish his parents would put him on medication.
- Mary just doesn't get it. Her parents aren't very bright, either.

Teachers express concern and frustration about their inability to reach all students (Farkas et al., 2003; Lortie, 1975), but at the end of the day they seldom take responsibility for children and adolescents who do not meet school standards. According to one study, teachers allocated about two-thirds of the blame for school failure that resulted in special education placement to child characteristics, about one-third to the home situation, and only 3.5% to school factors (Croll & Moses, 1985).

Teachers are not the only ones who express doubt that all children can learn. Administrators are also skeptical. One outspoken principal wrote a newspaper editorial comparing children in low-income schools to children with an incurable disease (Finley, 2002). Principals may confuse achievement with ability. Interviews with principals who had an unusually high incidence of children with problems in their schools revealed that they thought low-performing students had limited abilities caused by substandard homes and/or familial poverty (Allington, McGill-Franzen, & Schick, 1997).

The principals who were interviewed by Allington et al. (1997) had two primary solutions to learning problems—intervention through a separate program (e.g., preschool or special education) or waiting (e.g., delaying entry to school or retention). None of their solutions involved teaching changes, just changes in the way school was structured. In general, these administrators:

> explained the low achievement of children by calling up images of an unsatisfactory inventory shipped to the school by the manufacturers (parents). These school administrators would prefer a better inventory, but lacking that, will work vigorously to label the defective inventory they received and protect the reputation of the institution. (Allington et al., 1997, p. 230)

Alessi (1988) found similar sentiments among school psychologists. He identified five broad areas that could contribute to students' learning difficulties. The first is that students may be misplaced in a curriculum or the teaching materials may be of low quality (curriculum factors). This type of problem was described in the chapter on the myth of eclectic instruction (chapter 4). A second factor is that the teacher may not implement effective teaching procedures or behavior management strategies (teacher factors). This type of problem was described in the chapter on the myth of the good teacher (chapter 5). A third factor is that the principal or school leader may not implement effective schoolwide management practices or create a good climate for instruction (administrative factors). A fourth factor is that the parents may not provide enough support or the home environment is contributing to the learning problems (family factors). And the last factor is that the child may have veritable physiological or psychological disabilities that make learning difficult (child factors).

He conducted informal surveys with about 50 school psychologists around the country. First he asked them if they agreed that all five factors might play a primary role in learning or behavior problems and very few disagreed. He then asked them to identify the number of cases they'd had in the past year (usually about 100–120 per psychologist) where the referred problem was attributed to each of the five factors described above. His results indicated that curricula, teaching, and administrative factors were never mentioned. As Alessi (1988) put it, "All cases out of 5,000 examined confirmed that their schools somehow had been fortunate enough to have adopted only the most effective basal curricula . . . to have hired only the most skilled, dedicated, and best prepared teachers in the land . . . and retained only the nation's very best and brightest school administrators" (p. 148–149). When asked how many reports concluded that family factors were primarily responsible, the percentage ranged from 10% to 20%. Finally, when the school psychologists were asked how many referrals concluded that child factors were primarily to blame, 100% responded affirmatively. Clearly, the learners themselves are to blame for any learning problems.

Not too long ago there was a story making the rounds on the Internet called "The Blueberry Story" (Vollmer, 2002). As the story goes, Mr. Vollmer was an executive at an ice cream company that was noted for making the best blueberry ice cream in the country. He represented a group of businessmen committed to improving schools, who believed that public schools needed to change and that educators were a major part of the problem because they refused to change. One day while he was delivering his unpopular message to an unreceptive audience of teachers he had enlightenment. A high school English teacher asked him, "When you are standing on your receiving dock and you see an inferior shipment of blueberries arrive, what do you do?" Sheepishly he answered that he would send them back. "That's right!" the English teacher said, "and we can never send back our blueberries. We take them big, small, rich, poor, gifted, exceptional, abused, frightened, confident, homeless, rude and brilliant. We take them with ADHD, junior rheumatoid arthritis, and English as their second language. We take them all! Everyone one! And that, Mr. Vollmer, is why it's not a business. It's school!" With that revelation, the author began his transformation.

Teachers love this story, but I don't think it's very flattering. It shows that many teachers (and administrators) believe students with disabilities or disadvantages are damaged goods. They view teaching students who are imperfect, who are bruised, as a burden, not a challenge. It reminds me of the response given by Lester Maddox, the colorful governor of Georgia from 1967 to 1971, when he was asked what he proposed to do about the terrible prison system in Georgia. He replied, "There's not a lot more we can do unless we start getting a better class of prisoner" (quoted in Schneider, 1990, p. 872).

There is no doubt that many, many children face significant challenges in school. That's a fact. The myth is that those challenges make them uneducable, or worse, undesirable. These students may be more difficult to teach—it will take more skill and more time—but they are not uneducable.

FAULTY PREMISES

The myth of disability is based on the faulty premise that the only reasons for student academic failure are factors intrinsic to the student or demographic and family characteristics. Placing the blame for low academic achievement on students, their families, or their circumstances can create the false impression that there is little schools can do.

Blame the Student

Special education is the last stop on the educational train of excuses. There is always a slight chance that an individual can overcome difficult familial circumstances, but when the cause of the problem is a "bad brain," then there seems to be little hope of fixing the problem. There are several things that one must understand about special education to understand the myth of disability. First, the majority of students in special education have mild, not severe, disabilities and some disabilities are nonacademic. There is every reason to expect these students to achieve basic literacy in reading and mathematics. Second, although the label is *presumed* to identify intrinsic neurological dysfunction, there is seldom any objective evidence to justify that claim, especially for learning disabilities; rather, the label describes a set of symptoms, which leads educators to draw conclusions based on circular reasoning. Three, there is every indication that most reading disabilities, which are the cause of more than half of all referrals to special education, can be prevented or minimized through early intervention.

Most Disabilities Are Mild

Approximately 11% of the school-age population has disabilities that qualify them for special education. The Special Education Educational Longitudinal Study (SEELS) found that 75% of students in special education were labeled because they had either learning or speech and language disabilities. (They are grouped together here because they are often co-occurring.) The percentage for learning disabilities alone currently stands at 51%. 6% have severe emotional disturbance, 9% have mental retardation (the majority of which have mild mental retardation with IQs between 65 and 70), and 5% have other health impairments, which includes students with attention deficit disorder (National Dissemination Center, 2003). Those figures account for 95% of students in special education. The fact is that the majority of all students with disability labels have problems that should not prevent them from attaining basic or even advanced academic competencies. This is an important point that is often missing from discussions about whether or not schools should be held accountable for students in special education.

Identification Is Often Subjective

Another way to categorize students in special education is by high- versus low-incidence disabilities. Ninety percent of the students in special education have what might be called "high-incidence" disabilities. High-incidence disabilities depend on teacher referral and psychometric evaluation for identification. In other words, the diagnosis is subjective. Only 10% of students have sensory or neurological disabilities that are associated with obvious medical conditions (President's Commission, 2002) as shown in Figure 8.1. And many of that 10% have disabilities that should not reduce the potential for academic learning (e.g., attention deficit disorder or orthopedic handicaps).

The largest group of students in special education is students with learning disabilities (LD), who represent about half of all students in special education (U.S. Department of Education, 2002). Students identified with learning disabilities have increased 34% over the past decade (U.S. Department of Education, 2002). More than 80% of students with learning disabilities have difficulty learning to read (Lerner, 1989). According

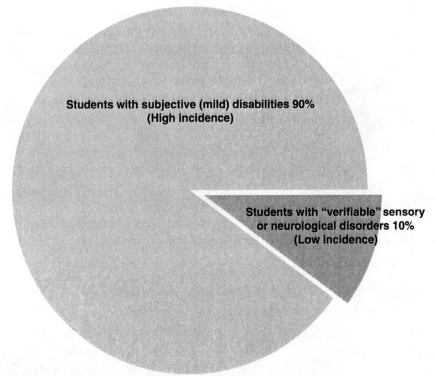

Source: President's Commission on Special Education (2002)

Figure 8.1.   Students in special education

to the federal definition for LD, the disability is presumed to have an intrinsic cause; however, there are no reliable neurological tests to determine if underlying biological factors exist. Students with LD are identified because they exhibit a discrepancy between their estimated potential on an intelligence test and their actual performance on an individual achievement test.

Professionals on the assessment team are supposed to rule out any possible environmental cause for the discrepancy, but applying exclusionary factors is difficult because it is often impossible to untangle the relative contribution of variables like poor instruction, poverty, or home environment. Students in special education are almost two times more likely to come from homes with incomes under $15,000 and half as likely as students in the general population to come from homes with incomes of over $75,000 (National Dissemination Center, 2003). In addition, it's impolitic to place the blame for underachievement on school or environmental factors. It's easier to blame poor performance on faulty brain wiring.

As a result, the assessment team usually rubber-stamps the referral and places the student in special education regardless of extenuating circumstances. A friend of mine, who is an LD teacher, told me about a recent referral she handled that illustrates the problem. She conducted an evaluation on a second-grade student and found that she was essentially a nonreader and she did, in fact, exhibit a discrepancy between IQ and reading achievement. However, this student had been attending a charter school that used very learner-directed teaching methods. As part of her evaluation, the teacher went and observed the child's reading lesson at the charter school. Not only was the lesson devoid of any instruction consistent with the recommendations of the National Reading Panel, but the time allocated to reading was about half of what is mandated by the state. The LD teacher was the lone dissenter at the team meeting and the child was placed in special education. This imprecise process of identifying "learning disabilities" describes a very heterogeneous group of individual children.

Supposedly there's a difference between students with reading disabilities that have a discrepancy (LD) and students with reading disabilities who don't have a discrepancy (garden-variety reading disabilities), but the line between them is indistinct. In fact, the growth curves of the two groups over time are virtually indistinguishable and neither group catches up with students who do not have reading disabilities at all (Lyon et al.,

2001). Some people think that when reading disabilities are called "dyslexia," they have an identifiable neurological cause and a unique learning profile, but that's not true. Dyslexia is just another label that describes specific problems in learning to read.

Another category of special education that has seen an increase in the number of referrals during the past decade is other health impaired (OHI), which includes students with attention deficit hyperactivity disorder (ADHD). The number of students identified with OHI has increased 351% (U.S. Department of Education, 2002). Although ADHD is presumed to have a biological basis, there is seldom a known neurological cause. Diagnosis of ADHD is based on behavioral rating scales and may be just as subjective as a diagnosis of LD.

The problem with accurate identification of both LD and ADHD is the result of circular reasoning. Circular reasoning is when a set of behaviors is described and labeled, and then the label is used as an explanation for the behavior. Consider these statements: "I'm right because I'm smarter than you. And I am smarter than you because I'm right." Circular reasoning in special education looks like this: "Students have learning disabilities because they can't learn to read. And they can't learn to read because they have learning disabilities." The symptom, not learning how to read, can be caused by many factors—some of them are environmental and some are intrinsic. Labeling the symptoms doesn't explain why the symptoms occurred.

The same is true of ADHD. It merely describes another set of symptoms. "Johnny is overactive and inattentive because he's got ADHD. And he has got ADHD because he's overactive and inattentive." Someday scientists may discover a cause for LD and dyslexia and ADHD, and design neurological tests that can be used for reliable diagnosis, but for now the label just describes the symptoms. Identification is subjective and prone to error. Students' poor reading skills or inattentive behaviors may be caused by intrinsic factors, home factors, school factors, or a combination. Circular reasoning is dangerous because it generally ignores the contribution of school factors.

Randy Sprick (1992), an educational consultant and author, told a wonderful story that describes the problem perfectly. He was working as a tutor to help a student named John who had finished first grade, but who wasn't reading. Mr. Sprick did some diagnostic work to figure out what the student did and didn't know about letters and words. When he informed the mother and father that he thought he could have John reading by the end of the summer, the parents were surprised.

> The mother looked incredulous and said, "That's great! But I do need to tell you that the school psychologist who tested John toward the end of the year thought he was probably hyperactive." Having worked with many students labeled hyperactive, I explained to the mother that although I could not comment on the validity of any other professional diagnosis, I said that I did not think that I would have any trouble helping him focus on the lessons, and I recommended that they delay acting on the psychologist's recommendation to have the child examined by their physician to explore medication.
>
> The mother then said that I should also be aware that the classroom teacher and the school psychologist concurred that John had a perceptual problems. I carefully explained that I could not comment on their diagnosis, but that I did not see anything that would prevent this child learning to read. Nobody had systematically taught him to blend the sounds together. We went through the same routine for the label Minimal Brain Dysfunction. The parents were ecstatic with my statement that I could effectively teach him, and they agreed to bring him in for tutoring.
>
> Later that afternoon, an angry school psychologist called me and demanded to meet with me immediately and demanded that I show her my diagnostic work that led me to the "unwarranted conclusion" that I could teach this child to read. I agreed to meet her an hour later. During our meeting she expressed that she thought I was raising false hope for this mother who had unreasonable expectations for her son. She then demanded that I show her the diagnostic tests. After looking at the work I had done with John, she pointed to a place on one of the tests and vehemently declared, "But look right here! Look where he wrote his name. You can see that this writing is direct evidence of this child's impairments!" At this point, I looked at her and informed her that that was the place where I had written his name—not John. (p. 11)

This humorous story illustrates the difficulty with ascribing neurological causes to academic behaviors (in this case, poor handwriting) in the absence of neurodiagnostic evidence.

Most Reading Disabilities Can Be Prevented

The third important point to understand about students in special education, especially students with learning disabilities, is that many of them are referred for reading problems, specifically decoding. Decoding is the act of recognizing printed words, not necessarily understanding them, just being able to interpret the squiggles on the page. Of all the problems that children experience in school, decoding problems are the easiest to fix. The research is unequivocal about the need for explicit, systematic instruction in phonemic awareness and phonics. Validated curricula with strong evidence of their effectiveness are available to do exactly that.

Decoding problems are easily prevented when instruction begins in kindergarten and first grade, but more difficult to remediate as children get older. Juel (1988) found that the probability of a poor reader at the end of first grade remaining a poor reader at the end of fourth grade was 87%, but the probability of a poor reader at the end of first grade being a good reader at the end of fourth grade was 15%. What's more, poor decoding creates a host of additional problems as children get older. Stanovitch (1986) has called this the *Matthew effect*. Students who get off to a good start in reading get into a positive cycle that provides opportunities for school success and increased cognitive ability. The opposite is also true.

Students who do not learn to decode in a timely manner quickly begin to hate reading. Because they hate to read, they don't read. Less practice causes them to fall further behind and often results in slow, halting oral reading. Slow reading, in turn, reduces the ability to understand what is read because all of the children's attention is devoted to figuring out what the words are, rather to what they mean. In other words, slow reading reduces reading comprehension. Poor reading comprehension reduces the amount of vocabulary and background knowledge that students can acquire when they read text, which further reduces reading comprehension. Less reading eventually leads to decreased cognitive ability (Cunningham & Stanovitch, 1998). Children who do not learn to decode in the early grades get into a failure cycle with devastating consequences, all of which are secondary to the initial, relatively trivial problem—decoding.

Unfortunately, the discrepancy model of identifying learning disabilities makes early identification almost impossible since it takes several years for discrepancies to get large enough for students to qualify. The majority of referrals for learning disabilities occur after second grade, at which point it is extremely difficult for them to catch up. In the past 10 years the number of students age 6–21 identified as LD has increased 34%, and the largest increase has come from adolescents between 12 and

17 years of age. Although students with learning disabilities comprise 40% of students in special education among 6–11-year-olds, they comprise 62% of those in the 12–17-year-old group (U.S. Department of Education, 2002). The system is designed to make students fail before providing any intensive remediation.

There are many reasons why children do not learn to read, or to do other academic tasks for that matter. It is likely that an interaction of factors contributes to reading disabilities. There is considerable evidence that all poor readers (not just those with learning disabilities) display brain patterns that differ from those of skilled readers, especially in the left hemisphere serving language (Lyon et al., 2001), but the atypical activity may be either a cause or an effect of being a poor reader. Many researchers believe that these differences reflect both biological and environmental influences. It is well known that reading disabilities tend to run in families (National Research Council, 1998), but the quality of reading instruction or early learning experiences may determine whether or not those tendencies turn into disabilities (Lyon et al., 2001).

Recent research has confirmed that effective reading instruction changes neural patterns. Learning to read is not natural; it must be taught. The quality of instruction matters most for those who, for whatever reason, do not learn to read easily. One way to look at it is that all children are born dyslexic, "it's just that some are easy to cure" (Fletcher, cited in Langland, 2004). The longer schools wait to identify students, the more difficult remediation becomes and the current model of identification favors a "wait until they fail" model of intervention.

Students with learning disabilities have been referred to as a "sociological sponge that attempts to wipe up general education's spills and cleanse its ills" (Lyon et al., 2001, p. 269). If teachers are not adequately prepared—if they don't know how to teach students with a wide variety of individual differences or how to manage the classroom, if they don't have a deep understanding of their subject (especially developmental reading), if they don't have access to well-designed, specific, and validated curriculum—then it is tempting to assume that nothing can be done. Applying a disability label makes chronic underachievement seem like a problem that is out of school hands. Although the disability label may be the most damaging of those assigned by education's Sorting Hat, the labels associated with socioeconomic or family factors affect the most students.

Blame the Family

Risk factors that are linked to poor achievement include speaking English as a second language, belonging to a minority culture, low parental educational levels, and poverty. Teachers also blame poor achievement on lack of parental support regardless of socioeconomic status. There is no doubt that all of these factors can contribute to low achievement, but do risk factors alleviate schools of responsibility for educational outcomes? Or do they heighten the school's responsibility by making what is learned in school even more important?

Effect of Risk Factors

Students with risk factors fall behind early and do not catch up. The Early Childhood Longitudinal Study (Rathbun, West, & Hausken, 2004) began studying over 22,000 children in over 1,200 schools when they entered kindergarten in 1998–1999. Currently, they are in fourth grade. Researchers identified four risk factors—a mother who has not completed high school, being on welfare, coming from a single-parent home, or speaking English as a second language. They found that children who had one risk factor were below their average peers at the beginning of kindergarten on indicators of early reading and mathematical competency. They gained some ground on very basic skills, but stayed behind on more advanced academic skills so that they still began first grade behind their more advantaged peers. The same was true for students who had two or more risk factors, only they were even further behind. The gap continued to widen for those with more risk factors throughout the primary grades.

It's important to reiterate that when children experience difficulty with beginning reading, or decoding, this trivial problem grows into a bigger one with each passing year. It doesn't really matter whether the cause of the poor reading is faulty brain wiring or environmental risk factors, early intervention can prevent, or at least minimize, the devastating secondary effects of reading failure that I described earlier. It's also important to keep in mind that the Early Childhood Longitudinal Study did not examine the effect of various interventions for helping children with risk factors catch up. The fact that children with risk factors lag behind does not necessarily mean that it is inevitable.

Children with risk factors tend to come from families with low incomes or incomes below poverty level. In 2004, the poverty level for a family of four was $18,850 and about 17% of the nation's 70 million children were believed to live in poor families. Another 38% of the children lived in low-income families with incomes of less than $37,700 for a family of four (Douglas-Hall & Koball, 2005). Schools are generally considered "low-income" when at least 40% of students qualify for free and reduced lunch. To qualify for free and reduced lunch, a family of four's income may be up to 130% of poverty level or $24,505 (free) or 185% of poverty level or $34,873 (reduced); plus there are other students (e.g., foster children) who are eligible based on formulas. The Department of Education's definition of poverty includes both poverty and low-income families plus some. In other words, schools that are considered low income include a lot of families with one or two hardworking parents who have high school diplomas. The stereotype of families on welfare evoked by the term "low-income school" is not accurate. It appears that the negative effects of poverty on school performance are most pronounced when poverty is long term and when students attend schools with a high concentration of students from poor families (National Research Council, 1998; Orland, 1990).

The way in which risk factors contribute to low achievement is unclear. On the whole, parental level of education seems to be the most predictive factor for school achievement. Students from homes with one or two college educated parents significantly outperformed students whose parents were not high school graduates (Orland, 1990; Grissmer, Kirby, Berends, & Williamson, 1994), but 75% of low-income children live in families with parents who have a high school diploma or more (Douglas-Hall & Koball, 2005). Minority status is another risk factor whose relationship to low achievement remains unclear. Two-thirds of all poor children are white, but the proportion living in poverty is much higher among blacks (four out of nine children) and Latinos (three out of eight children) (Five million children, 1994). Single-parent status does not seem to have a strong correlation to poor achievement (Orland, 1990).

It seems likely that demographic risk factors are not the real reason that poor and minority children fall behind early. I suspect they are indirect indicators of the literacy environment at home. This term includes things like the value that parents place on reading by reading themselves and the extent to which they express the expectation that children will also learn to read. The number of books in the house and the amount of time spent reading to children are also indicators of the literacy environment (National Research Council, 1998). Marvin and Mirenda (1993) found that children from low-income families experienced qualitatively different literacy experiences at home than children from more advantaged homes. Students from low-income families were less likely to go to the library or to hear rhymes and poems (which is important for developing phonemic awareness). Although they were just as likely to read with an adult, they were less likely to talk about the events in the books with an adult. Other researchers have documented fewer opportunities for verbal interactions (Hart & Risley, 1995), which can have a lasting negative impact on vocabulary and may depress reading comprehension in fourth grade and above (National Research Council, 1998). Marvin and Mirenda (1993) found that low-income parents also had lower expectations for their child's future academic success than more advantaged parents.

Affluent and educated parents place a high priority on learning to read. Consider the amount of time that middle-class parents spend reading aloud to children, especially alphabet books and Dr. Seuss books that emphasize the sounds of the language (alliteration and rhyming). Think of the time spent counting, arranging refrigerator magnets, singing alphabet songs, saying the sounds of the letters, and just talking. This informal instruction is an important determinant of readiness for academic learning. Low-income and welfare families may not have the time, the resources, or the wherewithal to engage in these type of activities.

Parent-Teacher Relationships

Teachers and parents have an uneasy relationship regardless of demographics. Large majorities of teachers feel that parents too often fail to do the kind of things at home that will enable teachers to do their jobs. One survey found that a majority of teachers perceive that parents do not provide children with structure at home, neglect discipline, perseverance, and good manners (Farkas, Johnson, & Duffett, 1999). Teachers also said that both suburban (67%) and inner-city (82%) parents don't know what's going on with their child's education and if they did, students would be more successful. Teacher resentment against parents who do not participate in their children's education crosses socioeconomic boundaries, but when socioeconomic factors are combined with lack of parental involvement, many teachers feel that they cannot overcome the negative effects. Forty-two percent of new teachers said that student achievement is mostly determined by parental involvement and socioeconomic factors, whereas only 54% said that teacher quality is just as important (Farkas et al. 2003).

I understand how frustrating lack of parental involvement can be for teachers, but I also think that many teachers and administrators lack empathy with low-income parents. One of the things that I learned during my years as a teacher was that school is a very intimidating place for many parents. It is a place that they associate with failure and inadequacy, and setting one foot across the threshold is difficult no matter how much they love their children. They feel judged, and often they are judged. What's more, many low-income parents may work the 3–11 shift, which interferes with popular after-school meeting times. What appears to be lack of support may actually be intimidation or lack of opportunity.

School can be intimidating even for parents who are well educated and affluent. A friend of mine, who has a Ph.D., has a daughter with a learning disability. She confessed that she spent years getting a stomach ache whenever she had to talk to one of her daughter's teachers because she knew that she was going to hear bad news or endure the negative comparisons with other children. Sometimes teachers forget that parental participation is a two-way street. When educators have negative feelings toward the parents, it can affect their interactions with students.

School Matters, Too

It's difficult to quantify the percentage of variance in student achievement accounted for by the school versus child and family factors, but school factors count for more than most teachers and administrators seem to believe. Scores in reading, mathematics, and science for students in the Early Childhood Longitudinal Study on measures of reading comprehension at the end of third grade were higher for children who attended private schools, even if they had more than two risk factors (Rathbun et al., 2004). Other research has also found higher achievement for children who attend Catholic schools, especially for black and Hispanic students and students with low socioeconomic status (Hoffer, Greeley, & Coleman,

1985). This result suggests that the school environment makes a difference in academic achievement. The most compelling reason, however, to believe that schools can make a difference in students' academic achievement regardless of familial and demographic variables is that some schools with a very high percentage of low-income and minority children have remarkable success.

Virtually every urban area boasts examples of schools that beat the odds. What I can't figure out is why more schools don't emulate those successful models. Successful low-income schools emphasize the factors over which they have control—amount of engaged time, teacher quality, curriculum and methods, and administrative leadership. They focus on the outcome, not the process; and they make no excuses. Many of them have had to fight the educational establishment to implement or establish their programs of high academic standards. Consider just a few examples from the thousands of successful low-income schools across the country.

Andrew Bennett Elementary. In 1974, when Nancy Ichinaga became principal, 95% of the student body at Andrew Bennett Elementary in southern California was illiterate. After four years, they went from the 3rd to the 50th median percentile rank in reading overall. They have kept improving so that now, after over 20 years, Andrew Bennett is one of the highest performing schools in Los Angeles County, even though 78% of its students are low income. One of the keys to their success is that they stress explicit, systematic decoding instruction in kindergarten. When California mandated whole language instruction in 1986, Ms. Ichinaga successfully enlisted parental support to lobby the State Curriculum Commission in order to obtain an exemption from the requirement to use whole language or lose funding for textbooks. She also gained an exception from the requirement to provide bilingual education because, although 30% of their student population speaks limited English, all instruction is in English (Carter, 2000).

Mabel B. Wesley Elementary. Wesley Elementary, named after a former slave girl who became a school principal, is the grandmother of comprehensive school reform in urban areas. The school is located in a very poor part of Houston called Acres Homes. It is 92% black, 7% Hispanic, and only 1% white; 87% of the students are on free or reduced lunch. When Thaddeous Lott, who grew up in Acres Homes and continues to live there, became principal in 1975 he implemented Direct Instruction, the model that did best among disadvantaged youngsters in Project Follow Through (Stebbins et al., 1977). At the time that he took over, most of the students read below grade level and many were nonreaders. By 1979, the third-, fourth-, and fifth-grade students were 2 years above where students had been before the implementation and by 1986 they were 2 years above grade level (Carter, 2000).

Despite the school's success, Lott ran afoul of district administrators when he refused to abandon his successful curriculum and replace it with whole language in the late 1980s (Palmaffy, 1998). Unable to believe that a school that was over 90% black and poor could outperform students in the suburbs, district administrators in Houston questioned Wesley's high test scores, although investigators never found *any* evidence of cheating. In 1991 Wesley was featured on the ABC news show *Prime Time Live* and in 1998 Wesley was featured on the *Oprah Winfrey Show*. In 2003, the *Dallas Morning News* raised new allegations of cheating, and Houston school officials hired an independent attorney to investigate. In May 2005, Wesley was once again exonerated (Spencer, 2005). It appears that many people find it hard to believe that poor, black children can achieve as much as white, middle-class children. As a result of both their success and publicity, Wesley has served as a model for many administrators seeking ways to raise achievement scores for black children living in poor urban areas, including City Springs.

City Springs School. This elementary school in Baltimore, with 95% of students considered low income, was one of the lowest performing public schools in the city. At one point, no students passed the third- or fifth-grade Maryland State test in either mathematics or writing. In 1997, principal Bernice Whelchel presided over a full immersion implementation of Direct Instruction. Scores for first-grade students on the Terra Nova test in reading went from the 28th percentile in 1998 to the 99th percentile in 2003 and from the 8th percentile to the 99th percentile in mathematics. For fifth graders the increase was almost as impressive, going from the 14th to the 87th percentile in reading and from the 9th to the 79th percentile in mathematics (Engelmann, 2003).

Morse Elementary. This school in Cambridge, Massachusetts, which is 65% low income, was in danger of closing because magnet schools had drawn off so many students in the Boston area. At the parents' request, Principal James Coady implemented a new curriculum called Core

Knowledge in all grades. Core Knowledge is based on the idea that all students need a specific, shared core of knowledge. It is much more specific about what to teach than how. The change was vigorously opposed by two teachers, who ended up leaving, and by the central administration. The strength of the opposition may have had something to do with the child-directed philosophy in influential institutions of higher education like Harvard's School of Education, which is located in Cambridge. The Core Knowledge curriculum strongly rejects the myth of process and fun and interesting. Now Morse is the highest performing elementary school in Cambridge with a median percentile rank in reading of 72 and 82 in mathematics (Carter, 2000).

KIPP Academy. The first KIPP (Knowledge Is Power Program) Academy was founded in Houston, and it now includes a network of academies. KIPP in the Bronx, however, was initially a public school from 1995–2000 (Thernstrom & Thernstrom, 2003) that was founded by David Levine after learning from Michael Feinberg at the original KIPP Academy in Houston. One of the interesting things about the KIPP Academy in the Bronx is that it shares a building with a regular public school that draws from the same population, which is 45% black and 55% Hispanic. Although the public school, I.S. 151, is the lowest performing school in the city; KIPP Academy is the highest performing middle school in the five districts that includes the Bronx (Carter, 2000). Interestingly, the district requires KIPP's test scores to be aggregated with another public school, making their success impossible to verify through public sources of data. Their own data suggests, however, that the average reading score for students who have attended for 2 years is at the 64th percentile and for students who have attended for 3 years it jumps to the 78th. The sixth- and seventh-grade students score at the 81st and 85th percentile rank in mathematics (Carter, 2000). KIPP Academies do not attribute their success to any particular curriculum. They attribute it to maximizing academic time; students at KIPP spent 67% more time in the classroom than public school students, in addition to high levels of teacher accountability.

Frederick Douglass Academy. This school for children in grades 7–12 is located in Harlem. The school is 80% low income and most students are drawn from the surrounding neighborhood, resulting in a racial composition of 79% black, 20% Hispanic, and 1% Asian American. In 1998, 93%

of the students who took the U.S. History Regents passed, compared with 58% across the city. In the Global History Regents, 95% passed compared to 54% citywide. Students achieved similar passing rates in English (88%) and precalculus (87%). Middle school students ranked 12th in reading and mathematics out of 235 schools in New York City. They use a knowledge-based curriculum that stresses liberal arts. The academy was founded on the idea that poor, urban students could be as successful as any other students and they seem to be proving that is true (Carter, 2000).

The teachers and administrators in the successful schools described above do not subscribe to the teaching myths. There is a clear focus on accountability and educational outcomes, a strong professional development component that turns good teachers into highly effective teachers, and reliance on sound instructional programs, not mushy eclectic instruction. Students may be grouped on the basis of performance, but they are not sorted or excused based on any learning style, risk factor, or special education label. Teachers and administrators have high expectations for student success.

Research on effective schools suggests that one of the differences between schools that transform themselves and those that do not is that school personnel believe that students can learn despite their disadvantages (Brock & Groth, 2003; Fashola & Slavin, 1998). The sense of inevitability that comes from blaming the student or the family gets in the way of establishing a vision of student academic achievement that includes all children.

THE HARM THAT IS DONE

The obvious harm that comes from ascribing school failure to child and/or family factors is the resulting low expectations. Low student achievement is perceived to be beyond the schools' control and little emphasis is placed on addressing the curricular, teaching, or administrative factors that might mitigate the risk factors. The confluence of these two factors heaps additional burdens on those who come to school behind academically. Teachers don't expect certain students to succeed, little effort goes into ensuring their success, and so the prophecy of failure is fulfilled.

Effect of Low Expectations

Self-fulfilling prophecies occur when expectations, even those that aren't warranted, come true. Self-fulfilling prophecies are common in the workplace, in business, in medicine, and unfortunately, in education. The landmark study of the effect of teacher expectations on student achievement was published in *Pygmalion in the Classroom* (Rosenthal & Jacobson, 1968). The study took place at Oak Elementary School in San Francisco. The authors randomly selected 20% of the students in the school so that the selected students were distributed among the teachers. The researchers then told the teachers that these particular students had been identified as late bloomers who had great potential to show academic gains during the upcoming school year. Achievement test data at the end of the year showed that targeted students made better gains than expected, especially children in first and second grades. Subsequent studies have shown that the relationship between teacher expectations and student performance is more complex than it may have seemed at first, but the power of expectations remains an important dynamic in the classroom (Good, 1982; 1987).

A self-fulfilling prophecy occurs when a person forms an expectation on the basis of some factor. Research has shown that teachers form expectations based on students' current achievement, conduct, socioeconomic status, race, risk factors, or special education labels (Barron, Tom, & Cooper, 1985). Once an expectation is formed, teachers communicate expectations through subtle behaviors. These include behaviors like singling students out for criticism, insincere or inappropriate praise, and less attention. If these behaviors occur consistently, students respond to the cues by engaging in behavior that matches the expectation and the expectation becomes true. The result is that high-expectation students will be encouraged to achieve at or above their potential but low-expectation students won't achieve as much as they could have. Expectations can affect the performance of individuals, groups, or whole schools (Good, 1987).

When teachers are asked if teachers in their school have high expectations for all students, 53% of elementary teachers and 39% of secondary teachers say that they do (Markow et al., 2001). Principals' estimates are always higher. Interestingly, when middle and high school students are asked if their teachers have high expectations, only 25% say yes. The percentage of teachers who have high expectations decreases for urban compared to suburban schools and for schools with over a two-thirds minority population. It appears that high expectations are not the rule, especially in schools with a high population of students with risk factors.

Both preservice and experienced teachers express negative attitudes about students in urban schools. Preservice teachers often use negative descriptions of children in urban settings (Schultz, Neyhart, & Reck, 1996; Wolffe, 1996). Estimates of the number of elementary teachers who express negative views about low-income students and their families range from 30–50% (Haberman, 1995) to 70% (Warren, 2002). Over half of high school teachers blame students and parents when students fail a test or assignment (Thompson, Warren, & Carter, 2004). If large numbers of teachers in a school hold negative views of the students they teach, it can affect school climate and lower expectations for students' success.

Teacher expectations for students in special education, especially students with learning disabilities, are similarly low. Teachers do not make disparaging comments about students with disabilities, for that would be considered unkind, but because they assume that the disability is intrinsic, they believe the prognosis for progress is poor. Logically, teachers' collective low expectations for an entire group of students, whether it is students with risk factors or with learning disabilities, exerts a more powerful influence on achievement than the low expectations of a single teacher for a single student because expectations for groups persist across teachers and over time.

My friend who has a daughter with learning disabilities has many stories about teachers with low expectations. Teachers seemed willing to reduce the amount of work for her daughter, but unwilling to teach her the skills she needed to know in order to succeed academically. For example, her daughter's second-grade teacher assigned fewer, and easier spelling words for her daughter. When my friend protested that she had to learn spelling rules and more difficult words, the teacher just looked at her blankly. This anecdote is particularly egregious since the primary disability was in mathematics, not reading or spelling.

There is some evidence that the teachers most likely to have low expectations for student success are those who lack confidence in their teaching abilities and who treat students as stereotypes, rather than as individuals (Thompson et al., 2004). A Public Agenda survey found that only 11% of teachers were very confident about achieving success with the "hardest-to-reach" kids in their own classroom and another 50% were somewhat confident, with elementary teachers expressing much more confidence than secondary teachers (Farkas et al., 2003). The teachers most likely to have high expectations for student success tend to be those with high levels of self-efficacy, who set reasonable goals for student success, and who have a pretty good idea of how to get them to the goal (Good, 1987). In other words, expectations are linked not just to student characteristics but also to feelings of teacher efficacy.

The low expectations associated with the myth of disability are partly a result of the failure to focus on academic outcomes (myth of process and myth of fun and interesting), inadequate teacher training and professional development (myth of the good teacher), and the use of ineffective and nonvalidated instructional programs (myth of eclectic instruction). It makes sense to predict that raising the level of professional competence would also raise teachers' expectations for the success of all students.

Ineffective Prevention and Remediation

When teachers and administrators have low expectations for student success and when they lack the professional competencies needed to raise achievement among hard-to-teach students, prevention and remediation efforts may fail. When student achievement remains low despite well-meaning but ineffective reform, low expectations get reinforced and the cycle of failure is perpetuated.

Millions of private, state, and federal dollars have been spent on prevention and remediation of the low achievement associated with disabilities and familial risk factors, with little success. The fact that programs haven't worked very well to this point should come as no surprise since the teaching myths dominate educators' thinking and perpetuate teaching practices that represent more of the same. Reform efforts have been primarily structural—earlier intervention, one-on-one instruction, and small class size—rather than functional changes in how and what to teach. Structural changes won't have the desired effect without accompanying changes in *how* and *what* to teach. When achievement outcomes are disappointing despite the investment of money, time, and effort; students and their families may get blamed.

Ineffective Special Education Programs

Students with learning disabilities do not close, or even narrow, the achievement gap. Special education is more like a black hole than the stepping-stone to success that it was meant to be. A review by Hanushek, Rivkin, and Kain (1998) found that special education does boost achievement of individuals with learning disabilities in mathematics and reading without detracting from the education of average students; however, the gains were so small (0.04 standard deviations in reading and 0.11 in math) that it would never allow students to close the gap (Lyon et al., 2001). In fact, they do not close the gap. In New York City, 3.5% of the eighth graders with learning disabilities passed the English exam and only 5% passed the math test (Lovett & Campanile, 2004).

The picture is worse at the high school level. Nationally, 30–50% fewer students with disabilities than average students pass high-stakes competency exams (Ysseldyke, Thurlow, Langenfeld, Nelson, Teelucksingh, & Seyfarth, 1998). Only 35% of high school students with learning disabilities graduate from high school with a regular diploma. Only 12% return to general education prior to graduation compared to 15% who drop out before they graduate (National Center for Educational Statistics, 2003a). Adults with learning disabilities, who comprise only 3% of the people in the National Adult Literacy Study, comprised 15% of those who scored at the very lowest levels of literacy (Kaestle et al., 2001). In light of statistics like these, it's hard to conclude that special education programs narrow the achievement gap.

The number of students with learning disabilities pursuing postsecondary education has increased, but it is still small. They are less likely than average students to attend a 4-year college and they are less likely to graduate. Murray, Goldstein, Nourse, and Edgar (2000) found that, among students with learning disabilities who graduated in the class of 1990, 17% had some kind of training after high school, 38% attended community college, and 9% attended a 4-year college. Five years after graduation, however, only 20% of students with LD who attended any type of postsecondary program had graduated, compared to 44% of average students. These data may not seem unexpected given their disability, but remember that students with LD have average or above-average intelligence and many have exceptional talents beyond the narrow area of disability.

Traditional remediation models for reading disabilities have been ineffective because they are "too little, too general, and too unsystematic"
(Lyon et al., 2001, p. 272). Even when they are effective, which is rare,
they are too late. Remediation typically does not begin until after students
are referred for special education, which does not occur until after second
grade. Lyon et al. (2001) estimated that if all students who score below the
25th percentile in reading received intensive, research-based, systematic
instruction in kindergarten and first grade, 70% of all reading disabilities
could be prevented (Lyon et al., 2001). This could only happen, however,
if teachers used effective, validated methods of reading instruction. Providing more minutes of ineffective instruction or doing it one-on-one
won't necessarily prevent or remediate reading disabilities.

Ineffective Programs for Learners with Risk Factors

Two entitlement programs for children of poverty have done little to alleviate the achievement gap. The first is Head Start, a program for children aged 3 to 5 years who come from poor families. Head Start was part
of President Lyndon B. Johnson's War on Poverty, and it received continued support in subsequent administrations, both Democrat and Republican. The rationale for Head Start was that early intervention could level
the playing field for children of poverty. In 1969, however, the Westinghouse Learning Corporation revealed that IQ gains made in Head Start
programs dissipated quickly once students went to school. A study in 1978
found the same thing, but reported that children who participated in Head
Start were less likely to need special education and less likely to be retained in a grade (Hacsi, 2002). Hundreds of research studies have examined various aspects of Head Start, but the core question, "Does it work?"
remains unanswered. Nevertheless, most people, including politicians, believe that Head Start works. At the request of Congress, the Government
Accounting Office reviewed 600 evaluation studies on Head Start. They
found that only 22 met their criteria for acceptability, and even many of
those studies had questionable control groups (Hacsi, 2002). After 40
years of research, it seems safe to conclude that children who attend Head
Start programs experience some benefits in terms of nutrition, better
health, social and emotional adjustment for kindergarten, but any academic benefits are minimal (Holden, 1990).

It's not too surprising that the results for Head Start in term of academic readiness are equivocal. It's naive to think that one year (sometimes two) in a program primarily staffed by poorly trained teachers with an emphasis on parental involvement, nutrition, health care, and socialization would produce significant academic gains. Studies have compared children who participated in Head Start to children who did not, which only shows that something is better than nothing. Studies have made no attempt to examine *what kind* of intervention at age 3 to 5 might result in higher literacy and mathematics achievement in the primary grades.

The second program for at-risk learners is called Title I. Title I was part of the Elementary and Secondary Education Act of 1965, which provided extra resources to high-poverty schools. The first and subsequent evaluations of Title I have been disappointing. Recent long-term trends in the National Assessment of Education Progress (NAEP) indicate that in 2002 the achievement gap in reading between students in Title I programs and those who were not stood at 26 points in fourth grade and 24 points in eighth grade (National Center for Education Statistics, 2003b). This indicates that they remain roughly two to three grade levels below peers, despite the fact that most have received extra instruction since first or second grade. Figure 8.2 shows the percentage of students who receive Title I services who scored below basic in fourth and eighth grades. The figure clearly shows that they do not catch up in any area, and in every area except reading the percentage below basic increases slightly from fourth to eighth grade (National Center for Education Statistics, 2003b).

Once again, it's not surprising to me that Title I programs have had little success. Until recently, there was not a concerted effort to examine what teaching methods work best with remedial readers or to intervene before high-risk youngsters start to fall behind. Teaching methods used by Title I teachers usually consist of the same kind of instruction that students had in general education. It takes more than extra minutes and smaller groups to help children with reading disabilities to catch up. It takes more skillful teaching and a more powerful curriculum to make a difference. It takes the science of teaching.

The one study that did attempt to examine the success of different teaching models for high-poverty children in the primary grades, Project Follow Through, found that two models, Direct Instruction and Applied Behavioral Analysis, were more successful than other models in produc-

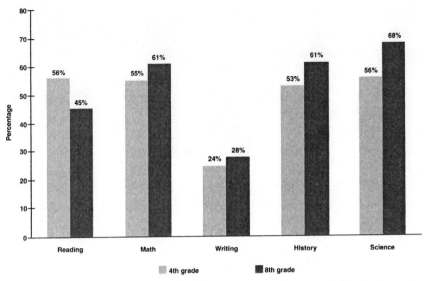

Figure 8.2. Percentage of students in Title I programs who score below basic on the NAEP in 4th and 8th grade

ing higher achievement in reading, written language, and mathematics by the end of third grade (Stebbins et al., 1977). What's more, analysis of the data from Direct Instruction sites indicated that young children with low IQs made just as much progress as those with higher IQs. They started lower and ended lower, but they were able to make approximately the same amount of gain (Gersten, Woodward, & Darch, 1986). Subsequent evaluations confirmed that "when this program is faithfully implemented, the results are stunning" (American Federation of Teachers, 1998). Unfortunately, the successful Follow Through models are generally rejected by reading teachers.

One of the models that did the worst in the Project Follow Through evaluation was similar to the popular whole language instruction that was widely used in Title I reading programs in the 1980s and 1990s, and that has now evolved into the balanced literacy that is popular in Title I programs. If students get more of the same, it is not surprising that they don't improve. More bad medicine doesn't improve academic achievement.

The most recent approach to improving academic achievement among low-income schools consists of financial incentives for whole-school reform. In 1998, Congress allocated $145 million for the Comprehensive

School Reform (CSR) Demonstration project, which became fully authorized with the passage of NCLB. The idea behind CSR is to help schools combine financial resources (state, Title I, etc.) to implement research-based reform models. To qualify for CSR funds, schools must implement a so-called research-based model of school reform, provide accountability measures, and include a strong element of staff development, among other things. It appears that CSR can significantly increase achievement among low-income students, although the effects are variable (Borman, Hewes, Overman, & Brown, 2002). Private efforts to support whole-school reform such as the Rand Corporation's New American Schools have also met with mixed results (Berends, Bodilly, & Kirby, 2002).

One of the reasons for the mixed results is that schools do not select the most promising models. The list of eleven "approved" models for CSR includes only three models (two at the elementary level and one high school) that received a positive rating by the American Institutes for Research (1999) in their evaluation of promising models. The percentage of grants going to CSR models that received a positive rating actually declined from 20.2 in 1998 to 8.1 in 2002 (Viadero, 2004). Go figure! A meta-analysis of student achievement indicated that only three CSR models have established their effectiveness across contexts and research designs (Borman et al., 2002). Interestingly, the American Federation of Teachers (1998) and the American Institutes for Research (1999) also gave positive ratings to two of the successful models in the meta-analysis, Direct Instruction and Success for All.

The way in which comprehensive school reform is implemented also contributes to uneven success. Wide variations in the fidelity of implementation exist even among schools that have adopted the same model (Vernes, Karam, Mariano, & DeMartini, 2004). Brock and Groth (2003) conducted a longitudinal study of 54 schools in Utah that qualified for grant money for school improvement. Initial grant awards focused on efforts to reduce class size, but later efforts encouraged schools to implement CSR. Out of 54 schools, only 15 adopted a CSR model, 19 adopted some curricular reforms that included parts of a CSR model, and 20 dabbled in various other innovations. The authors, who were evaluators for the state, visited the schools over a 4-year period. They found that "those schools that expressed confidence in their ability to improve student achievement outcomes in spite of student demographic factors took an entirely different approach from those schools that stated that they could not greatly impact student achievement outcomes because of student demographic factors" (p. 12). The schools that were most successful adopted CRS models with strong research support that were highly teacher directed, and the implementation included ongoing professional development, a high degree of staff involvement, a strong commitment to student learning, continuous monitoring and evaluation of student achievement, reallocation of resources to support the plan, and strong leadership from the principal. All the CSR reform models included intensive training for teachers and ongoing coaching.

Research on school characteristics confirms that effective school reform must go beyond changes in structure (like class size or more teachers' aides) to include changes in instructional methods and curriculum, intensive and ongoing professional development, and a focus on academic outcomes. In other words, as long as the teaching myths dominate educators' thinking, reforms will fall short. It's not possible to reverse the cycle of failure by doing more of the same—uninspired in-service training, homegrown eclectic instruction rather than validated curricula, half-hearted commitment to research-based practices, cloudy vision of learner outcomes, no systematic and ongoing evaluation, and lack of confidence in the ability to raise academic achievement. Elmore (2002b) suggested that "low performing schools, and the people who work in them, don't know what to do. If they did they would be doing it already." As long as educators cling to the myths, real and lasting change will elude them.

Effective special education programs and effective comprehensive school reform initiatives have to use powerful instructional practices that "teach more in less time" (Kameenui and Simmons, 1990, p. 11). Figure 8.3 shows the expected progress of average learners versus at-risk learners. At-risk learners start out lower and lose ground over time. It's easiest to close the gap in the primary grades because the gap is smaller, but to close or even narrow the gap requires a steeper learning curve. There is only one way to close or narrow the gap for students with disabilities or risk factors. Educators have to use scientific research to identify the teaching practices that teach more in less time, and then they need to faithfully implement them in kindergarten and first grade.

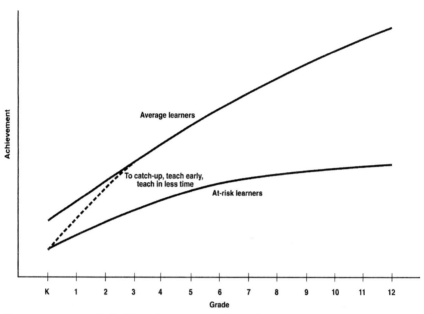

Figure 8.3. Hypothetical learning curves and "catch-up curve" for average versus at-risk learners

SUMMARY

Low expectations and ineffective prevention and remediation are the debilitating result of the myth of disability. Rather than focus on the alterable factors that the school can control, the blame for school failure shifts to students and their families. As long as the myths of process, fun, good teachers, and eclectic instruction persist, teachers will feel inadequate and overwhelmed by students who are hard to teach. They will play the blame game, lower their expectations, and insist that it's *not fair* to expect so much from students with disabilities and disadvantages. Unsuccessful students will get sorted into some category that, once assigned, will explain away school failure. The serious consequences of the labeling trap for students can hardly be overstated. Every year 40% of the school-age population will be labeled and perceived to be incurable. Millions of children will slowly die of a poor education and the "professionals" who were hired to cure them will dismiss their academic death as inevitable.

9

The Origins of Myths

We have met the enemy and he is us.

—Pogo

The American teaching myths obscure the academic purpose of formal education, devalue the science of teaching, and minimize the importance of teacher training. As a result, too many underperforming students get sorted into various categories of uneducability. On the surface, the teaching myths appear to be cloaked in egalitarian sentiment, but the teaching myths actually deny educational opportunities to many children and adolescents.

To some extent, the triumph of myth over science was inevitable given the evolution of the field of education. There are three categories of factors that created the conditions for the myths to take root. The first were historical factors that saw the emergence of the differentiated curriculum over the traditional academic curriculum in the early twentieth century. With the influx of immigrants at the turn of the century, young people were sorted into different curriculum tracks to better prepare them to function in society. Differentiation laid the foundation for the "Sorting Hat" model of public education. Educators have never successfully addressed the real problem, which is how to mitigate the academic side effects of disability, poverty, and cultural differences.

The second category of factors was the various social, economic, and educational forces that maintained teachers' *bricoleur* status. Compulsory school laws created an unceasing demand for teachers; but the limited supply and the high turnover created a revolving door. The forces of supply and demand required that teachers be trained in the most expedient, rather than the most demanding, manner. The unique sociology of teaching—the almost universal exposure of the population to the classroom, the peculiar status of schoolteachers, the characteristics of those who choose to teach, and the ways in which their experience in the classroom shape them—all created a set of circumstances that influenced how society viewed teachers and how teachers viewed themselves.

The third category of factors rests on the reluctance of individuals in higher education to embrace a science of teaching that might have launched the field in a different direction. As a result of their learner-directed idealism, education researchers have expressed little interest in validating teaching practices that work because they equate scientific interventions with one-size-fits-all methods of instruction that interfere with the natural developmental trajectory of intellectual growth. Teacher educators perpetuated the belief that teaching was an intuitive occupation that could not be reduced to practical skills or empirically validated principles of teaching and learning. The dearth of science and the unwillingness to impart what little there was had a negative impact on the quality of curricula and teacher preparation.

DIFFERENTIATED CURRICULUM

In the early 19th century, Horace Mann promoted publicly financed, locally controlled schools through the eighth grade that would provide all children with access to a common body of knowledge. He advocated common schools, as he called them, with religious zeal. "It is a free school system, it knows no distinction of rich and poor . . . it throws open its doors and spreads the table of its bounty for all the children of the state. . . . Education then, beyond all other devices of human origin, is the equalizer of the conditions of men, the great balance wheel of the social machinery" (quoted in Mondale & Patton, 2001, p. 29). Mann's idea was radical at the time and many citizens vigorously opposed it; however, Americans take public education for granted because the common school movement succeeded. The goal of the common schools was to give all children the opportunity to develop their minds and to provide access to careers and opportunities that lay beyond their current social status. The initial function of public education, then, was to level the playing field and to allow all children to rise based on their own merit. This idealistic view of public education, however, did not endure into the 20th century.

Although common schools supported a traditional curriculum that stressed learning for learning's sake, many educational leaders rebelled against the rigid traditional high school curriculum that stressed liberal arts and Western civilization. A variety of related reform movements became known as progressivism, but they had very different goals. The movement most often associated with progressivism is pedagogical progressivism, which focused on the process of teaching using learner-directed (child-centered) methods. The movement that exerted a stronger influence on 20th-century education was the social efficiency movement, which focused on organizing schools to promote curriculum differentiation and social efficiency (Langermann, 1989)

Social efficiency progressives maintained that schools should be organized to meet the economic and social needs of society. One aspect of this philosophy was the principle of differentiation. It held that very few children needed a traditional education. Only college-bound students, less than 10% of the population until after World War II (National Center for Educational Statistics, 1993), needed to study academic subjects, and some experts doubted that anyone needed to study a traditional curriculum. Experts who adhered to the theory of social efficiency believed that a differentiated curriculum could better meet the diverse needs of immigrant children who needed to learn life skills or prepare for a vocation. Social efficiency progressives wanted to offer a broader array of vocational, life-skills, and agricultural courses in high school. Some believed that offering a more differentiated curriculum might entice more adolescents to stay in school. A less charitable view of the social efficiency movement is that it sought to prepare a compliant cadre of workers for the menial jobs suited to their class status.

The social efficiency movement became aligned with the testing movement in psychology and, beginning in the 1920s, IQ tests were used to determine who should receive an academic curriculum and who should receive a vocational curriculum (Ravitch, 2000). These efforts were the beginning of what would later be known as tracking. The advocates of social efficiency had a huge influence on how schools were organized. During the first half of the century, high school curricula became increasingly vocational and differentiated (Labaree, 2004). In other words, schools turned into sorting machines rather than educational ladders.

In 1908, Charles W. Eliot, who had previously been a defender of the need to provide all students with a classical education, delivered an address to the National Society for the Promotion of Industrial Education in which he said "the teachers of the elementary schools ought to sort the pupils and sort them by their evidence of probable destinies" (Eliot, 1961, p. 19–20). Social theorist Pitirim Sorokin (1927) took it a little further.

> The essential social function of the school is not only to find out whether a pupil has learned a definite part of the textbook or not; but . . . to discover . . . which of the pupils are talented and which are not . . . to eliminate those who do not have desirable mental and moral qualities, . . . and to promote those who happen to be the bright students in the directions of those social positions which correspond to their general and specific abilities. Whether successful or not, these purposes are some of the most important functions of the school. From this standpoint the school is primarily a testing, selecting and distributing agency. (p. 188)

The procedure of tracking students in eighth or ninth grade was common by the 1930s and 1940s (Mondale & Patton, 2001). In the 1940s, reformers suggested that schools could better accommodate unmotivated students by implementing what was called the life adjustment curriculum. The life adjustment movement further deemphasized academic subjects in favor of practical endeavors. Advocates proposed that 20% of the student population should be prepared for college and 20% for skilled occupations, and rest should be prepared with basic living skills. "Life adjustment education was based on the assumption that 60% of the nation's youth lacked the brains for either college or skilled occupations" (Ravitch, 2000, p. 329).

The life adjustment movement went too far, however, and parents, teachers, school board members, and higher education professors reacted negatively to the life adjustment movement. Tracking came under increased scrutiny following the *Hobson v. Hansen* suit in 1967, which found that the tracking system was discriminatory because black students were overrepresented in the low tracks. The Passow Report (1967), a study of the Washington, D.C., public school district, concluded that tracking was ineffective and should be abandoned. Educators increasingly viewed tracking as inequitable and studies showed that tracking did not result in increased achievement or higher self-esteem (Oakes, 1985). However, the alternative, providing the same education for everyone in mixed ability groups, did not solve, or even the address, the problems created by individual differences in academic performance.

In my view, there is nothing inherently wrong with differentiated curriculum per se. In many ways special education is all about differentiating instruction. Differentiation becomes a problem, however, when instruction is differentiated for groups rather than individuals, when it is not dependent on performance, and when it is fixed rather than flexible. When differentiation essentially lowers expectations instead of providing opportunities to learn, then it is not beneficial.

Some critics of the differentiated curriculum argue that it denies access to a general body of knowledge, and that a shared body of knowledge is necessary to maintain democracy (Hirsch, 1996; Ravitch, 2000). I agree with these arguments, but I think there is another important point. The differentiated curriculum was a way to deal with an increasingly heterogeneous school-age population, all of whom had to attend school. Educators have always attempted to use organizational solutions (e.g., differentiation versus whole-group instruction) to address what is fundamentally a teaching problem. Differentiation has allowed educators to ignore the question of *how to teach more effectively* in order to mitigate the low achievement associated with risk factors such as poverty or minority status.

Academic achievement for all is a relatively new priority (Graham, 1993). A higher percentage of adolescents graduate from high school now than in the past, but this has not lead to higher levels of achievement. That's because increased access has meant more students with a variety of risk factors that make them prone to low achievement. Rather than trying to find more powerful instructional interventions to help learners *overcome* risk factors, educators have *accommodated* the risk factors by making organizational changes or watering down the curriculum. Organizational changes, whether it is tracking or smaller class size or block scheduling, do not increase academic achievement unless they are accompanied by changes in teaching practices. All the myths provide ways to either avoid the issue or to sugarcoat it. Despite educators' recognition that it is wrong to sort children based on class or other noninstructional variables, education's Sorting Hat continues to function.

TEACHERS AS *BRICOLEUR*

A number of factors have kept the status of teachers low throughout the 20th and into the 21st century. The demand for teachers has almost always exceeded the supply. This situation created a need for administrators to fill teaching positions with warm bodies rather than well-qualified ones. The high turnover rate, caused partially by high mobility and partially by restrictions on performing the dual roles of family and job, exacerbated the problem of finding enough teachers to staff the public schools. Finally, unlike other professions, the process of acculturation into the teaching profession, both before certification and after, relies heavily on experiential learning. All of these factors taken together gave teaching its "special, but shadowed" status (Lortie, 1975). Teachers are admired but do not have the status of other professionals with similar education.

Supply and Demand

Massachusetts passed the first compulsory school law in 1852, but it took another 50 years before most states followed suit. By 1918, all states had passed some form of compulsory school attendance law, and the trend was to keep students in school for increasingly longer periods of time (Violas, 1978). The ban on child labor in the early 20th century also had the effect of sending more children to school. At first students attended only elementary school, but over the years more and more children also attended junior high or high school. Compulsory schooling created an unrelenting demand for teachers. The number of teachers grew from 425,000 in 1900 to 800,000 in 1930 (Warren, 1985). Despite brief periods of surplus (such as during the Depression in the 1930s), teacher shortages have been the rule throughout the 20th century, especially in rural areas and in specific subject areas (Sedlak & Schlossman, 1986).

The high demand for teachers and the minimal requirements for entry were mutually reinforcing. In the early part of the 20th century, normal schools, which were a combination of high school and teacher preparation, offered the best preparation for teaching, but they did not have a monopoly. Normal schools faced competition from certification by examination (which could be as simple as a few personal questions from the president of the school board), short summer institutes, or high school courses in pedagogy. If normal schools were too selective, they would go out of business and other, even less rigorous, avenues of teacher certification would become dominant (Labaree, 2004). In addition, the shortage of teachers created pressure to turn out enough teachers to meet the demand. Although normal schools became State Teacher's Colleges, which eventually were absorbed as schools of education within liberal arts colleges, the tradition of easy access to teacher certification was established.

High Turnover

Even after the supply and demand should have stabilized, the high turnover of teachers ensured that the teaching force was minimally qualified. Rather than address the problem of high turnover, educational leaders tried to solve the problem by focusing on attracting fresh recruits to the teaching profession.

In some cases, the turnover was created by movement within the ranks, such as elementary teachers moving up to high school or rural teachers moving to the cities, but most of the turnover occurred as teachers left to get married or have children. It was common for local school boards to put many restrictions on female teachers' behavior, including forbidding marriage or child rearing. Although these restrictions began to weaken in the 1920s when there was a severe teacher shortage, the prohibition against marriage and children and the restrictions on behavior persisted until after World War II, especially in rural areas.

My mother's experience was fairly typical. She graduated from high school in 1938 and obtained a teaching certificate after attending a small liberal arts college for 2 years. Her first job was in a very small rural community where she recalled walking through a cornfield for her interview because the president of the school board was out plowing his field. Dating, dancing, driving, smoking, and drinking were done in secret and in the next town. She taught in a two-room elementary school for 2 years before moving to a larger community to take a job teaching mathematics in a junior high school. In 1945, she left teaching altogether and went to

Chicago to work for the government. There she met my father, got married, and quit working to become a full-time mother and homemaker.

Little is known about teacher turnover prior to World War II except what can be gleaned from the National Survey of the Education of Teachers, which was conducted by the U.S. Office of Education in the early 1930s. Based on the median for years of teaching experience, the authors of the study concluded that young teachers left the field at a high rate. The report stated "this fact may also be taken as an indication that teaching is not considered by many of the young people entering it as a permanent career. To the extent that teaching is regarded as a 'stepping stone' or 'stop-gap' occupation, *its progress toward professional status is definitely retarded*" (italics added; cited in Lazerson, 1987, p. 101).

More information is available about turnover after World War II. A study of college graduates found that only 36% of the education graduates remained in education and nearly one-half of the women who left teaching were not in the labor force at all (Wolffe, 1954; Morris, 1957). Compare that to male-dominated professions such as engineering (64%), medicine and dentistry (96%), law (74%), business (51%), or agriculture (48%). It should be noted that had this study included teachers who did not have a college degree, the retention rate probably would have been slightly higher. Other studies reported a 20–30% turnover rate during this period (Sedlak & Schlossman, 1986).

Although men left teaching to become administrators, women left to get married and raise children. Mason (1961) found that 71% of male teachers said they planned to leave teaching in order to become an administrator. Sixty-five percent of female teachers indicated that they planned to leave the classroom within 5 years. Of those who planned to leave, 80% stated that the reason had to do with family matters. Pavalko (1970) found that 40% of Wisconsin women teachers between 1959 and 1960 had left teaching, and marriage was strongly related to leaving the field. Ninety percent of single women were still teaching, compared to only 46% of married women.

The turnover rate of teachers has decreased in recent years, but it is still higher than other professions. Data from the Bureau of National Affairs (1998) reveal a turnover rate of 11% across all professions, and turnover rate for teachers of 15% in 1988–1989, 13.2% in 1991–1992, and 14.3% in 1994–1995. This is only a little higher than other female-dominated professions such as nursing, which has a 12% turnover rate. Although the decrease in turnover during the past decade is encouraging, a 2001 study by the Center for the Study of Teaching and Policy (Ingersoll) found that "teacher turnover is a significant phenomenon and a dominant factor behind the demand for new teachers and the difficulties schools encounter adequately staffing classrooms with qualified teachers" (p. 5).

There are also indications that the most capable women leave the profession. Pavalko (1970) found that women with higher IQs were more likely to leave teaching than women with lower IQs. More recent also data suggest that the best and brightest leave teaching. U.S. Department of Education data indicate that teachers who scored in the top quartile of the ACT or SAT are twice as likely to leave teaching within 5 years as they are to remain in the field (Quality counts, 2000).

In short, high turnover prevents teaching from becoming a profession where the initial investment and the continuing career rewards attract and retain the most capable candidates. A more prolonged and demanding preparation and a career structure more conducive to conveying and developing a specialized body of knowledge might help make teaching a profession worthy of meeting the difficult educational challenges of the 21st century.

Acculturation Before Certification

One of the things that sets teaching apart from almost every other occupation is that virtually every man, woman, and child has spent many years sitting in a classroom, immersed and yet removed from the culture of teaching. This unique situation has two profound effects. First, the familiarity makes teaching look easy. Second, the experiences leave an indelible impression on future teachers that instill deeply held, and often false, beliefs about the nature of teaching.

A friend of mine once complained, "Everybody thinks they know how to teach because everybody's gone to school." What is taught in school is common knowledge to all high school graduates. People assume that if you know it, you can teach it. Both teachers and the general public seem to subscribe to this view. What is perceived as difficult is the subject matter itself (science, history, etc.), not how to teach it, and subject matter is seen as the domain of college professors and other experts, not teachers.

The view that teaching is easy is particularly prevalent among intelligent people from affluent families for whom school *was* relatively easy.

The misconception that teaching is easy comes from the "apprenticeship of observation" (Lortie, 1975) that everyone experiences during their K–12 education. Lortie suggested that being a student is like serving an apprenticeship because it involves extended face-to-face contact. He wrote that "teachers start their professional preparation early in life, their entire school experience contributes to their work socialization" (p. 56). It is different from a normal apprenticeship, however, in that the student is the client, not the understudy.

Lortie compared it to watching a play from the audience. A person in the audience knows nothing of the actor or director's intentions or reflections, the hours of practice, the interpretation, staging, or the skills required to perform. The perception of a child in the audience is very different from the perspective of a novice learning from the master. No trade secrets are shared, but the audience thinks they understand what teaching is all about. Teachers entering the field think they know a lot about teaching, whereas people entering other occupations know that their knowledge is limited. "What students learn about teaching then, is intuitive and imitative rather than explicit and analytical; it is based on individual personalities rather than on pedagogical principles" (Lortie, 1975, p. 62). It's a little like deciding to become an actress or actor because of some famous film star that you liked. Teachers decide to become teachers based on a simplistic idea of what it involves, unaware that it is considerably more complicated than it looks.

Research studies have confirmed that teachers' beliefs are deeply rooted in their childhood recollections of school (Richardson, 1996). These beliefs appear to have far more impact on their eventual teaching practice than do their teacher certification programs. A review of the literature by Kagan (1992) confirmed that college students enter teacher education programs with preconceived ideas of how to teach be based on their memories and images of themselves as teachers. These images remain unchanged by their teacher certification programs. A common thread in all the research about college students who want to become teachers is that they are optimistic, service oriented, and believe that experience is the best teacher (Richardson, 1996). This faith in experiential learning begins during the long apprenticeship of observation and continues throughout their teaching career.

Acculturation Following Certification

Lortie provided an apt description of the beginning teacher's entrance into the field by comparing it to Robinson Crusoe's struggle for survival.

> As for Defoe's hero, the beginning teacher may find that prior excellence supplied him with some alternatives for action, but his crucial learning comes from his personal errors; he fits together solutions and specific problems into some kind of whole and at times finds leeway for the expression of personal tastes. Working largely alone, he cannot make the specifics of his working knowledge base explicit, nor need he, as his victories are private. (cited in Feiman-Nemser, 1983, p. 153)

Induction into the teaching profession tends to be a solitary venture of trial-and-error learning. Ironically, the relative autonomy so valued by teachers in their classrooms has the negative effect of limiting the amount of social reinforcement they receive from peers and administrators. This lack of validation from peers can contribute to feelings of self-doubt as they wonder if they are really making a difference.

The lack of a more formal mediated entry into teaching is more typical of unskilled than of skilled occupations. Contrast a taxi driver to a racecar driver, a food service worker to a chef, or a retail salesperson to a manager. When the process of entering a profession is prolonged and intense, skills and knowledge associated with the profession become more important than predispositions. "Occupations with highly developed subcultures — that is, with rich, complex bodies of knowledge and technique — differentiates entrants from outsiders, laying the basis for a special sense of community among the initiated" (Lortie, 1975, p. 56). The abrupt sink-or-swim entry into the teaching profession may be related to the historical need to keep entrance requirements low in order to ensure a steady supply of teachers to meet the demand. However, this autonomy is unlikely to elevate or hone professional teaching skills. "There is a growing body of research to show that the typical experience of teachers in school is noneducative at best and miseducative at worst" (Lanier & Little, 1986, p. 527).

The transformation from student to teacher is based on an abiding faith that trial-and-error learning will provide sufficient professional development to meet most classroom challenges. There are three stages to this experiential learning process. First, teachers are shaped by their 16 years spent on the other side of the desk. Second, aspiring teachers engage in several guided field experiences during their college preparation, culminating in student teaching. Three, teachers embark on journey of discovery in the largely isolated environment of their own classroom. The practical knowledge that results from these experiences is idiosyncratic and contextual. It is not based on a shared body of scientific knowledge about teaching and learning. Interestingly, the contribution of college education course work, which has the potential to provide a generalizable knowledge base for teaching, is less important than any of the other stages of experiential learning. Says Richardson (1996), "most researchers involved in life history and socialization research also agree that the experiential effects of personal life, previous schooling, and student teaching are more powerful in building conceptions of teaching than the formal pedagogical education received in teacher education programs" (p. 106).

But is this situation desirable or inevitable? I argued in chapter 6 that the myth of good teachers has a negative impact on the teaching profession because it minimizes the importance of teacher training and ignores the science of teaching. The fact that certification programs have little impact on teaching behavior and student achievement is not desirable. Whether it is inevitable remains to be seen.

Teaching myths are formed during childhood and adolescence, reinforced by field experiences during college, and solidified by experiential learning on the job. This process explains why teaching today looks a lot like yesterday, and it underscores the difficulty of change. David Britt, former president of the Children's Television Network, noted that "schools today are one of the few places in our society that our grandparents would easily recognize" (cited in Latham, 2002, p. 11).

HIGHER EDUCATION'S DUBIOUS CONTRIBUTION

Schools of education, by which I mean any unit in a college or university devoted to teacher preparation, lie at the bottom of the university food chain. Teacher education has been characterized as a nonintellectual profession where those with academic inclinations find few rewards (Lanier & Little, 1986). Teacher education programs are widely recognized to have serious credibility problems, but numerous studies and recommendation have not prompted significant change. This situation has led to disillusionment among education reformers and efforts to bypass colleges and universities by deregulating teacher certification (e.g., Finn & Kanstoroom, 2000). There is no doubt in my mind that schools of education shoulder a large part of the blame for creating an environment that supports myth over science.

It is no secret that education professors have had an enduring attraction to the teaching philosophy that I call learner-directed, which originated with John Dewey's philosophical focus on the child rather than the curriculum. Although early reformers associated with social efficiency (the testing and differentiated curriculum movement) exerted a stronger influence on K–12 education than reformers who advocated learner-directed teaching methods (Langermann, 1989), Dewey's philosophy, with its gentler message of individuality and opportunity, exerted greater influence on professors in schools of education.

Labaree (2004) suggested that Dewey's learner-directed philosophy offered a more inspirational mission and vision than the cold, scientific approach of social efficiency. "It was a vision of education that could really get an education professor's blood pumping. Pedagogical progressivism proposed to do a lot more than just make schools efficient. It called for turning education upside down, by having the purposes and interests of the student drive the curriculum rather than forcing the curriculum onto the student" (p. 157).

Teacher educators' and researchers' stubborn adherence to learner-directed philosophies have affected the way that they fulfill their professional responsibilities. Education professors have two obligations—to prepare teachers and to conduct research that will advance the field. Regarding their first obligation, our survey found that only 16% of education professors believed that education and training was more important than experience. Regarding their second obligation, only 23% thought that scientifically conducted research was the best way to determine how and what to teach (see Table 2.2). In my opinion, education professors have failed in both their obligations, and the consequences of those failures have kept public education stuck in time. Education professors have perpetuated the myths by overreliance on experiential learning at the expense of validated teaching methods and deep content knowledge (e.g., requirements for early reading instruction) and by eschewing a research agenda to identify empirically validated curricula and methods.

Teacher Preparation

Learner-directed philosophies dovetail nicely with the myth of process and the myth of fun. Teacher educators who believe in learner-directed methods convey the message that learning is a naturalistic process of discovery and that lessons should build on student interests. In keeping with their philosophy, teacher educators prefer to facilitate rather than to impart knowledge about how to teach. As a result of these indirect teaching methods, many prospective teachers never find out about the scientific evidence that informs teaching practice. I have even heard teacher educators argue that critical teacher behaviors such as behavior management skills cannot be taught, that they can only be learned through experience. One professor freely admitted that her teaching style with college students was "improvisational" (Commeyras, 2002), and she considered that to be a good thing. Some education professors believe that an emphasis on technical expertise limits, rather than enhances, the opportunity for future teachers to develop their full potential (Feiman-Nemser, 1983). True to their convictions, teacher educators function as guides who provide field experiences where preservice teachers can, through trial and error, embark on a lifelong career of reflection and insight that will eventually make them into good teachers (if they have the right dispositions).

A 1997 survey by Public Agenda and the Fordham Foundation confirmed this description of education professors' priorities (Farkas et al., 1997). When asked what skills were "absolutely essential" to impart to prospective teachers, 84% said that being a "lifelong learner" was essential whereas only 37% said it was important for prospective teachers to know how to "maintain discipline." Asked about their philosophy of the role of teachers, 92% said, "teachers should see themselves as facilitators of learning who enable their students to learn on their own" and only 7% said that "teachers should see themselves as conveyors of knowledge who enlighten their students with what they know." As a result of this idealistic vision of learning as painless inquiry, education courses are sometimes perceived as free of content.

Education courses have been described as "puerile, repetitious, dull, and ambiguous" (Koerner, 1963), "Mickey Mouse" (Lortie, 1975), "useless" (Farkas et al., 2000), "shallow and stultifying" (Sowell, 1993), "naive," "simplistic," "shallow," "a joke" (Latham, 2002), and "deadly dull" (Kramer, 1991). The curriculum of teacher education programs has been described as "intellectually thin" (Keller, 2003; Labaree, 2004) and professors are described as out of touch (Farkas et al., 1997). The research is unequivocal about the lack of cohesion and mediocrity of the course work provided for teachers (Lanier & Little, 1986, p. 549). Administrators in highly successful, low-income schools express unanimous frustration with the poor quality of teachers who graduate from teacher education programs (Carter, 2000). Even education insiders agree. The Holmes Group (1995), which consisted of school of education insiders, said in its third report, "Education schools that fail to ground their work in well-studied practice inhabit a make-believe land, a Potemkin village of reassuring facades" (p. 90).

My own experience as an undergraduate preservice teacher confirms this portrait. Having transferred to a large university from a small liberal arts college, the ease with which I was able to get As surprised me. My test scores on the ACT, SAT, and GRE were average, and yet I graduated Phi Beta Kappa. Years later, my mother asked me why I never seemed proud of that accomplishment and I remember my answer distinctly: "Because it wasn't hard." The only thing I remember learning about how to teach was that teachers should be "firm, fair, friendly, and consistent." Good advice, but hardly worth the thousands of dollars my father spent to send me to college.

Teacher educators are unapologetic about their emphasis on field experience rather than course work or pedagogy. "Educators tend to support John Dewey's conviction that the main purpose of experiential learning is to make the preservice teacher a true student of teaching rather than an apprentice seeking to imitate a master" (Ishler, Edens, & Berry, 1996, p. 359). Field experiences should be a critical component of teacher education programs *but* (and here is my fundamental disagreement with learner-directed philosophies) they should be for generalization and extension, not for discovery of facts and principles that are already known. To ignore scientific research in teacher education (most notably in the area of beginning reading or behavior management) is as unconscionable as ignoring scientific breakthroughs in medical education.

Teacher preparation programs tend to be heavily experiential, filled with reassuring rhetoric about lifelong learning and the teachers' role as a facilitator. To the extent that there is substance, it is related to foundations of education (i.e., John Dewey) and child development (i.e., Piaget). Methods courses generally do not emphasize research-based principles of classroom management or effective teaching principles. The course titles may be listed, but the content is often missing. For example, Steiner and Rozen (2004) examined 59 syllabi for pedagogy courses at a variety of universities. All but four courses were linked to a field experience. They found that only six included explicit instruction of strategies such as reciprocal teaching, scaffolded instruction, and content-area reading strategies. Many syllabi also failed to include specific information about lesson planning, assessment, curriculum models, or state standards. They also found little evidence that college course work provided prospective teachers with more than a cursory knowledge about the extensive research base for teaching reading or remediating reading problems. In general, schools of education are not "congenial to use of research-based teaching practices or sympathetic to public concern about schooling outcomes." (Preparing teachers, 2003).

As things stand now, the net effect of teacher preparation on young teachers is to reaffirm their faith that experience will teach them all they need to know about teaching and reinforce their idealistic notion that learning will occur naturally as long as they retain their sense of calling. Although beginning teachers have a vague sense that there might be more to know about teaching than they've been told, there is little awareness that technical skills are important, that learning can or should be measured, that a knowledge base for teaching exists, or that scientific research can make them more successful. Teachers cannot raise their expectations for student achievement if they have not acquired the knowledge and skills that might help them to become more effective, especially with students who have disabilities or other risk factors.

Scholarly Research

The second professional obligation of education professors, especially at large universities, is to engage in scholarly activity that will advance the knowledge base for teaching. Generally, education researchers enjoy higher status than teacher educators in the higher education hierarchy (Goodlad, 1990; Judge, 1982), which gives them a louder voice. There is currently a lot of discussion among education researchers about the need for and value of research aimed at figuring out which teaching practices work and which ones don't (Mayer, 1999). An increasing number of education researchers reject this type of scientifically credible research in favor of anecdotal evidence (Levin & O'Donnell 1999). Meanwhile, the public is clamoring for answers to questions like how to teach children to read effectively in a timely manner or which curricula provide the best opportunity to reduce the achievement gap. Although historically much of the research in education has been quantitative (numerical), it has seldom been experimental or designed to answer questions about effectiveness. Arguments against engaging in scientific research generally fall into two categories—they *shouldn't* and they *can't*.

Education researchers argue that they *shouldn't* engage in experimental research because it is limiting and devalues the entire educational enterprise. They equate "useful" research with the legacy of the social efficiency movement and with social control (Dunseath, 2000). Teaching and learning, the theory goes, are too complex to be subjected to scientific investigation. Education professors' affiliation with learner-directed philosophy means that they do not believe that answers can lie in one-size-fits-all programs, textbooks, methods, principles, or rules of teacher behavior. Because every child's education is unique, no one curriculum or method will work all the time.

Some education researchers seem to reject certainty and are content to live with ambiguity. Any attempt to find solutions to educational problems is considered untenable because the problems are so multifaceted that any single, or even multiple, solution would be incorrect. Better to study the problem from every angle in order to detect the nuances of teacher-learner-context interactions than to reduce the problem down to one that could be investigated scientifically. Postmodern relativism, the idea that there is no truth beyond that constructed by each individual, is a good fit for education researchers. If physicists were like education researchers, there would be no theory of gravity, relativity, or string theory. Time, matter, and energy would remain blissfully random.

Arguments that education researchers *can't* conduct experimental research basically consist of refuting the comparison to medical research. Criticism of the scientific method in education include the practical drawbacks associated with random assignment and the difficulties associated with controlling multiple variables like class size, socioeconomic status, teacher quality and management skills, school climate, leadership, and so on. Educational interventions are complex, involving both specific content (curriculum) and teacher procedures (methods); variations in any of those components can affect the outcome. Furthermore, critics suggest that it's impossible to make assumptions about causality in education research because the relationship between teaching and learning is filtered through individual teachers and students, which changes the outcome. In other words, the outcome is relative.

Critics of scientific research also point to controlled studies that have been done in the past that reveal conflicting results. For example, studies on the effect of class size have yielded different effect sizes in Tennessee as compared to California. Based on these arguments, some education researchers conclude that medical-type scientific research is not useful for addressing educational issues. Researchers who support scientific research in education point out that contradictory findings are often the result of weak conceptual foundations (Levin & O'Donnell, 1999).

Neither of these arguments has substance. What is lacking among education researchers is the will. That is, the "can't do" arguments are red herrings and the "shouldn't do" arguments are ideological. Although there is no denying that many variables must be controlled in education research, there are variables that must be controlled in any scientific experiment. The way those variables are ultimately controlled is through replication. It would be a mistake to limit education research to just one type of research because the methodology depends on the research question. Early theory-building research is exploratory (Level 1) and requires different methodologies than research-designed to confirm if the theory works. Education researchers seem to heap theory on theory without ever moving to the next phase where the theory is tested for applicability and an instructional intervention is compared with another viable intervention. If the outcome shows the intervention is effective, then it must be validated through replication and alternative explanations for the result must be ruled out. Eventually, Level 3 large-scale implementation research will yield convincing evidence of an intervention's effectiveness if the previous steps in the research process have been followed.

SUMMARY

There are many mutually reinforcing factors that have influenced the way in which teaching has evolved, or failed to evolve, during the 20th century. Public schools have never operated with the goal of helping all students achieve specified learning outcomes. Educators watered down the curriculum for certain groups of students, but they never addressed the possibility that different, more powerful, instruction might allow low-performing students to enjoy more success in school. In the absence of overt sorting like tracking, labels associated with learning styles, disabilities, and demographics provide a covert sorting mechanism that can explain school failures.

The unique sociology of teaching has conspired to keep teaching an occupation, rather than a profession. High demand for teachers coupled with high turnover and easy entry requirements created a supply of less-qualified teachers. The perception that teaching is easy and a highly personalized view of teaching keeps the focus on good teachers rather than good teaching. Reliance on experiential learning impedes development and acquisition of a shared set of empirically validated professional practices that might advance teachers' *bricoleur* status.

Finally, teacher educators have expressed little interest in teaching prospective teachers how to identify and use effective teaching practices, and education researchers have shown little interest in validating teaching practices through experimental research. The science of teaching has not found a home in the very place where one might expect to find it. These historical, sociological, and philosophical conditions create a conundrum for people who wish to see the field of education move from myth to science.

10

From Myth to Science

If I were seriously ill and in desperate need of a physician, and if by some miracle I could secure either Hippocrates, the Father of Medicine, or a young doctor fresh from the Johns Hopkins School of medicine, with his equipment comprising the latest developments in the technologies and techniques of medicine, I should, of course, take the young doctor. On the other hand, if I were commissioned to find a teacher for a group of adolescent boys and if, by some miracle, I could secure either Socrates or the latest Ph.D. from Teachers College, with his equipment of the latest technologies and techniques of teaching, with all due respect to the College that employs me and to my students, I am fairly certain that I would jump at the chance to get Socrates.

—William C. Bagley, *Education and Emergent Man* (1934, p. 195)

Professionals can be differentiated from people in occupations by their recognition of the complexity of their field, a desire to understand the underlying principles and rules that make sense of the complexity, and the need to know how to apply those principles to reliably accomplish their shared goals. Professionals respect not only the creative passion that defines excellence but also the technical and scientific knowledge that supports it. Teachers, on the other hand, rely on interpretation of general principles and intuition, which means that some children, especially those who come to school with disabilities or risk factors, will falter despite the teacher's best efforts.

For a variety of historical, sociological, and philosophical reasons, teachers remain *bricoleur* rather than professionals. The public appears to admire teachers, but not to respect them. Seven out of ten Americans said that teaching is an occupation of either very great (47%) or considerable (23%) prestige (Johnson, Duffet, Vine, & Syat, 2003), but less than 50% would like to have their son (31%) or daughter (43%) enter the teaching profession (Gallup, 1985). When asked to rank-order 12 professions, the general public ranked teaching third in terms of its contribution to society and seventh in prestige. Teachers rated their profession first in terms of its contribution to society, but last in prestige (Elam, 1989)—which indicates that teachers have either a very high or very low collective self-esteem, depending on how you look at it. Both teachers and the public ranked physicians number one.

The medical profession may or may not deserve their top-ranking status, but the respect garnered by physicians highlights their status as a mature profession. Carnine (2000) suggested that education, unlike the medical profession, has not yet evolved into a mature profession. This is evident when one considers some of the characteristics of professional people.

1. Professionals are accountable for the work they do. The myth of process and the myth of fun and interesting stand in the way of agreement on the goals of education and acceptance of objective measures of success. Most people would probably agree that returning the patient to good health is more important than a doctor's bedside manner. There is less agreement, however, that improving academic achievement is more important than a personable teacher who can entertain students with her lessons.

2. Professionals share a consensus about best practice that is based on the best available scientific evidence. Educators seem to value craft knowledge over research knowledge, use intuition instead of evidence, and rely on expert opinion rather than data. The field of education experiences fads, rather than scientific breakthroughs. Teachers prefer eclectic instruction, but they need validated curricula. A shared body of knowledge should lead to some standardization of practices and procedures that have implications for preparing new people to enter the profession.

3. Professionals require a high level of education and training in order to do their job well. Teacher preparation needs to begin with rigorous course work that conveys a body of knowledge based on theory-building and classroom research. Course work should be accompanied by supervised, structured opportunities for application in field experiences. Teacher preparation should be intentional rather than accidental. Many educators object to the idea that teacher preparation is "training" (they prefer to call it education), but certain aspects of teaching are highly technical. Doctors don't object to training. Why should teachers?

4. Professionals enjoy solving difficult problems and completing difficult tasks. They do not view difficult cases as anomalies, nor do they use labels to shift the blame for their failures. Professionals start by selecting an intervention based on the knowledge base for their field, not whimsy. If the intervention doesn't work, then they examine all the variables to figure out why it didn't work, how to make it work, or how to change it. Without a validated intervention in place to begin with, and without data, efforts to solve educational problems amount to nothing more than chance attempts.

In short, the failure to develop a science of teaching keeps teachers *bricoleur*.

Latham (2002) randomly selected 20 engineers, 20 physicians, 20 lawyers, and 20 educators and asked them to describe a problem that they commonly encountered in their work. Then he asked them how they would go about solving the problem and what formed the basis for their solution. Engineers referred to laws, principles, and formulas related to physics. Physicians generally referred to their knowledge of physiology, anatomy, microbiology, and chemistry. Lawyers referred to constitutional law, statutes, precedent, and logic. Educators gave responses such as the following:

> "It seemed at the moment to be a good way to handle the situation."
> "I've used it before, and it's worked well."
> "It was suggested to me by a [teacher/supervisor/professor/principal]."
> "That's the way the teacher's manual said to do it."
> "I was taught to do it that way at the University."
> "I don't really know, I never thought much about it." (p. 15)

Imagine if doctors based their decisions on hunches and hearsay rather than on scientific evidence. After an emergency hospitalization for a pulmonary embolism, Diane Ravitch described what would have happened if her doctors had been education researchers instead of doctors. "Among the raucous crowd of education experts, there was no agreement, no common set of standards for diagnosing my problem. They could not agree on what was wrong with me, perhaps because they did not agree on standards for good health" (Ravitch, 1998, p. 34). The education researchers could not reach a consensus on a cure, either.

> Each had his own favorite cure, and each pulled out a tall stack of research studies to support his proposals. One group urged a regimen of bed rest, but another said I needed vigorous exercise. One prescribed a special diet, but another said I should eat whatever I wanted. One recommended Drug X, but another recommended Drug Not-X. Another said that it was up to me to decide how to cure myself, based on my own priorities about what was important to me. (p. 34)

Although medical science is imperfect, doctors base decisions on the best available research to ensure that patients will be protected from irresponsible treatments. Why shouldn't school children have similar protections?

Some people do not believe that the scientific model of research can work in the social sciences (e.g., Postman, 1992), but I disagree. I have heard educators argue that it's easy to control variables in medical experiments, but that there are too many variables to control in educational experiments. It seems to me, however, that there is every bit as much variability among doctors as teachers, and as much heterogeneity among patients as school children. Life-style choices affect the incidence of disease just as surely as demographic factors affect school achievement, but medical professionals don't give up on patients who don't take care of themselves.

Physicians did not always base their practice on empirically validated procedures. The professionalization of medicine took centuries. The late Dr. Lewis Thomas (1979), former president of the Memorial Sloan-Kettering Cancer Center, described how the field of medicine looked a century ago.

> It is hard to conceive of a less scientific enterprise among human endeavors. Virtually anything that could be thought up for treatment was tried out

at one time or another, and, once tried, lasted decades or even centuries before being given up. It was, in retrospect, the most frivolous and irresponsible kind of human experimentation, based on nothing but trial and error, and
usually resulting in precisely that sequence. (p. 159)

It sounds a lot like the field of education today.

If the field of medicine is 100 years ahead of the field of education, perhaps educators can learn something from them to speed the process of
professionalization. To be sure, there are differences between medicine
and education that limit the comparison. The most important difference is
that the medical model of diagnosis cannot be applied to education. The
medical model is based on diagnosing a cause, which implies a cure. For
example, streptococcus bacteria cause strep throat. If the cause is bacter-
ial, then the disease can be cured with antibiotics. When the medical
model is applied in education, it results in circular reasoning as shown
earlier with the label *learning disabilities*. Learning disabilities are caused
by . . . by what? We don't know. There is seldom a known cause and even
if there were, it would probably not be alterable. Educators can only treat
the symptoms, and the treatment is the same regardless of the cause. For
example, whether reading disabilities are caused by intrinsic or environmental factors, the intervention must consist of specific components and
procedures based on the research base for teaching beginning reading.

Medical problems such as obesity and alcoholism are more similar to
educational problems because a combination of genetic or biological factors interacts with life-style choices, and there is rarely a single identifiable cause. These medical conditions, like educational problems, are
much more difficult to treat than diseases like strep throat, which have a
single known cause and cure.

A second important difference is that based on the medical model, the
treatment of choice in medicine is pharmacological whereas in education
the treatment consists of behavioral and cognitive interventions. There are
no drugs that can magically cure reading disabilities or any other academic disability.

The final difference between education and medicine is that medical
failures are more immediate and more obvious than educational failures.
Chronic or acute illness commands more urgency than illiteracy, although
I would argue that not learning to read puts lives at risk just as surely as

disease. Despite these differences, however, the history of medical education is instructive.

HOW MEDICINE BECAME A MATURE PROFESSION

The Flexner report catapulted the medical profession into the 20th century. It is generally credited with standardizing medical education and establishing a scientific model of practice (Asera, n.d.). In 1908 the American Medical Association Council commissioned the Carnegie Foundation for the Advancement of Teaching to study medical training facilities across the country. Ironically, the person who conducted the study was an educator, not a physician. At that time, there were three ways to become a doctor: an apprenticeship under a local physician, a proprietary system in which doctors who owned a medical college gave instruction for profit, and a university system (Beck, 2004). Prior to 1900, there was little concern about the lack of standardization in training and medical procedures, but a series of scientific breakthroughs revealed the inadvisability of treatments such as blistering, bleeding, and purging (Beck, 2004) and created a pressing need for rigorous training and practices based on research.

Flexner visited all 155 medical schools in the United States and Canada and concluded that all medical schools should be shut down except those that were associated with a university and that had an affiliated teaching hospital. He advocated strict admission standards including 2 years of general education. Medical schools were to include 2 additional years of related subject matter study such as anatomy and 2 years of hospital-based fieldwork (Flexner & Pritchett, 1910). He believed that the government should enforce standardization and very soon after he issued his report licensing boards started requiring hospitals to meet the requirements or shut down.

There have been numerous calls for reform in teacher education, but none have had the impact on teacher education that the Flexner report had on medical education. The Carnegie Corporation of New York and the Rockefeller Foundation produced a document entitled *What Matters Most* (NCTAF, 1996) that some people compared to the Flexner report, but there was no rush to implement the recommendations. The Carnegie Corporation tried again in 2002 (Hinds, 2002) with little effect. It seems doubtful that any report will change teacher education the way the Flexner report changed medicine.

WHY THERE WILL BE NO FLEXNER REPORT IN EDUCATION

There are several reasons why it is unlikely that any Flexner-type report in education will standardize teacher preparation and set standards for best practice in the teaching profession, at least in the foreseeable future. The first is that the conditions are different now in education than they were in medicine 100 years ago. The second is that the role of the leadership in the process of change is quite different. The third reason is that university-based teacher preparation linked to field experience is already the rule and part of the problem. The final, and most compelling, barrier to change, however, is what I call Dewey's legacy.

At the turn of the century, there was an oversupply of physicians in this country with one doctor for every 600 people, compared to the next highest ratio of one doctor for every 1,800 people in England. What's more, some physicians feared that improvements in hygiene would further reduce the demand for doctors (Our prospects as a profession, 1898). Reducing the number of institutions in the name of preserving quality didn't create a serious shortage of doctors except in certain areas (predictably areas with low-income and minority populations). On the other hand, there has always been a chronic shortage of teachers. Reducing the number of universities that could offer teacher preparation, implementing more selective admission requirements, or requiring more and more demanding course work followed by one or two years of supervised field experience would have the effect of reducing the number of graduating teachers, at least in the short term. A radical reduction in the number of teachers, even for a short time, would wreak havoc with the public school system.

Another factor is that Flexner's investigation occurred at the behest of the leadership in the medical community, whereas the impetus for changes in teacher education has come primarily from outside the educational establishment. In 1900, the hierarchy of the medical establishment wanted changes to occur in the medical profession. The American Medical Association (AMA) lobbied for standardization of training. What's more, it started out as a scientific-driven organization, with the study and clarification of science as its charter purpose. Contrast this to the recalcitrance of education leaders in response to calls for reform in teacher education and their reluctance to promote promising results or embrace a science of teaching.

Third, the Flexner report made university-based training coupled with teaching hospitals a new requirement for medical education, but university-based training and supervised field experiences are already the rule in teacher education. What's more, some of the university medical schools and teaching hospitals (e.g., Johns Hopkins) in 1900 provided an existing model of best practice where residents could learn research-based medicine. Even if schools of education agreed tomorrow on a set of best practices for teaching, efforts to implement residency programs in education would suffer from a shortage of exemplary field placements. Teacher preparation programs would be hard pressed to provide enough exemplary school-based field experiences because very few K–12 schools provide models of research-based practice. It would be like training doctors in the most up-to-date techniques, and then having them complete their residency in outdated hospitals. Residencies are the lynchpin of medical education, but they are the missing link in teacher preparation. Residencies, clinical experiences, induction programs, internships, student teaching, mentorships—whatever you want to call them—are only as good as the role models.

K–12 schools that are affiliated with universities have been around for a long time in the form of campus schools, lab schools, or professional development schools. The problem is that, in the absence of a science of teaching, university-affiliated schools tend to reflect the same fuzzy thinking of the university professors who helped established them. Rather than setting a higher standard of professional practice, the teaching myths just get more firmly embedded. There may be some university teacher preparation programs affiliated with schools that model best practice based on scientific research, but there aren't enough to meet the nationwide need for K–12 and special education teachers. When there are more effective schools in operation (i.e., those that get good achievement outcomes even from students with disabilities and risk factors), collaborative relationships between universities and schools will strengthen teacher preparation.

Although the Flexner report helped standardized medical education, it is unlikely that any call to action will improve teacher preparation in a way that leads to higher student achievement. Dewey's legacy ensures that the science of teaching will take a back seat to the art.

DEWEY'S LEGACY

Critics, such as Diane Ravitch (2000) and E. D. Hirsch (1996), have argued that education's demise is rooted in the domination of learner-directed approaches (also known as child-centered, progressive, developmentally appropriate, holistic, and constructivist) to education throughout the twentieth century. The origin of these approaches can be traced to John Dewey and the teaching practices he experimented with at the Laboratory School at the University of Chicago between 1896 and 1904, which burgeoned into the child-study movement. Although the rhetoric, especially among education professors and education "experts" has been loud and influential, the reality is that these methods are seldom used in actual classrooms (Cuban, 1993; Kliebard, 1986). The teaching myths represent the trappings of Dewey's ideal, but not the actual implementation.

That being said, I would hasten to add that curriculum-based methods (also called traditional, teacher-directed, positivist, and behavioral) have not dominated classrooms either. With only vague philosophical moorings and in the absence of shared goals and a science of teaching, teachers have operated like independent artisans rather than members of a profession. Dewey's *lasting legacy* is the highly idiosyncratic and contextualized perspective reflected in the teaching myths.

Every student, every teacher, every classroom, and every school are perceived to be unique in ways that defy shared goals and standardized procedures. Dewey (1929) argued that reform could not be achieved by research findings that reveal best practices. He did not believe that laws and facts yielded rules of practice. Instead, he believed that "scientific results furnish a rule for the conduct of *observations and inquiries*, not a rule for overt actions" (p. 30). In Dewey's view, the purpose of science in education was to provide tools for thinking about teacher-student interactions, not to verify that certain teaching practices worked. The belief, which is inherent in the teaching myths, that children's differences are more important than their similarities and that there are no *best* teaching practices has done more to harm to the field of education than any single method or curriculum.

To their credit, teacher educators are beginning to see the need for a consensus about professional practices (Darling-Hammond & Bransford, 2005), but they still resist specificity, standardization, and reliance on what is generally referred to as scientifically based research. Teacher educators who want to reform teacher preparation suggest that education is similar to other professions such as medicine, law, or engineering in their quest to develop a common curriculum for beginning teachers (Darling-Hammond & Bransford, 2005), but any similarity is superficial. I think that teacher educators want to emulate the *form* of medical preparation; they want to control licensing, accreditation, and certification. Modeling the form, however, will not produce better teachers and higher student achievement because education lacks the *substance*. By substance I mean profession-wide shared methodologies for research, strategies for teaching, and knowledge base of curricula and methods that work. The knowledge base in education is too contextual, too generic, and too untested to be useful.

Too Contextual

Educators are careful to maintain a "learner-centered lens" on instruction (Bransford, Derry, Berliner, Hammerness, & Beckett, 2005, p. 52) and they avoid any appearance of advocating a single "cookie-cutter" formula (Bransford, Darling-Hammond, & LePage, 2005, p. 5). Teacher educators urge teachers to consider individual differences (especially learning style) in planning curriculum, to consider the cultural context of the school, and to take their lead from observing students. As long as teaching practices are contextual and personal, they can never be validated except with a single individual. They cannot have wide applicability.

Teacher educators justify this subjective perspective by pointing to the use of clinical judgment in medicine. They don't seem to understand that in medicine, clinical judgment is applied when the standard treatment doesn't work or when there is a reason to believe that it won't. The situation that teachers find themselves in is applying clinical judgment in the *absence* of standard practices based on scientific research. Ideally, differentiation and individualization in education occurs after a research-based educational program is in place, just as it does in medicine.

Too Generic

This highly subjective view of curricula and methods leads to recommended teaching practices that are very general and open to interpretation. For example, highly effective teachers engage learners in "instructional discourse" (Highly effective teachers, 2004). First of all, everyone's definition of instructional discourse is probably a little different, but beyond that is the fact that engaging students in discourse is a lot harder than it sounds. Even at the college level it is extremely difficult to get students to talk in class, especially in any instructionally relevant or intellectual way. A prescriptive curriculum that specifies teaching procedures, explanations, questions, correction for wrong answers, and activities would increase the probability of promoting instructional discourse. Educators, however, want to be able to operate freely and reject prescriptive curricula as too confining, even when such curricula help teachers achieve the desired teacher behavior.

It's a little like telling doctors to listen to the patient's heart without teaching them exactly what to listen for or telling a surgeon to make an incision without giving specific guidance about what to do next. Without specificity, it is up to the individual to figure out what works through trial and error.

Too Untested

The Committee on Scientific Principles for Education Research (Shavelson & Towne, 2002) concluded that the "set of guiding principles that apply to scientific inquiry in education are the same set of principles that can be found across the full range of scientific inquiry" (p. 51–52). Certainly there are many factors that make education research somewhat more difficult than research in the physical sciences, not the least of which is the failure to agree on the goals of education, but I agree with Shavelson and Towne that science is applicable to education. They suggest that there are three types of questions to ask in education research. What is happening? Is there a systematic effect? And why or how is it happening? I believe that many of the problems in education can be traced to the failure to ask or heed the answers to the second question, "Is there a systematic effect?" This question addresses cause-effect issues related to student achievement. All Level 3, wide-scale implementation research, and some of Level 2, small-scale classroom research, is designed to answer the question, "Is there a systematic effect?"

The "what works" question is best answered with scientifically based research, especially randomized designs, that compare one approach to another approach. The dilemma for advancing the science of teaching is that in order to validate a particular teaching practice, it must necessarily be standardized, not contextual, so that it can be shown to have wide applicability. Yet educators reject standardized practices as "cookie-cutter" approaches that are insulting to teachers and insensitive to student differences. Validated teaching practices must also be prescriptive, not general or loosely defined, in order to test them in controlled studies. But educators reject prescriptive procedures as too rigid. This situation results in a catch-22 where acceptable teaching practices are too contextual and generic to be subjected to scientific research and validated teaching practices are rejected as unacceptable. This catch-22 is what prevents the field of education from developing a science of teaching.

Not Useful

The lack of credible research and lack of consensus leads to a situation where it is very difficult to create useful standards for teacher certification. Many schools of education seek accreditation from an organization like the National Council for Accreditation of Teacher Education (NCATE), which evaluates institutions based on the extent to which prospective teachers meet specified teaching standards. At this time, there is no convincing evidence that NCATE accreditation improves the quality of graduating teachers (Allen, 2003). Many states have adopted the Interstate New Teacher Assessment and Support Consortium (INTASC, 1992) core standards for all teacher preparation programs. Prospective teachers and practicing teachers must now document how they meet the INTASC standards. They put evidence of their efforts (called artifacts) into a binder notebook or in an electronic file (called a portfolio) and write brief essays describing the importance of their work (called a reflection).

Teaching standards suffer from the fact that they are based on research that is too contextual, too generic, and too untested. Therefore, the standards are based more on beliefs than on scientific evidence. The teaching myths are embedded in the standards that perpetuate the status quo. In addition, the standards are vague and completely unmeasurable. Consider the following examples taken from the INTASC standards:

1. The teacher understands how students differ in their approaches to learning and creates instructional opportunities that are adapted to the diverse learners (myth of learning style, myth of disability)
2. The teacher . . . uses a variety of instructional strategies (myth of eclectic instruction)
3. The teacher . . . creates a learning environment that encourages positive social interaction, active engagement in learning, and self-motivation (myth of process, myth of fun and interesting)
4. The teacher . . . is a reflective practitioner . . . who actively seeks out opportunities to grow professionally (myth of the good teacher)

All of these examples describe desirable teaching behaviors in the abstract, but they could describe either effective or ineffective instructional practices depending on how they are interpreted. There is no way to use a portfolio to determine whether or not a teacher will be effective or will be able to inspire high achievement outcomes among students, especially among students who pose significant challenges. The portfolio ends up being a process in and of itself with very little useful outcome.

Schools of education seem to be on the cusp of change, but Dewey's legacy makes it unlikely that educators will agree on anything resembling a true science of teaching in the near future. I can understand the level of uncertainty that exists in the education. Teaching and learning are complex and methodologies for scientific research are extraordinarily difficult to execute. What I cannot understand is the way that educators seem to wrap uncertainty around themselves like a cloak. Unlike medicine, there will be no report that revolutionizes teacher preparation. Change in education will be much more arduous.

SUMMARY

The teaching myths are insidious because there is a grain of truth in all of them. Sometimes the process can be more important than the eventual

outcome, but without accountability there may be no discernable outcome. Interesting lessons do promote student engagement, but interesting lessons do not ensure that students will learn. Eclectic instruction can
help teachers individualize instruction, but it can as easily create confusion. Some people seem to have innate qualities that make them natural
teachers, but the right kind of education and training can make everyone
a better teacher. People have unique strengths and abilities, but learning
styles shouldn't be misconstrued to deny educational opportunity. Some
individuals have disabilities that necessitate more and better instruction,
but too often the label lowers expectations. Certain risk factors contribute
to low academic achievement, but they do not make low achievement inevitable.

Despite their appeal, the teaching myths perpetuate a view of teaching that obscures the goals of education and encourages teachers to
adopt intuitive, idiosyncratic teaching practices that are ineffective with
large numbers of children and adolescents. Teachers may not recognize
that their freewheeling teaching style contributed to student failure. The
myth of learning style and myth of disability excuse teachers from taking responsibility for the students who inevitably fail. The myths are not
conducive to development of a science of teaching that might provide
answers to persistent educational problems. In addition, such a subjective and situational perspective keeps teachers *bricoleur* rather than true
professionals.

The *myth of process* and the *myth of fun and interesting* encourage
teachers to use teaching methods that distribute youngsters in a naturalistic normal curve that leaves learners at the bottom without hope, learners
in the middle without the skills for future success, and learners at the top
without a sense of accomplishment. Without specific benchmarks for
progress or objective measures of success, the problem gets ignored until
it's too late to do anything about it. The focus on process has obscured the
primary purpose of education, which is to develop intellectual skills.
Without a shared sense of purpose, scientific research directed at improving academic achievement has been fragmented or neglected.

The *myth of eclectic instruction* allows teachers to believe that designing curriculum is a way to express their creativity and individualize instruction. In fact, eclectic methods and curriculum tend to be ineffective,
haphazard, and incohesive. This is especially true at the elementary level

where the requirements of beginning reading, writing, and mathematics instruction may be completely counterintuitive to an educated adult. Embracing eclectic instruction precludes the need for scientific research that might validate specific interventions that increase achievement for many students.

The *myth of the good teacher* overestimates the role of innate characteristics and underestimates the importance of education and training in determining teacher quality. The truth is that having a good heart is a necessary, but not sufficient, condition for being an effective teacher; although teaching must be artful, there is no art form that doesn't rely on technique. This myth has left teachers stumbling for quality through a combination of luck, trial-and-error learning, and experience.

The last two myths, the *myth of learning style* and the *myth of disability*, provide excuses for student failure by labeling students. The self-fulfilling prophecy of labels can be devastating to students who already possess a variety of risk factors that make school challenging. Labels like tactile/kinesthetic or right-brain learner may describe unique intrinsic strengths, but they can also describe students who have weak verbal or analytic skills. These weaknesses may be intrinsic or the result of poor instruction, but in either case they should be addressed, not bypassed. Similarly, labels like learning disabilities, at risk, and low socioeconomic status may cause teachers and administrators to write off certain groups of learners rather than to recognize that they need more and better instruction. These labels can have the effect of lowering expectations for individuals and groups and denying them the instruction they need to succeed in school.

Taken together, the myths promote an idiosyncratic and contextual view of teaching that hinders development of a science of teaching. Curricula and methods that have been validated through systematic evaluation can provide powerful tools for increasing academic achievement for all students teachers. Rigorous and ongoing teacher training can transform the science of teaching into effective teaching practices.

External pressure from outside groups can sometimes jump-start change or encourage a more scientific approach. For example, in the wake of birth defects caused by pregnant women taking the drug Thalidomide, the Food and Drug Administration and politicians exerted pressure on the medical community that eventually led to the Kefauver-Harris Drug Control Act of 1962. This law imposed federal controls on the sale of danger-ous drugs and required substantial scientific evidence that a drug was safe as well as mandatory disclosure to physicians about the effectiveness and side effects. After the Kefauver Act, clinical testimony by experts was no longer sufficient evidence for approval. Similarly, external pressure may eventually motivate educators to use validated teaching practices that are based on objective evidence rather than expert opinion.

Public pressure for accountability for student achievement will keep the focus on outcomes rather than process. I suspect that it will become in-creasingly difficult for schools to meet adequate yearly progress goals if they cling to the myths and resist validated teaching practices. I sincerely hope that the public does not allow the economic and political difficulties associated with NCLB to weaken its original intent. The federal require-ment to disaggregate test score data for traditionally low-performing groups—children of poverty, individuals with disabilities, minorities and second-language speakers—provides a powerful incentive to raise expec-tations for children who might otherwise be ignored.

The Comprehensive School Reform Program holds promise for helping schools mitigate the risk factors associated with poverty, but only if schools adopt validated models and implement them with fidelity. Although Dewey's legacy and the teaching myths suggest that only context-specific teaching practices can lead to higher achievement, "the early success of CSR, which has broadened the use of replicable technologies driven by scientific knowl-edge, stands in stark contrast to these beliefs about schools, educational change, and evaluation" (Borman et al., 2002, p. 38).

The Education Sciences Reform Act (U.S. Congress, 2002) is also based on the premise that scientific research is relevant to education and that it is important to answer the question of "what works" to raise student achievement. The National Academy of Sciences (2004) suggests that the federal government can help promote scientifically based research de-signed to establish whether or not curricular innovations and teaching methods actually work. Under the weight of evidence, the educational es-tablishment may eventually change. High-quality curricula and effective instructional methods will result in more excellent teachers. More excel-lent teachers will produce higher achievement for all students.

The myths create a self-perpetuating cycle that leads in circles instead of leading forward. Teachers caught in the loop do not attain full professional status; they remain *bricoleur*. Learners who experience little success in school do not need indirect process approaches, fun activities, eclectic procedures, or self-taught teachers with low expectations. They need accountability, basic skills, direct teaching, validated curriculum, and well-trained teachers with high expectations for the success of *all* students. They need a science of teaching that can complement the art.

References

60 Minutes. (2004, October 3). "Bill Parcells: On the couch" [television broad-cast]. Retrieved October 5, 2004, from http://222.cbsnews.com/stories/ 2003/08/28/60minutes/main570622.shtml

Adams, G. L., & Engelmann, S. (1996). *Research on direct instruction: 25 years beyond DISTAR.* Seattle, WA: Educational Achievement System.

Adams, M. J. (1990). *Learning to read: Thinking and learning about print.* Cambridge, MA: MIT Press.

Alberto, P. A., & Troutman, A. C. (2003). *Applied behavior analysis for teachers* (6th ed.). Upper Saddle River, NJ: Merrill Prentice Hall.

Alessi, G. (1988). Diagnosis diagnosed: A systemic reaction. *Professional School Psychology, 3*(2), 145–151.

Allen, M. (2003). *Eight questions on teacher preparation: What does the research say? A summary of the findings.* Denver, CO: Education Commission of the States.

Allington, R. L., McGill-Franzen, A., & Schick, R. (1997). How administrators understand learning difficulties: A qualitative analysis. *Remedial and Special Education, 18*(4), 223–232.

American Federation of Teachers. (1998). *Building on the best learning from what works.* Washington, DC: Author.

American Institutes for Research. (1999). *An educator's guide to school reform.* Arlington, VA: Educational Research Service.

Anderson, J. R., Reder, L. M., & Simon, H. A. (2000, Summer). *Applications and misapplications of cognitive psychology to mathematics education.* Texas Educational Review. Retrieved February 6, 2005, from http://act-r.psy.cmu.edu/ people/ja/ja-vita#.pubs

Anderson, R. C., & Freebody, P. (1981). Vocabulary knowledge. In J. T. Gurthrie (Ed.), *Comprehension and teaching: Research review* (pp. 71–117). Newark, DE: International Reading Association.

Armbruster, B., Lehr, F., & Osborn, J. (2001). *Put reading first.* Washington, DC: National Institute for Literacy.

Arter, J. A., & Jenkins, J. R. (1977). Examining the benefits and prevalence of modality considerations in special education. *The Journal of Special Education, 11,* 281–298.

Asera, R. (n.d.). American Association of Colleges for Teacher Education. Retrieved December 1, 2004, from http://www.aacte.org/Research/flexnerrpt.pdf

Aukerman, R. C. (1971). *Approaches to beginning reading.* New York: J. Wiley & Sons.

Ausubel, D. P. (1968). *Educational psychology: A cognitive view.* New York: Holt, Rinehart, & Winston.

Bagley, W. C. (1934). *Education and emergent man.* New York: T. Nelson and Sons.

Barron, R., Tom, D., & Cooper, H. (1985). Social class, race and teacher expectations. In J. Dusek (Ed.), *Teacher expectancies* (pp. 251–269). Hillsdale: NJ: Earlbaum.

Bateman, B. (1971). Reading: A controversial view research and rationale. In L. Tarnopol (Ed.), *Introduction to educational and medical management* (pp. 289–304). Springfield, IL: Charles C. Thomas.

Baumann, J., Hoffman, J. V., Moon, J., & Duffy-Hester, A. M. (1998). Where are teachers' voices in the phonics/whole language debate? Results from a survey of U.S. elementary classroom teachers. *Reading Teacher, 51*(8), 636–651.

Baumeister, R. F., Campbell, J. D., Krueger, J. I., & Vohs, K. D. (2003). Does high self-esteem cause better performance, interpersonal success, happiness, or healthier lifestyles? *Psychological Science in the Public Interest, 4*(1), 1–44. Retrieved June 3, 2003, from http://www.psychologicalscience.org/journals/pspi/4_1.html

Beck, A. H. (2004). The Flexner report and the standardization of American medical education. *Journal of the American Medical Association, 291*(17), 2139. Retrieved December 1, 2004, from http://jama.ama-assn.org/cgi/content/full/291/17/2139

Becker, W. C. (1977). Teaching reading and language to the disadvantaged— What we have learned from field research. *Harvard Educational Review, 47,* 518–543.

Berends, M., Bodilly, S. J., & Kirby, S. N. (2002). *Facing the challenges of whole-school reform. New American schools after a decade.* Santa Monica, CA: Rand Corporation. Retrieved March 10, 2005, from http://www.rand.org/publications/MR/MR 1498/

Berliner, D. C., & Biddle, B. J. (1995). *The manufactured crisis: Myths, fraud, and the attack on America's public schools.* Reading, MA: Addison-Wesley.

Bestor, A. (1953). *Educational wastelands: The retreat from learning in our public schools.* Urbana, IL: University of Illinois Press.

Biederman, I., & Shiffrar, M. M. (1987). Sexing day-old chicks: A case study and expert systems analysis of a difficult perceptual learning task. *Journal of Experimental Psychology: Human Learning Memory and Cognition, 13,* 650–645.

Biemiller, A., & Slonim, N. (2001). Estimating root word vocabulary growth in normative and advantaged populations: Evidence for a common sequence of vocabulary acquisition. *Journal of Educational Psychology, 93,* 498–520.

Binder, C., Haughton, E., & Bateman, B. (2002). Fluency: Achieving true mastery in the learning process. Retrieved May 8, 2004, from http://curry.edschool .virginia.edu/go/specialed/papers/

Borman, G. D., Hewes, G. M., Overman, L. T., & Brown, S. (2002). *Comprehensive school reform and student achievement: A meta-analysis.* (Report No. 59). Baltimore, MD, Johns Hopkins University, Center for Research on the Education of Students Placed at Risk. Retrieved May 18, 2005, from http://www .csos.jhu.edu/CRESPAR/techReports/Report/59.pdf

Bradbury, R. (2001, August 29). Retrieved March 16, 2005, from http://archive .salon.com/people/feature/2001/08/29/bradbury/index2.html

Brand, S., Dunn, R., & Greb, F. (2002). Learning styles of students with attention deficit hyperactivity disorder: Who are they and how can we teach them? *The Clearing House, 75*(5), 268–273.

Bransford, J., Darling-Hammond, L., & LePage, P. (2005). Introduction. In L. Darling-Hammond & J. Bransford (Eds.), *Preparing teachers for a changing world: What teachers should learn and be able to do* (pp. 1–39). San Francisco: Jossey-Bass.

Bransford, J., Derry, S., Berliner, D., Hammerness, K., & Beckett, K. L. (2005). Introduction. In L. Darling-Hammond & J. Bransford (Eds.), *Preparing teachers for a changing world: What teachers should learn and be able to do.* (pp. 40–87). San Francisco: Jossey-Bass.

Brock, K. J., & Groth, C. (2003). "Becoming" effective: Lessons from one state's initiative in schools serving low income children. *Journal of Education for Students Placed at Risk, 8*(2), 167–190.

Bruer, J. T. (1998). Brain science, brain fiction. *Educational Leadership, 56*(3), 14–18.

Bureau of National Affairs. (1998). *BNA's quarterly report on job absence and turnover. Bulletin to management.* Washington, DC: Author.

Burress, L. (1989). *Battle of the books: Literary censorship in the public schools, 1950–1985.* (ERIC Document Reproduction Service No. ED 308508).

Carbo, M. (1982). *The reading style inventory*. Roslyn Heights, NY: Learning Research Associates.

Carbo, M. (1984). Research in learning style and reading: Implications for instruction. *Theory into Practice, 23*(1), 72–76.

Carbo, M. (1987a). Deprogramming reading failure: Giving unequal learners an equal chance. *Phi Delta Kappan, 69*(3), 197–202.

Carbo, M. (1987b). Reading styles research: What works isn't always phonics. *Phi Delta Kappan, 68*(6), 431–435.

Carbo, M. (1987c). Matching reading styles: Correcting ineffective instruction. *Educational Leadership, 45*(2), 55–58.

Carbo, M. (1990, October). *How to triple reading progress with recorded books*. Paper presented at the Wisconsin Education Association Council Convention, Madison, WI.

Carnine, D. (2000). Why education experts resist effective practices (and what it would take to make medicine more like education). Washington, DC: Thomas B. Fordham Foundation.

Carroll, J. B., Davies, P., & Richman, B. (1971). *The American heritage word frequency book*. Boston: Houghton Mifflin.

Carter, S. C. (2000). *No excuses: Lessons from 21 high-performing, high-poverty schools*. Washington, DC: The Heritage Foundation.

Chall, J. S. (1967). *Learning to read: The great debate*. New York: McGraw-Hill.

Chall, J. S. (1983). *Stages of reading development*. New York: McGraw-Hill.

Chall, J. S. (2000). *The academic achievement challenge: What really works in the classroom?* New York: Guilford Press.

Chall, J. S., Jacobs, V. A., & Baldwin, L. E. (1990). *The reading crisis: Why poor children fall behind*. Cambridge, MA: Harvard University Press.

Chall, J. S., & Mirskey, A. (1978). Education and the brain. In J. S. Chall and A. F. Merskey (Eds.), *Seventy-fifth yearbook of the National Society for the Study of Education* (pp. 371–378). Chicago: University of Chicago Press.

Chen, M. (2001, May 16). Seeking Edutopia. *Education Week, 20*(36), 42, 56.

Chi, M. T. H., Glaser, R., & Farr, M. J. (1988). *The nature of expertise*. Hillsdale, NJ: Lawrence Earlbaum Associates.

Cohen, M. (2002). Unruly crew. *Education Next, 2*(3), 42–47.

Collins, J. (1997, October 27). How Johnny should read. *Time Magazine, 150*, 78–82.

Commeyras, M. (2002, May). The improvisational in teaching reading. *Reading Online, 5*(9). Retrieved February 11, 2004, from http://www.readingonline.org

Community Action Forum. (n.d.). *Prevent reading failure in Oregon*. Retrieved February 26, 2005, from http://www.ori.org/-keiths/caf/read-fact.html

COMPASS, Inc. (2003). *The state of the teaching profession in Ontario, 2003.* Retrieved on September 24, 2003, from http://www.oct.ca/en/Collge Publications/news-archive/20030903_e.asp

Cook, T. (2001). Sciencephobia. *Education Next, 1*(3), 62–68. Retrieved September 8, 2002, from http://www.educationnext.org

Cooley, W. W., & Leinhardt, G. (1978). *The instructional dimensions study. The search for effective classroom process.* Pittsburgh, PA: Learning Research and Development Center. (ERIC Document Reproduction Service No. ED 167580)

Council for Learning Disabilities (1986). Measurement and training of perceptual and perceptual motor functions. *Learning Disability Quarterly, 9,* 247.

Crawford, D. B., & Carnine, D. (2000). Comparing the effects of textbooks in eighth-grade U.S. History: Does conceptual organization help? *Education & Treatment of Children, 23,* 387–423.

Crawford, D. B., & Snider, V. E. (2000). Effective mathematics instruction: The importance of curriculum. *Education & Treatment of Children, 23,* 122–143.

Croll, P., & Moses, D. (1985). *One in five: The assessment and incidence of special educational needs.* London: Routledge & Kegan Paul.

Cuban, L. (1993). *How teachers taught: Constancy and change in American classrooms; 1890–1990.* New York: Teachers College Press.

Cunningham, A. E., & Stanovitch, K. E. (1998). What reading does for the mind. *American Educator, 22,* 8–15.

Cunningham, G. K., & Stone, J. E. (2005). Value-added assessment of teacher quality as an alternative to the National Board for Professional Teaching Standards: What recent studies say. In Robert Lissitz (Ed.), *Value added models in education: Theory and applications.* Maple Grove, MN: JAM Press.

Curry, L. (1983). *An organization of learning styles, theories and constructs.* Paper presented at the Annual Meeting of the American Educational Research Association, Montreal, Canada (ERIC Document Reproduction Service No. ED 235185)

Dahl, K. L., Scharer, P. L., Lawon, L. L., & Grogan, P. R. (2001). *Rethinking phonics: Making the best teaching decisions.* Portsmouth, NH: Heinemann.

Darling-Hammond, L. (2002, September). Research and rhetoric on teacher certification. A response to "Teacher Certification Reconsidered." *Policy Analysis Archives, 10*(36). Retrieved October 11, 2004, from http://epaa.asu.edu/epaa/v10n36.html

Darling-Hammond, L., & Bransford, J. (2005). *Preparing teachers for a changing world: What teachers should learn and be able to do.* San Francisco: Jossey-Bass.

DelFattore, J. (1992). *What Johnny shouldn't read: Textbook censorship in America.* (ERIC Document Reproduction Service No. ED 349550)

Dewey, J. (1916). *Democracy and education: An introduction to the philosophy of education.* New York: Macmillan.

Dewey, J. (1929). *The sources of a science of education.* New York: Horace Liveright.

Douglas-Hall, A., & Koball, H. (2005, February). Basic facts about low-income children in the United States. *National Center for Children in Poverty.* Retrieved March 3, 2005, from http://www.nccp.org

Drucker, P. (n.d.). Retrieved April 5, 2005, from http://www.quotegarden.com

Dunn, R. (1982). Teaching students through their individual learning styles: A research report. In Learning Styles Network (Ed.), *Student learning styles and brain behavior* (pp. 142–151). Reston, VA: National Association of Secondary School Principals.

Dunn, R., Dunn, K., & Price, G. E. (2000). *Learning styles inventory.* Lawrence, KS: Price Systems.

Dunseath, K. (2000). *Defending educational research in changing times.* Proceedings of the ASET-HERDSA Conference. Toowoomba, Australia: University of Queensland. Retrieved December 1, 2004, from http://www.aset.org.au/confs/aset-herdsa2000/procs/dunseath-k.html

Edmondson, A. (2001, June 19). Watson kills reform model for city schools. *The Commercial Appeal,* p. A1.

Ehrenberg, R. G., & Brewer, D. J. (1994). Do school and teacher characteristics matter? Evidence from "high school and beyond." *Economics of Education Review, 13*(1), 1–17.

Elam, S. M. (1989). The second Gallup/Phi Delta Kappa poll of teachers' attitudes toward the public schools. *Phi Delta Kappan, 70*(10), 785–799.

Eliot, C. W. (1961). Industrial education as an essential factor in our national prosperity. In E. A. Krug (Ed.), *Charles W. Eliot and popular education* (pp. 19–20). New York: Teachers College Press.

Ellis, A. K., & Fouts, J. T. (1993). *Research on educational innovations.* Princeton Junction, NJ: Eye on Education.

Ellis, E. S., Worthington, L. A., & Larkin, M. J. (1994). *Executive summary of the research synthesis on effective teaching principles and the design of quality tools for educators* (Tech. Rep. No. 6). Eugene: University of Oregon National Center to Improve the Tools of Educators.

Elmore, R. F. (2002a, September/October). The limits of "change." *Harvard Education Letter Research Online.* Retrieved October 11, 2004, from http://www.edletter.org/current/limitsofchange.shtml

Elmore, R. F. (2002b). Unwarranted intrusion. *Education Next, 2*(1). Retrieved March 21, 2005, from http://educationext.org/

Engelmann, K. (2003, fall). City Spring sets the standard . . . again. *Direct Instruction News, 3*(2), 12–16.

Engelmann, S. (1992). *War against the schools' academic child abuse.* Portland, OR: Halcyon House.

Engelmann, S., & Bruner, E. C. (2003). *Reading mastery classic.* Columbus, OH: SRA/McGraw-Hill.

Esar, E. (n.d.). Retrieved February 24, 2005, from Michael Moncur's (Cynical) quotation Web site available from http://www.quotationspage.com/subjects/education

Facts about illiteracy (2001). Retrieved February 10, 2005, from SIL international Web site at http://www.sil.org/literacy/LitFacts.htm

Farkas, S., Johnson, J., & Duffett, A. (1997). *Different drummers: How teachers of teachers view public education.* Washington, DC: Public Agenda.

Farkas, S., Johnson, J., & Duffett, A. (1999). *Playing their parts: Parents and teachers talk about parental involvement in schools.* Washington, DC: Public Agenda.

Farkas, S., Johnson, J., & Duffett, A. (2003). *Stand by me: What teachers really think about union, merit pay, and other professional matters.* Washington, DC: Public Agenda.

Farkas, S., Johnson, J., & Foleno, T. (2000). *A sense of calling: Who teaches and why.* Washington, DC: Public Agenda.

Fashola, O. S., & Slavin, R. E. (1998, January). Schoolwide reform models: What works? *Phi Delta Kappan, 79,* 370–379.

Feiman-Nemser, S. (1983). Learning to teach. In L. S. Shulman & G. Sykes (Eds.), *Handbook of teaching and policy* (pp. 150–170). New York: Longman.

Finley, D. (2002, December 10). Legislation won't make children learn. *The Arizona Republic,* p. B9.

Finn, C. (1991, May 27). Accounting for results—Problems of American education. *National Review.* Retrieved February 22, 2005, from http://www.findarticles.com

Finn, C. E., & Kanstoroom, M. (2000, Summer). Education: Solutions improving, empowering, dismantling. *The Public Interest, 140,* 64–73. Retrieved May 15, 2004, from http://thepublicinterest.com

Five million children: A statistical profile of our poorest young citizens. (1994). *National Center for Children in Poverty. Columbia University.* Retrieved March 14, 2005, from http://www.nccp.org

Fletch, R. (1955). *Why Johnny can't read—and what you can do about it.* New York: Harper.

Flexner, A., & Pritchett, H. S. (1910). *Medical education in the United States and Canada: A report to the Carnegie Foundation for the Advancement of Teaching.* New York: Carnegie Foundation for the Advancement of Teaching.

Friedman, T. L. (2005, May 13). Where have you gone, Joe DiMaggio? *The New York Times*. Retrieved May 13, 2005, from http:www.nytimes.com/2005/05/13/opinion/13friedman.html

Frisby, C. L. (1993). One giant step backward: Myths of black cultural learning styles. *School Psychology Review, 22*(3), 535–558.

Fry, E. (1996). Data raise doubts about whole language. *Reading Today, 13*(3), 33.

Gallup, A. (1985). The Gallup poll of teachers' attitudes toward the public schools part 2. *Phi Delta Kappan, 66*(5), 323–330.

Gardner, H. (1983). *Frames of mind: The theory of multiple intelligences*. New York: Basic Books.

Gardner, H. (1993). *Multiple intelligences: The theory into practice*. New York: Basic Books.

Gardner, H. (1999). *Intelligence reframed: Multiple intelligences for the 21st century*. New York: Basic Books.

Gersten, R., Woodward, J., & Darch, C. (1986). "Direct instruction: A research-approach to curriculum design and teaching." *Exceptional Children*, 53.

Goldhaber, D. (2002, Spring). The mystery of good teaching. *Education Next 2*(1). Retrieved October 28, 2004, from http:www.educationnnext.org/

Good, T. (1982). How teachers' expectations affect results. *American Education, 18*(10), 25–32.

Good, T. (1987). Two decades of research on teacher expectations: Findings and future directions. *Journal of Teacher Education, 38*(4), 32–47.

Goodlad, J. I. (1990). *Teachers of our nation's schools*. San Francisco: Jossey-Bass.

Goodman, K. S. (1965). *A linguistic study of cues and miscues in reading*. (ERIC Document Reproduction Service No. ED 011482)

Gould, S. J. (1981). *The mismeasure of man*. New York: W.W. Norton.

Graham, P. A. (1993). What America has expected of its schools over the past century. *American Journal of Education, 101*(2), 83–98.

Grissmer, G. W., Kirby, S., Berends, M., & Williamson, S. (1994). *Student achievement and the changing American family*. Santa Monica, CA: Rand Corporation.

Grossman, K. N. (2005, February 21). City schools to ax scripted reading program despite gains. *Chicago Sun-Times*. Retrieved February 21, 2005, from http://www.suntines.com

Haberman, M. (1995). *Star teachers of children in poverty*. West Lafayette, LA: Kappa Delta Pi Publications.

Hacsi, T. (2002). *Children as pawns: The politics of education reform*. Cambridge, MA.

Hanushek, E. A., Rivkin, S. G., Kain, J. F., (1998). Does special education raise academic achievement for students with disabilities? Working Paper 6690. Cambridge, MA: National Bureau of Economic Research.

Hart, B., & Risley, T. (1995). *Meaningful differences.* Baltimore: Paul H. Brooks.

Herszenhorn, D. M. (2004, May 5). City made deal without bids for training of teachers. *The New York Times,* B1, 4.

Heward, W. L. (2003). Ten faulty notions about teaching and learning that hinder the effectiveness of special education. *Journal of Special Education, 36*(4), 186–205.

Highly effective teachers study. (2004). Retrieved May 12, 2005, from http://www.pefchattanooga.org/www/docs/5.261

Hinds, M. D. (2002). *Carnegie challenge 2002: Teaching as a clinical profession: A new challenge for education.* New York: Carnegie Corporation of New York.

Hirsch, E. D. (1996). *The schools we need and why we don't have them.* New York: Doubleday.

Hirsch, E. D. (2000). "You can always look it up" . . . or can you? *American Educator, 24*(1), 4–9.

Hirsch, E. D. (2003). Reading comprehension requires knowledge — of words and the world. *American Educator, 27*(1), 10–13, 16–22.

Hoffer, T., Greeley, A. M., & Coleman, J. S. (1985). Achievement growth in public and Catholic schools. *Sociology of Education, 58,* 74–97.

Holden, C. (1990). Head start enters adulthood. *Science, 247,* 1400–1402.

Holmes Group (1986). *Tomorrow's teachers.* East Lansing, MI: Author.

Holmes Group (1990). *Tomorrow's schools.* East Lansing, MI: Author.

Holmes Group (1995). *Tomorrow's schools of education.* East Lansing, MI: Author.

Holt, C. R., Denny, G., Capps, M., & DeVore, J. B. (2005, February 25). Teachers' ability to perceive student learning preferences: "I'm sorry, but I don't teach like that." *Teachers College Record.* Article 11767. Retrieved March 3, 2005, from http://www.tcrecord.org

Howell, K. W., & Nolet, V. (2000). *Curriculum-based evaluation: Teaching and decision making.* Belmont, CA: Wadsworth/Thomson Learning.

Hunter, M. (1982). *Mastery teaching.* El Segundo, CA: TIP Publications.

Ingersoll, R. M. (2001, January). Teacher turnover, teacher shortages, and the organization of schools. *University of Washington Center for the Study of Teaching and Policy.* Retrieved January 10, 2005 from http://www.ctpweb.org

Interstate New Teacher Assessment and Support Consortium (INTASC) (1992, September). *Model standards for beginning teacher licensing and development: A resource for state dialogue.* Washington, DC: Council of Chief State School Offices.

Irvine, J. J., & York, D. E. (1995). Learning styles and culturally diverse students: A literature review. In J. A. Banks & C. A. McGee Banks (Eds.), *Handbook of research on multicultural education*. New York: Macmillan.

Ishler, R. E., Edens, K. M., & Berry, B. W. (1996). Teacher education: Elementary education curriculum. In J. Sikula, T.J. Buttery, and E. Guyton (Eds.), *Handbook of research on teacher education* (2nd ed., pp. 348–377). New York: Simon & Schuster Macmillan.

Jesness, J. (2000, November 8). You have your teacher's permission to be ignorant. *Education Week, 29*(10), 49, 52.

Johnson, J., & Duffet, A. (2003). *Where we are now.* Washington, DC: Public Agenda.

Johnson, J., Duffet, A., Vine, J., & Syat, B. (2003). *Attitudes about teaching.* New York: Public Agenda.

Johnson, J., Duffett, A. Vine, J., & Moye, L. (2003). *Where we are now. Twelve things you need to know about public opinion and public schools.* Washington, DC: Public Agenda.

Johnson, J., & Farkas, S. (1997). *Getting by: What American teenagers really think about their schools.* Washington, DC: Public Agenda.

Judd, C. H. (1908). The relation of special training to general intelligence. *Educational Review, 36,* 28–42.

Judge, H. (1982). *American graduate schools of education: A view from abroad.* New York: Ford Foundation.

Juel, C. (1988). Learning to read and write: A longitudinal study of fifty-four children from first through fourth grade. *Journal of Education Psychology, 80,* 437–447.

Kaestle, C. F., Campbell, A., Finn, J. D., Johnson, S. T., & Mikulecky, L. J. (2001). *Adult literacy and education in America* (NCES 2001-534). Washington, DC: National Center for Education Statistics.

Kagan, D. M. (1992, Summer). Professional growth among preservice and beginning teachers. *Review of Educational Research, 62*(2), 129–169.

Kalsbeek, D. (1989). Linking learning style theory with retention research. *The Association for Institutional Research, 32,* 1–9 (ERIC Document Reproduction Service No. ED 304964)

Kameenui, E. J., & Simmons, D. C. (1990). *Designing instructional strategies: The prevention of academic learning problems.* Columbus, OH: Merrill.

Kavale, K. A., & Forness, S. R. (1987). Substance over style: Assessing the efficacy of modality testing and teaching. *Exceptional Children, 54,* 228–239.

Keller, B. (2003, November 12). Education school courses faulted as intellectually thin. *Education Week, 23*(11), 8.

Kirsch, I. S., Jungeblut, A., Jenkins, L., & Kolstad, A. (n.d.). Executive summary of adult literacy: A first look at the results of the National Adult Literacy Survey. Retrieved April 4, 2005, from http://www.nces.gove/naal/resources/execsumm.asp

Kirst, M. (2004, November 18). *Education politics and policy: Retrospect and prospect.* Paper presented at the Virgil E. Herrick Memorial Lecture Series. Madison, WI.

Klahr, D., & Nigam, M. (2004). The equivalence of learning paths in early science instruction: Effects of direct instruction and discovery learning. *Psychological Science, 15*(10), 661–667.

Kliebard, H. M. (1986). *The struggle for the American curriculum 1983–1958.* Boston: Routledge & Kegan Paul.

Koerner, J. (1963). *The miseducation of American teachers.* Boston: Houghton Mifflin.

Kohn, A. (1993). *Punished by rewards: The trouble with gold stars, incentive plans, A's, praise, and other bribes.* New York: Houghton Mifflin.

Kohn, A. (1997, September 3). Students don't "work"—they learn. *Education Week.* Retrieved February 4, 2005, from http://www.alfiekohn.org/teaching/edweek/sdwtl.htm

Kolb, D. A. (1985). *The learning style inventory.* Boston, MA: McBer.

Kramer, R. (1991). *Ed school follies.* New York: Free Press.

Labaree, D. F. (2004). *The trouble with ed schools.* New Haven: Yale University Press.

Langermann, E. C. (1989). The plural worlds of educational research. *History of Education Quarterly, 29*(2), 185–214.

Langland, C. (2004, November 5). Provocative report issued at dyslexia conference. *The Philadelphia Inquirer.* Retrieved November 10, 2004, from http://www.philly.com/mld/inquirer/living/education/10103035.htm

Lanier, J. E., & Little, J. W. (1986). Research on teacher education. In M. C. Whitrock (Ed.), *Handbook of research on teaching* (pp. 527–569). New York: Macmillan.

Latham, G. (2002). *Behind the schoolhouse door: Managing chaos with science, skills, and strategies.* North Logan, UT: P and T Ink.

LaVoie, R. (1994). *Last one picked—first one picked on.* Alexandria, VA: PBS Video Greater Washington Educational Telecommunication Association.

Lazerson, M. (Ed.). (1987). *American education in the twentieth century: A documentary history.* New York: Teachers College Press.

Lerner, J. (1989). Educational intervention in learning disabilities. *Journal of the American Academy of Child and Adolescent Psychiatry, 28,* 326–331.

Levin, J., & O'Donnell, A. M. (1999). What to do about educational research's credibility gaps. *Issues in Education, 5*(2), 177–230.

Levine, M. (2002). *A mind at a time.* New York: Simon & Schuster.

Levi-Strauss, C. (1966). *The savage mind.* Chicago: University of Chicago Press.

Liberman, I. Y. (1985). Should so-called modality preferences determine the nature of instruction for children with reading disabilities? In F. H. Duffy & N. Geschwind (Eds.), *Dyslexia: A neuroscientific approach to clinical evaluation.* Boston: Little Brown & Company.

Lindsley, O. (1992). Why aren't effective teaching tools widely adopted? *Journal of Applied Behavior Analysis, 25*, 21–26.

Linksman, R. (2000). The fine line between ADHD and kinesthetic learners. *Latitudes (1)*6. Retrieved July 13, 2000, from http://www.latitudes.org/learn 01.html

Lloyd, J. W., Forness, S. R., & Kavale, K. (1998). Some methods are more effective than others. *Intervention in School and Clinic, 33*(4), 195–200.

Loewen, J. (1995). By the book. *American School Board Journal, 182*(1), 24–27.

Lombardi, V. (n.d.). Retrieved September 10, 2005, from the Illinois Loop Web site at http://www.illinoisloop.org

Lortie, D. C. (1975*). Schoolteacher: A sociological study.* Chicago: University of Chicago Press.

Lovett, K., & Campanile, C. (2004, May 19). Staggering fail rate in special ed. *The New York Times.* Retrieved May 23, 2004, from http://www.nytimes.com

Lyon, G. R., Fletcher, J. M., Shaywitz, S. E., Shaywitz, B. A., Torgesen, J. K., Wood, F. B., Schulte, A., & Olson, R. (2001). Rethinking learning disabilities. In C. E. Finn, A. J., Rotherham, & C. R. Hokanson (Eds.), *Rethinking special education for a new century* (pp. 259–287). Washington, DC: Fordham Foundation.

Mandeville, G. K., & Rivers, J. L. (1991). The South Carolina PET study: Teachers' perceptions and student achievement. *Elementary School Journal, 91*(4), 377–407.

Markow, D., Fauth, S., & Gravitch, D. (2001). *MetLife survey of the American teacher: Key elements of quality schools.* New York: MetLife.

Markow, D., & Scheer, M. (2002). *MetLife survey of the American teacher: Student life: School, home, and community.* New York: MetLife.

Marvin, C., & Mirenda, P. (1993). Home literacy experiences of preschoolers enrolled in Head Start and special education programs. *Journal of Early Intervention, 17*(4), 351–367.

Mason, W. S. (1961). *The beginning teacher.* Washington, DC: U.S. Department of Health, Education, and Welfare, Office of Education, Circular no. 644.

Mayer, R. (1999). To foster meaningful learning is science still relevant? *Issues in Education, 5*(2), 255–260.

McCarthy, B. (1987). *The 4MAT system: Teaching to learning styles with right/left mode techniques.* Barrington, IL: Excel.

Meister, D. G., & Melnick, S. A. (2003). National new teacher study: Beginning teachers' concerns. *Action in Teacher Education, 24*(4).

Moats, L. C. (1995). The missing foundation in teacher preparation. *American Educator, 19*(9), 43–51.

Moats, L. C. (1999). *Teaching reading is rocket science: What expert teachers of reading need to know.* Washington, DC: American Federation of Teachers.

Moats, L. C. (2000). *Whole language lives on: The illusion of "balanced" reading instruction.* Washington, DC: Thomas B. Fordham Foundation.

Mondale, S., & Patton, S. B. (2001). *School: The story of American public education.* Boston: Beacon Press.

Morris, C. N. (1957). Career patterns of teachers. In L. J. Stiles (Ed.), *The teacher's role in American society* (pp. 247–263). New York: Harper and Brothers.

Murnane, R. J., & Phillips, B. R. (1981). What do effective teachers of inner-city children have in common? *Social Science Research, 10,* 83–100.

Murray, C. Goldstein, D. E., Nourse, S., & Edgar, E. (2000). The post-secondary school attendance and completion rates of high school graduates with learning disabilities. *Learning Disabilities Research and Practice, 15,* 119–127.

Myers, I. B., McCaulley, M., Quenk, N. L., & Hammer, A. L. (1998). *MBTI manual: A guide to the development and use of the Myers-Briggs type indicator* (3rd ed.). Palo Alto, CA: Consulting Psychologists Press.

National Academy of Sciences (2004). *Executive Summary.* Retrieved May 11, 2005, from http://www.nap.edu/catalog/11112.html

National Center for Educational Statistics. (1993). *120 years of American education: A statistical portrait.* Washington, DC: Author.

National Center for Educational Statistics. (2003a). Table 109. *Number of students with disabilities exiting special education by basis of exit, age, and type of disability.* Retrieved March 21, 2005, from http://nces.ed.gov/

National Center for Educational Statistics. (2003b). *The nation's report card.* Washington, DC: U.S. Department of Education. Retrieved March 17, 2005, from http://nces.ed.gov/nationsreportcard/reading/results2003/

National Commission on Excellence in Education. (1983). *A nation at risk.* Washington, DC: Author.

National Commission on Teaching and America's Future (NCTAF). (1996). *What matters most: Teaching for America's future.* New York: Author.

National Dissemination Center for Children with Disabilities. (2003). *Who are the children in special education?* Retrieved May 3, 2005, from http://www.nichy.org/pubs/research/rb2text.htm

National Education Association. (2000–01). *Status of the American public school teacher.* Washington, DC: Author. Retrieved October 22, 2004, from http://www.nea.org

National Institute of Child Health and Human Development. (2000). *Report of the national reading panel: Teaching children to read.* Washington, DC: Author.

National Public Radio (1997). Body and soul. *All things considered.* Retrieved March 28, 2003, from http://nl.newsbank.com

National Research Council. (1998). *Preventing reading difficulties in young children.* Washington, DC: National Academy Press.

Nelson, J. (1993, April 21). What's your learning style? *New York Times Magazine, 142,* 78.

Nikiforuk, A. (1994). *If learning is so natural, why am I going to school?* Toronto, ON: Penguin Books.

Oakes, J. (1985). *Keeping track: How schools structure inequality.* Birmingham, NY: Vail-Ballou Press.

Oregon Reading First Center. (2004, March). *Review of comprehensive programs.* Retrieved April 20, 2005, from http://reading.uoregon.edu/curricula/or_rfc_review_2.php

Orland, M. (1990). Demographics of disadvantage: Intensity of childhood poverty and its relationship to educational achievement. In J. Goodlad & P. Keating (Eds.), *Access to knowledge: An agenda for our nation's schools* (pp. 43–58). New York: The College Board.

Our prospects as a profession. (1898). *Journal of the American Medical Association, 31,* 932–935,

Our view. (2003, December 16). *Rockford Register Star.* Retrieved February 22, 2005, from http://www.rrstar.com

Palmaffy, T. (1998, January–February). No excuses. *Policy Review,* no. 87. Retrieved February 21, 1998, from http://www.policyreview.org/jan98

Parents of nasal learners demand odor-based curriculum. (2000, March 15). *The Onion.* Retrieved March 18, 2000, from http://www.theonion.com/

Passow, A. H. (1967). *Executive summary: Toward creating a model urban school system: A study of Washington, D.C. Public Schools.* New York: Teachers College. (ERIC Document Reproduction Service No. ED 013288)

Pavalko, R. M. (1970). Recruitment to teaching: Patterns of selection and retention. *Sociology of Education, 43,* 340–353.

Pear, R. (2005, February 28) Governors of 13 states plan to raise standards in high schools. *The New York Times*. Retrieved March 1, 2005, from http://www .nytimes.com/2005/02/28/politics/28govs.html

Pinker, S. (1994). *The language instinct.* New York: William Morrow.

Policy statement: Learning disabilities, dyslexia, and vision. (1998, September). Retrieved December 16, 2004 from http://www.aao.org/aao/member/policy/ disability.cfm

Popham, J. W. (1971). Teaching skill under scrutiny. *Phi Delta Kappan, 53*(1), 599–602.

Postman, N. (1992). *Technopoly: The surrender of culture to technology.* New York: Knopf.

Preparing Teachers: Are American Schools Up to the Task? (2003). From a consumer perspective: Briefings on eduucational research from the Education Consumers Network. Retrieved March 4, 2005 from http//www.education-consumers.com/briefs/nov2003.shtm

President's Commission on Excellence in Special Education. (2002). *A new era: Revitalizing special education for children and their families.* Washington, DC: U.S. Department of Education.

Public Agenda: Reality check. (2002, March 6). *Education Week, 21*(25), pp. S1–S8. Retrieved May 10, 2005, from http://www.edweek.org/reports/

Quality Counts (2000): Attracting the best and the brightest? (2000). *Education Week, 19*(18). Retrieved May 10, 2005, from http://www.edweek.org/reports/

Rathbun, A., West, J., & Hausken, E. G. (2004). *From kindergarten through third grade: Children's beginning school experiences.* Washington, DC: U.S. Department of Education.

Ravitch, D. (1998, December 16). What if research really mattered? *Education Week, 18*(16), 33–34.

Ravitch, D. (2000). *Left back: A century of failed school reforms.* New York: Simon & Schuster.

Ravitch, D. (2005, March). Failing the wrong grades. *The New York Times*. Retrieved March 16, 2005, from http://www.nytimes.com/2005/03/15/opinion/ 15ravitch.htm

Ravitz, J. L., Becker, H. J., & Wong, Y. T. (2000). *Constructivist-compatible beliefs and practices among U.S. teachers.* (Irvine: Teaching, Learning, and Computing: 1998 National Survey, Report #4). University of California, Irvine and University of Minnesota. (ERIC Document Reproduction Service No. ED 445 657)

Reading between the lines of rigidity. (2004, November 29). *Wisconsin State Journal*, p. A9.

Reed, E. W. (1997–98). Projects and activities: A means, not an end. *American Educator, 21*(4), 26–27, 48.

Reiss-Weimann, E., & Friedman, R. (1997). *The land of letter people: Teacher resource unit.* Waterbury, CT: Abrams.

Rice, J. (2003). *Teacher quality: Understanding the effectiveness of teacher attributes.* Washington, DC: Economic Policy Institute.

Richardson, V. (1996). The role of attitudes and beliefs in learning to teach. In J. Sikula, T.J. Buttery, & E. Guyton (Eds.), *Handbook of research on teacher education* (2nd ed., pp. 102–119). New York: Simon & Schuster Macmillan.

Rose, L. C., & Gallup, A. M. (2001). The 33rd annual Phi Delta Kappa/Gallup poll of the public's attitudes toward the schools. *Phi Delta Kappan, 83*(1), 41–48.

Rosenshine, B. R. (1976). Classroom instruction. In N. L. Gage (Ed.), *The psychology of teaching methods: Seventy-fifth yearbook of the National Society for the Study of Education* (pp. 335–371). Chicago: University of Chicago Press.

Rosenshine, B. V. (1986). Synthesis of research on explicit teaching. *Educational Leadership, 43*(7), 60–69.

Rosenshine, B. V., & Berliner, D. C. (1975) Academic engaged time. *British Journal of Education, 4*, 3–11.

Rosenthal, R., & Jacobson, L. (1968). *Pygmalion in the classroom.* New York: Holt, Rinehart, & Winston.

Rowling, J. K. (1998). *Harry Potter and the sorcerer's stone.* New York: A. A. Levine Books.

Rude, R. (2002). The road to interest and curiosity. *American Educator, 26*(1), 39–40.

Ruggiero, V. R. (2000). Bad attitude. *American Educator, 24*(2), 10–15, 44–48.

Schmidt, W., Houang, R., & Cogan, L. (2002). A coherent curriculum: The case of mathematics. *American Educator, 26*(2), 10–26.

Schmidt, W., McKnight, C. C., Houang, R., HsingChi, W., Wiley, D. E., Cogan, L. S., & Wolfe, R. G. (2001). *Why schools matter.* New York: Jossey-Bass.

Schneider, W. (1990, April 7). The trivializing of American politics. *National Journal, 14*, 872.

Schroeder, C. C. (1993). New students—new learning styles. Retrieved November 12, 2004, from http://www.virtualschool.edu/mon/Academia/Kiersey1.Learning Styles.html

Schultz, E., Neyhart, T., & Reck, U. (1996). Swimming against the tide: A study of perspective teacher attitudes regarding cultural diversity and urban teaching. *Western Journal of Black Studies, 20*(1), 1–7.

Sedlak, M. W., & Schlossman, S. L. (1986). *Who will teach? Historical perspectives on the changing appeal of teaching as a profession.* Santa Monica, CA: Rand Corporation.

Seethaler, P. M., & Fuchs, L. S. (2005). A drop in the bucket: Randomized controlled trials testing reading and math interventions. *Learning Disabilities Research & Practice, 20*(2), 98–102.

Sewall, G. T. (2000). Bad attitude. *American Educator, 24*(2), 4–9, 42–43.

Sewall, G. T. (2003). *Senate testimony.* Retrieved December 1, 2004 from http://www.historytextbooks.org/senate.htm

Shanker, A. (1995, June 25). Debating the standards. *The New York Times.* Retrieved May 20, 2005, from the Illinois Loop Web site at http://illinoisloop.org

Shavelson, R. J., & Towne, L. (Eds.). (2002). *Scientific research in education.* Washington, DC: National Academy Press.

Silberman, C. (1970). *Crisis in the classroom.* New York: Random House.

Sizer, T. (1997, June 25). On lame horses and tortoises. *Education Week.* Retrieved February 9, 2005, from http://www.educationweek.org

Slavin, R. E. (1987). The Napa evaluation of Madeline Hunter's ITIP: Lessons learned. *Elementary School Journal, 87*(2), 165–171.

Slavin, R. E. (1989). PET and the pendulum: Faddism in education and how to stop it. *Phi Delta Kappan, 70*(10), 752–759.

Slavin, R. E., & Madden N.A. (2001). *One million children: Success for all.* Thousand Oaks, CA: Corwin.

Smith, L. (2001). Can schools really change? *Education Week, 20*(21), 30.

Snider, V. E. (1992). Learning style and learning to read: A critique. *Remedial and Special Education, 13*(1), 6–18.

Sorokin, P. (1927). *Social mobility.* New York: Harper.

Sowell, T. (1993). *Inside American education.* New York: Free Press.

Spencer, J. (2005, May 5). Probe finds 4 schools cheated on TAKS test. *The Houston Chronicle.* Retrieved May 17, 2005, from http:www.chron.com

Spilich, G. J., Vesonder, G. T., Chiesi, H. L., & Voss, J. F. (1979). Text processing of domain-related information for individuals with high and low domain knowledge. *Journal of Verbal Learning and Verbal Behavior*, 18, 275–290.

Sprick, R. (1992). Myths, misconceptions, and the thief at the door. *ADI News, 11*(4), 9–11.

Stahl, S., & Kuhn, M. R. (1995). Does whole language or instruction matched to learning styles help children learn to read? *School Psychology Review, 24*(3), 393–404.

Stahl, S. A., Osborn, J., & Pearson, P. D. (1994). *Six teachers in their classrooms: A closer look at beginning reading instruction.* (Technical Report No. 606). Champaign, IL: Center for the Study of Reading. (ERIC Document Reproduction Service No. ED 376451)

Stallings, J. (1985). A study of implementation of Madeline Hunter's model and its effects on students. *Journal of Educational Research, 78*, 325–37.

Stallings, J., & Krasavage, E. M. (1986). Program implementation and student achievement in a four-year Madeline Hunter follow-through project. *Elementary School Journal, 87*, 117–38.

Stanovich, K. E. (1984). The interactive-compensatory model of reading: A confluence of developmental, experimental, and educational psychology. *Remedial and Special Education, 5,* 11–19.

Stanovich, K. E. (1986). Mathew effects in reading: Some consequences of individual differences in the acquisition of literacy. *Reading Research Quarterly, 21*, 360–407.

Stanovich, K. E. (1993). Romance and reality. *The Reading Teacher, 47*(4), 280–291.

Stanovich, K. E., West, R. F., & Freeman, D. J. (1981). A longitudinal study of sentence context effects in second-grade children: Tests of an interactive-compensatory model. *Journal of Experimental Child Psychology, 32*, 185–199.

Stebbins, L. B., St. Pierre, R. G., Proper, E. C., Anderson, R. B., & Cerva, T. R. (1977). *Education as experimentation: A planned variation model* (Vol. 4-A). Cambridge, MA: Abt Associates.

Steiner, D. M., & Rozen, S. D. (2004). Preparing tomorrow's teachers: An analysis of syllabi from a sample of America's schools of education. In F. M. Hess, A. J. Rotherham, & K. Walsh (Eds.) *A qualified teacher in every classroom?* (pp. 119–148). Cambridge, MA: Harvard Education Press.

Stone, J. E. (1999). Learning requires more than play. *Education Matters, 5*(12), p. 1, 8.

Tarver, S. G., & Dawson, M. M. (1978). Modality preference and the teaching of reading: A review. *Journal of Learning Disabilities, 11,* 17–29.

Tarver, S. G., & Hallahan, D. P. (1974). Attention deficits in children with learning disabilities: A review. *Journal of Learning Disabilities, 7*, 560–569.

Teachers to learn about the latest reading research (2003, June 5). University of Wisconsin—Milwaukee Press Release. Retrieved January 24, 2004, from http://www.uwm.edu/News/PR/03.06/reading.html

Temes, P. (2001, April 4). The end of school reform. *Education Week, 20*(29), 36.

Thernstrom, A., & Thernstrom, S. (2003). *No excuses: Closing the racial gap in learning.* New York: Simon & Schuster.

Thomas B. Fordham Foundation. (1998). *A nation still at risk: An education manifesto.* Washington, DC: Author.

Thomas, L. (1979). *The medusa and the snail.* New York: Viking Press.

Thompson, G. L., Warren, S., & Carter, L. (2004). It's not my fault: Predicting high school teachers who blame parents and students for students' low achievement. *High School Journal, 87*(3), 5–15.

Thorndike, E. L. (1917). Reading as reasoning: A study of mistakes in paragraph reading. *Journal of Educational Psychology, 8*, 323–332.

Twain, M. (1899). *Pudd'nhead Wilson and those extraordinary twins*. New York: Harper & Brothers.

Tyack, D., & Cuban, L. (1995). *Tinkering toward utopia*. Cambridge, MA: Harvard University Press.

Tyson-Bernstein, H. (1988). *A conspiracy of good intentions: The textbook fiasco*. Washington, DC: The Council for Basic Education.

U.S. Congress. (1994). *Goals 2000*. Washington, DC: Author.

U.S. Congress. (2001). *No Child Left Behind Act of 2001*. Washington, DC: Author.

U.S. Congress. (2002). *Education Sciences Reform Act HR 3801*. Washington, DC: Author.

U.S. Department of Education. (2002). Office of Special Education Programs. *The twenty-third annual report to Congress on the implementation of IDEA*. Washington, DC: Author.

U.S. high schools are obsolete, Gates tells governors group. (2005, February 27). *The Philadelpia Inquirer.* Retrived March 15, 2005, from Knight Ridder Database.

Vandevoort, L. G., Amrein-Beardsley, A., & Berliner, D. (2004). Board certified teachers and their students' achievement. *Education Policy Analysis Archives, 12*, (46). Retrieved March 4, 2005, from http://epaa.asu.edu/epaa/v12n46/v12n46.pdf

Veenman, S. (1984). Perceived problems of beginning teachers. *Review of Educational Research, 54*(2), 143–78.

Vernes, G., Karam, R., Mariano, L., & DeMartini, C. (2004). *Assessing the implementation of comprehensive school reform models*. Working paper prepared for the U.S. Department of Education. Santa Monica, CA: Rand Corporation.

Viadero, D. (2004, April 21). Reform programs backed by research find fewer takes. *Education Week, 23*(32), 1, 18.

Violas, P. C. (1978). *The training of the urban working class. A history of twentieth century education*. Chicago: Rand McNally College.

Vollmer. J. R. (2002, March 6.). The blueberry story: A business leader learns a lesson. *Education Week, 21*(25), 42.

Walsh, K. (2001). *Teacher certification reconsidered: Stumbling for quality*. Baltimore, MD: Abell Foundation. Retrieved October 11, 2004, from http://www.abelfoundation.org

Warner Brothers. (1988). *Stand and deliver*. Playhouse Theatrical Film No. 11805, Color, 103 minutes.

Warren, D. (1985). Learning from experience: History and teacher education. *Educational Researcher, 14*(10), 5–12.

Warren, S. (2002). Stories from the classrooms: How expectations and efficacy of diverse teachers affect the academic performance of children in poor urban schools. *Educational Horizons, 80*(3), 109–116.

Watkins, C. (1997). *Project Follow Through: A case study of contingencies influencing instructional practices of the educational establishment.* Cambridge, MA: Cambridge Center for Behavioral Studies.

Watters, C. (2005, January 26). Approach to reading argued. *Rockford Register Star.* Retrieved January 27, 2005, from http://www.rrstar.com

Westinghouse Learning Corporation. (1969). *The impact of Head Start: An evaluation of the effects of Head Start on children's cognitive and affective development.* Athens: Ohio University.

White, M. A. T. (1988). Meta-analysis of the effects of Direct Instruction in special education. *Education and Treatment of Children, 11,* 364–374.

Willingham, D. (2004). Reframing the mind. *Education Next, 3*(3). Retrieved February 7, 2005, from http://www.educationnext.org/pastissues.html

Wisconsin Public Radio. (2002, August 3). *Michael Feldman's Whad'ya know?* Retrieved February 11, 2005, from http://www.notmuch.com/show/Archive.pl?s_id=107

Witkin, H., & Goodenough, D. (1981). *Cognitive styles: Essence and origins.* New York: International Universities Press.

Wolf, A. (2005, January 21). A lesson from the heartland. *The New York Sun.* Retrieved January 27, 2005, from http://www.nysun.com

Wolffe, D. L. (1954). *America's resources of specialized talent. The report of the commission on human resources and advanced training.* New York: Harpers.

Wolffe, R. (1996). Reducing preservice teachers negative expectations of urban students through field experience. *Teacher Education Quarterly, 23*(1), 99–106.

Ysseldyke, J. E., Thurlow, M. L., Langenfeld, K. L., Nelson, J. R., Teelucksingh, E., & Seyfarth, A. (1998). *Educational results for students with disabilities: What do the data tell us* (Technical Report 23). Minneapolis, MN: National Center on Educational Outcomes. (ERIC Document Reproduction Service No. ED 425590)

Zahorik, J. A. (1996). Elementary and secondary teachers' reports of how they make learning interesting. *The Elementary School Journal, 967*(5). 551–564.

Zalud, G. G., & Richardson, M. V. (1994). The top 10 materials and methods of reading instruction used by teachers in a rural state. *Rural Educator, 16*(1), 26–29.

Zigmond, N. (2005, February 18). *The seven habits of highly effective special education teachers.* Paper presented at the Oshkosh Special Education Conference. Oshkosh, WI.

Index

accountability, 10–11, 40–44, 118,
187, 189–190; lack of, 40–44;
teaching to the test, 28, 41
acculturation to teaching; before
certification, 163–164; after
certification, 165–166
achievement gap, 6–7, 44, 148,
149–150, 153–154; vocabulary,
33–35; reading comprehension, 34,
135
apprenticeship of observation, 164
assessment:
authentic, 41, 46; progress
monitoring, 19; standardized, 28
attention:
attention deficit hyperactivity
disorder. *See* disabilities; attention
span, 53; selective attention, 53–55

background knowledge, 6, 29–33, 36,
39, 44, 56, 65, 110–111, 113, 135
beginning reading, 5–7, 35–37, 100;
fluency, 70, 72; letter–sound
correspondences, 53–54, 76–77,
79–80; phonemic awareness, 70,
71, 75–77, 81, 135, 139; phonics,
37, 70–74, 115; rhyming, 100; use
of context clues, 74–75, 77–78. *See
also* National Reading Panel
behaviorism, 150; applied behavior
analysis, 18, 150. *See also* teacher-
directed philosophy
beliefs about teaching and learning:
administrators, 127; origins, 146;
professors, 25, 28, 49, 88, 90, 168;
school psychologists, 127–128;
teachers, 22–26, 28, 45, 62, 88, 90,
107, 126–127, 139, 164, 167
blueberry story, 128–129
bricoleur, 24, 26, 69, 95, 155, 160,
173, 175–176, 187, 190

Carnegie Foundation. *See* Flexner
report
classroom management, 19, 49–50,
94, 103–104, 119, 128, 168–169
chick-sexing experiment, 38–39
child-centered (learner-directed)
philosophy, 17–18, 30, 55, 65, 90,
157, 167–169, 171, 182; in higher

211

About the Author

Vicki E. Snider has been a professor in the Department of Special Education at the University of Wisconsin–Eau Claire for 20 years. Before moving into higher education, Dr. Snider taught students with disabilities in the public schools for 12 years. She still spends time in classrooms supervising student teachers, consulting, and running a summer clinic. Her research interests and consuming passion revolve around the need to provide effective instruction for students who are at-risk for school failure.